For Marcy and Gabriel
With gratitude for all the ways you support and contribute to the teachings. Blessings

Buddha and the Art of Intimacy

Martin Lowenthal
July 2009

OTHER BOOKS BY MARTIN LOWENTHAL

Heart to Heart, Hand in Hand, Shoulder to Shoulder

Alchemy of the Soul

Dawning of Clear Light

Embrace Yes

Opening the Heart of Compassion

Buddha and the Art of Intimacy

weaving sacred connections of love

Martin Lowenthal, Ph.D.

Dedicated Life Publications

Published in the United States by

Dedicated Life Publications

Printed by BookSurge LLC, an Amazon.com company

Robert Bly has generously given permission to use his translation of the poem "The Holy Longing" by Johann Wolfgang Von Goethe as it appears in *The Soul is Here For Its Own Joy*, page 209.

ISBN: 1-4392-3736-0

Cover and book design by Grace E. Pedalino

Acknowledgments

There are many people who directly and indirectly assisted in the development and completion of this book.

I want to thank the hundreds of students, families and counseling clients I have worked with who let me into their worlds and showed me not only their pains, but their courage and their determination to connect, to love, and to grow.

I am grateful to the members of the Dedicated Life Institute for their support and encouragement. The Dedicated Life Institute is an organizational vehicle for presenting these teachings and for students to support their spiritual growth together.

Special gratitude is due Grace Pedalino for her helpful editing and her wonderful aesthetic sensibility that she brought to the design and layout of the entire book.

Lastly, but not least, I am grateful for the support, encouragement, and editorial comments of my wife Karen Edwards.

CONTENTS

Preface

At the heart of sacred experience and in the teachings of spiritual traditions, the radiant jewel of intimacy reaches out beyond the walls of appearance and superficiality to connect us to each other, to life, and to the world. The experience takes us out of ourselves even as it resonates in the core of our very sense of being. In the blush of its fullness, we are transported beyond time into the eternal and beyond separation to communion. This communion is not confined to religious mystics but is a part of the human capacity for emotions. It has been the subject for great poets as well as numerous writers of self-help books. Intimacy, while highly valued, has often been misunderstood by both religious and popular commentators.

Buddha and the Art of Intimacy is a celebration of this profound experience and of the critical role of intimate connections in both everyday and spiritual life. Intimacy as a relational dynamic occupies a central space in our hopes and fears, in our popular conversations, and in our attempts to feel at home in life. Yet beyond the simplistic understandings we often come across and may settle for, more significant voices seek to be heard. The intention of this book is to find and express these deeper resonances.

This book does not provide a comprehensive or thorough exploration. The experience of intimacy and the relationships that give ongoing form to intimate bonding are simply too complex and diverse to cover completely in what I consider to be an introduction to the subject. My hope is that you, the reader, will enjoy what is discussed and are inspired to examine your own experiences and to experiment with new possibilities. I have also written a companion book that is a handbook for practicing deeper intimacy in our family relationships, *Heart to Heart, Hand in Hand, Shoulder to Shoulder: A Guide to Strengthening Intimate Relationships.*

As I have written and rewritten this work, the subject made three demands on me that I have labored to address with varying degrees of success. The first demand was spiritual. The substance of what I have to say has not been dictated by the spiritual teachings of Buddhism or any other tradition on the nature, importance, or role of emotions and the dynamic of human connection. My own experience, the reports of the experiences of others in my counseling with couples and families, my observations as both a pastoral counselor and as a former academic sociologist and researcher, combined with a review of the literature have provided the guide and been the litmus test of authenticity for what is shared in this book.

The second demand was intellectual. Intimacy is both a common and mysterious experience. What is it? What is the role intimacy plays in human relations and in our sense of the sacred? What distinctions are useful in describing and working with the various experiences of intimacy? How does the personal experience of intimacy translate into collective experience and manifest over time in patterns of communication, the culture of a relationship, and in the functioning of a relationship as a social system? While not exhaustively covering each of these questions, I have addressed them in a way that intends to convey a picture of the subject without becoming too academic or too simplistic.

The third demand was psychological/emotional. More than a dynamic of life, intimacy is an experience that is surrounded by hopes, fears, pleasures, pains, love, accumulated patterns of reaction, and desires. In our psychological landscape, the depths of our connections unfold not in the conceptual realm but in the terrain of emotions. The possibilities and the challenges of an intimate life in these times of rampant superficiality and increasing narcissism place those of us who would be lovers of life and of the sacred in conflict with our culture. In addition, the close relationships we create and nurture often are confronted by the demands of an insatiable work and career life, voracious consumer appetites, the increasing focus of family life on the fears for and the injunctions to protect and accommodate children, of a polarizing, regressive religious and political scene, segmented and fragmenting social life, and a numbing substitution of entertainment for authentic cultural participation. This book also examines the hazards of these conflicts and seeks to encourage you in your sacred quest for connection, meaning, home, and a richer life.

Prelude

In the fall of 1976, sitting meditation on the screened porch of an old, converted farm house in the woods of Maine with a view of the colorful foliage that precedes the release of leafy growth of spring and summer, I struggled to become more present with my rich surroundings and with a core of equanimity that seemed like a distant hope. My marriage had recently ended. I was burnt out as director of a university research institute trying to keep dozens of researchers employed while teaching a full load and had decided to resign that position to concentrate on teaching and taking care of my three children, who lived with me half of the time. Dropping my work with the institute also meant diminished income at a time when I would be financially supporting two households instead of one with virtually no savings. During that year, I had also spent considerable time taking care of my parents in San Francisco because my father had had a stroke and the initial stages of Alzheimer's disease and my mother was recovering from an injury.

I was taking a long weekend solo retreat to deepen my Buddhist practice and to navigate through the stormy seas of my fears, disappointments, frustrations, and longings. The peace I sought was elusive and remained a concept in my mind that inspired hope and effort but also perpetuated a conflict in my consciousness between my mental commentator on whatever was arising and the relaxation that developed in my continued sitting. At the close of a mindfulness practice on the second day, I dedicated the benefits of my practice, rang a small bell, unfolded my legs from their half-lotus configuration (a full lotus was never sustainable owing to various knee injuries), and simply sat comfortably releasing any struggle to maintain correct posture and disciplined attention.

Without effort a sense of oneness emerged, a union with everything and with life that transcended time and space. I remained in that state for an unknown length of time but the experience was timeless, like I was inside eternity. I had a fundamental sense of love that included the sensibilities of romantic and parental love and yet felt more generic, unconditional, and inclusive. The fullness of presence, the sense of being simultaneously me and everything, the profound feeling of home, the clarity of perception, and the experience of resting inside a sacred way of being and that this sacredness was inside me as well as everywhere were not identified conceptually at the time but only on reflection afterward.

This experience of sacred intimacy was so intense that it unhinged my sense of myself, my ideas about love, purpose, life and the impossibility of bridging the divide that separated me from everyone and everything else. While I had no thought of these issues during the experience, when my self-consciousness returned and my mind sought to understand what had happened and to identify the implications of the experience and its residue, I became acutely aware of having received a gift and that my life would never be quite the same. I tried to recreate the experience for months after that day without success. Yet I could tell that a seed had been planted that would need to blossom in its own time. Experiences of that sacred intimacy arose from time to time over the next couple of years and took much deeper root about five years later.

Besides coming to understand that such gifts of

consciousness do not arise from a simple formula, I also realized that I had habitual patterns of thinking and feeling that reactively hijacked me and frequently kept me on the surface of life. These reactive habits included a longing for connection as if love would solve the problem that was my life, fears of dying alone, addiction to working, confusions about the relationship of sexuality to intimacy, desires for approval and validation, and wanting everyone to like me.

As I consciously worked to become freer of these reactive agendas, my life became more engaged and I experienced becoming increasingly connected to all of life. I began to welcome the challenges of having my "buttons" pushed so I could get clearer and work to unhook the content of emotional charges and intentionally channel that energy. My erotic energies broke out of the confines of sexuality to vitalize my work, my connections in nature and my spiritual practices, and my relationship to my children, my friends, and years later to the woman who became my wife.

My heart broke out of the walls of numbness, opened the bars of frustration, grief, and fear, and moved on past the guards of reaction. I learned to celebrate what was present in my life as a way of being intimate rather than bemoan what was missing as a confirmation of inadequacy or having been victimized. In the early 1980s when I started teaching spiritual retreats and leading meditation groups, I called this work "celebrational meditation." I came to make a distinction between the problem-solving frame of the therapeutic context and the celebrational frame of sacred work that calls on us to be present with *what is*, to appreciate the gifts of life, to cultivate our capacities for love and wisdom, and to serve larger purposes through creating benefit and beauty.

In addition to this book exploring and celebrating the

landscape of intimacy, it also seeks to highlight elements of spiritual work that are often discounted or misunderstood.

In Buddhism for example, many people have rejected intimacy out of a misinterpretation of the principle of non-attachment. Disassociating from reactive emotions is meant as a strategic practice not as a goal. It is designed to gain perspective and break old habits so we are free to be fully present with the people and things in our life. The authentic purpose is to engage and rejoice in the gift of life, to cultivate the sense of connection with everyone and everything, and to mature into an embracing wisdom that informs our loving and compassionate service to others. In other words, the practices are meant to release the grip of unexamined beliefs and reactive feelings and to cultivate the integration of the head and the heart in the embodiment of a sacred way of loving and living. In this way relationships become a training ground for spiritual practice as well as an evolving context of connection that matures as we mature.

I also want to suggest that the sacred states that are supported by Buddhist practices, as well as those of other mystical traditions, are only part of a practical and complete approach to good relationships and the development of healthy intimate bonds. Buddhist philosophy provides little guidance for life cycle human development and mostly ignores the developmental stages and challenges of close relationships except those involving a student and the guru. Expanding our view to include these significant domains of modern life bridges a gap between the personal stages of emotional development and the requirements of cultivating spiritual capacity and between individual experience and the development of collective consciousness.

The first part of this book is concerned with the role of intimacy in the development of sacred states and ways of being and connecting. I explore how this conscious development leads to personal development and maturity. In the context of relationships, intimacy naturally leads to a sense of *we* and to our personal emotional and social growth as well as the development of our relationships as social systems. I then examine the personal and collective challenges we face in these times of superficial and narcissistic culture and of a fractious economic, political and social world.

I suggest that developing sacred intimacy leads to wisdom, love/compassion, and service that can strengthen, enrich, and enhance intimate bonds in social relationships. Wisdom, love and dedicated service, in turn, can inspire a re-visioning of the possibilities in our society and have critical roles to play in raising the level of our collective consciousness.

1.

The Heart of the Sacred

Fundamentally speaking...we are intrinsically Buddha and we are intrinsically good. Without exception...we can say that we automatically have Buddha within us. That is known as Buddha-nature, or bodhichitta, the heart of the Buddha.

CHÖGYAM TRUNGPA RINPOCHE[i]

Two disciples once asked their master, "The teachings say that we should rejoice in our afflictions and be grateful for the bad just as we feel blessed by the good. How is that possible?" The master looked at them and sent them to another teacher in a nearby village.

As they approached this master, they saw his broken-down hut and him sitting peacefully on his porch. They, like everyone else, knew he was poor and had had a life of sickness and pain. Yet he always glowed with peace and joy.

Even as they asked their question—"How can one be grateful, even for the bad things?"—they experienced the fullness of the master's presence and the embrace of his loving connection in their hearts.

He said to them, "Why did your master send you here? I have never experienced anything bad in my whole life! I only know the ease of always being at home, the joy of aliveness, and the love of intimacy with everyone and everything."

Books often begin with some fundamental problem in our lives and then pose their particular solution. In this book, I want to begin, not with a problem but with the promise of intimacy, love, beauty, and home. The wonder of intimacy does not need to be a solution for it directly penetrates to the heart of our aliveness and the potential for sacred vision.

Inner Wisdom

When the spiritual traditions talk about inner wisdom, they are referring not so much to what is inside us as to the wisdom that arises from inside the sacred, a sacred way of being, seeing, and acting. In Tibetan, *tag nang* refers to the experience of *sacred outlook* and literally means "pure perception." As my first Buddhist teacher, Chögyam Trungpa Rinpoche said, "Sacred outlook means perceiving the world and oneself as intrinsically good and unconditionally free."[ii]

The sacred is not a thing, not apart from the world or us. It is a way of perceiving, relating, and engaging with life. The sacred dimensions of our being are not visible but are a way of seeing, are not tangible but can be felt and are not heard but resonate in the core of our being.

It is our soul that invests the world and our lives with meaning and each time we make meaning we are connecting to what we make meaning of. That drive to connect is the vitalizing impulse of love that places us in the world and the world in us. The soul is a lover.

Heart Postures

What we experience is very much determined by what we attend to and what heart postures we bring to each situation and relationship. If we hold the heart posture of being able to learn new skills throughout our life and attend to improving our communications, we will find that our interactions with others are more enjoyable and connective. On the other hand, if we operate from a belief that we are too damaged to learn and attend to our fear of making a mistake, we will avoid difficult conversations with others and simply add evidence to our indictment of our own inadequacy.

Our heart posture is our sense of the nature of reality as we have come to know it and experience it. It includes our attitudes about ourselves and the world and determines much of our perceptions and ways of relating. If our heart posture is governed by fear and the idea that we are vulnerable and the world is a dangerous place, we will look for threats, behave defensively, and may be reserved in our relationships. If our heart posture is governed by love, we see ourselves as a lover of life, seeking opportunities for relationships and engaging intimately in the world with all of its challenges.

Whenever we feel imprisoned in a limiting and isolating heart posture, one of the most difficult tasks we face in breaking out of our confinement is having to realize how much of what we think we know about ourselves, human nature, emotions, love, and intimacy "isn't necessarily so." All of us come face to face with the realization that what we thought we understood is fundamentally colored by our reactive feelings of fear, anger, sadness and hope.

When we take on a new heart posture, it is like living in a different culture with its own codification of reality, its own guidelines for maturity, and its own possibilities for transformation. A new heart posture takes work and is based on opening to the direct experience of reality as it is. It requires that our relationship with life become fresh, allowing our deeper nature to emerge.

Love as Heart Posture

The love referred to here is not so much an emotion as a

way of being, a way of perceiving, an attitude, or what I am calling a *heart posture*. The emotion is an expression of that heart posture and perception. Love is a perception of what? It is a perception of connection and oneness—a perception and heart posture of the essential connectivity and unity of reality. Love shifts boundaries. It connects us to the world.

I invite you to recall times when you experienced the excitement and beauty of being in love. All of us desire to be at home in life and feel the aliveness that arises from being in love. The experience of romantic love in its ecstatic blush models a much deeper lesson on the spiritual path—namely the profound sense of connection, the vividness of perception where everything looks more colorful and rich, and the fullness of aliveness.

Living within a sacred view, we meet life and are met in the core of our being, experiencing a fullness of presence, intimate connectedness, dynamic aliveness, and profound belonging. Life freshly opens to each moment, revealing the often hidden radiance of the world. Oneness and the beauty of diversity arise simultaneously. We know a deep intimacy with each other and life.

The relation between the sacred and life is like a snail whose shell-home is part of its own being. No matter where we are, we are always within a sacred embrace. No matter what we do, we are still embraced. No matter what we may think and feel, our very being is always embraced by sacred reality and we need only to become aware and live in a sacred heart posture.

What keeps us from this wholehearted, erotic, sacred engagement with life? How can we learn to live from that deep place in our being where everything is seen as sacred and our very way of being manifests an embracing love?

Sacred Vs. Superficial

The opposite of the sacred is not the material or evil. It is being superficial. We are called to move beyond the superficiality of our limiting reactive habits to live spontaneously, our own authentic, unique lives as a contribution to the lives of others. We are called to remember that we are the environment for other people. Becoming freer and finding the light that is hidden in our particular darkness enables us to see with sacred eyes and to live in a heart posture of love.

When we cling to superficial views and addictions, we do not sense all the opportunities for experiencing joy.

> Once, an accomplished fiddler stood in the town center playing joyfully with passion. The passing crowd stopped to listen and, engulfed by the beauty of the music, began to dance. They were so engrossed, they lost themselves in the sweetness of this world of sound.
>
> A deaf man happened to come along, and unable to hear the entrancing music, was utterly appalled by the bizarre scene. Since he could not perceive why the people were dancing, he concluded that they were actually mad.
>
> When we hear the resonance and magnificence of the sacred, how can we keep from dancing?

The teachings and practices of all religious traditions are aimed at transporting us into the Sacred and rooting us in our own sacred nature as well as all life. Whether we explore the sacred heart of Christianity, the Divine spark in Judaism, or the open and compassionate presencing in Buddhism, we enter an intimate path into the world of the Sacred.

Intimate Nature of the Sacred

Intimacy points to a way of being that is unconditional, a way of relating that is loving and always eternally present, and an approach to action that is obedient to the sacred service of creating benefit and beauty. The nature of the sacred dimension of life is to be intimate—fully present, unconditionally embracing and connected—namely loving, dynamically alive and inclusively unitive. The intimate aspect of our fundamental nature cuts through and transcends whatever we are doing, whether we feel good or bad, and who we think we are. This loving intimate nature is eternally open, joyfully present, always at home, and simply "is," as in all there is is *is*.

At the same time, our nature is paradoxical in that it is both beyond all that is and is all that is, both beyond and immanent. It is always opening and always forming; always formless, formative, and form; always no-thing and yet all things; not our feelings and our feelings. All feelings are a way of relating to something, all relating is a form of connecting, and all connection is a form of love—the impulse to manifest the intimate meaning that each person, event or thing has for us.

This open, loving nature is always there whether you are talking with a friend, arguing with your spouse, playing with your children, making plans, planting a magnolia tree, napping, or watching a sunset. Each moment is an opportunity to experience the always-fresh recognition of open, inseparable loving presence.

In this book, I am not only sharing the promise of intimacy. I reveal the dedicated effort that is required to realize that promise. I give concrete suggestions about how to make those efforts effective. Every description of the splendor of intimacy mentioned in this volume represents the conscious work of years. It is not that we cannot experience the wonders of intimacy immediately, but to cultivate a heart posture that transforms our being and our entire experience of life takes dedication, effort, and time.

I invite you to become intimate with the subject of intimacy by letting its deeper nature speak to your heart through this book. Such an exploration of intimacy brings you into a sacred conversation that requires a new way of speaking. Familiar words are used in unfamiliar ways to reveal deeper qualities of life than our modern usage normally conveys. In this process, ancient wisdom and ideas are given back their power to awaken us and expand our awareness and sense of connection. We, who are willing to engage in this conversation, are constantly challenged to go beyond our limiting perspectives, beliefs, and attitudes and listen from the place of our deepest wisdom nature.

Rather than acquiring some particular knowledge, this is meant to be practiced in life and taken to heart. We want to realize intimacy in our lives, not become encyclopedias of concepts, thoughts, and words.

Paradox of Our Nature

As we travel through the landscape of intimacy and its spiritual and social nature, we will encounter how paradoxical we are. Paradox can be defined as an *apparent* contradiction in that it combines two or more realities that don't *appear* to belong together.

One core paradox of human spirituality is the haunting sense of separateness that comes with having a distinct body and a personal identity even as we know we are a member of a community that we are intimately connected to, dependent upon, and always contributing to as part of a larger social, physical, and spiritual ecology.

Awakening to the possibilities of intimacy with all of life, we can invite the truth of reality to speak to us with its authentic voice and demand of us that we genuinely listen. Initially, the voice may appear through the language of a presentation such as this. Then it may emerge in our conversations with others committed to the same exploration. Eventually, we learn to hear this voice in the sounds that resonate throughout the world of our experience. When we are mindful and present, we recognize this voice in the chaotic symphony played moment to moment and we become intimate with this sacred Reality.

Pioneers of Intimacy

The dissolution of close-knit village communities combined with the loss of traditional guidance on navigating the life cycle and relationships, and the multitude of pressures of modern life, all challenge us to make our way through a variety of social interactions to find and sustain the intimacy our heart's desire. Our souls need to feel at home in the world. Particularly in America, where the culture of the frontier required the creation of a community among strangers, so many of us live, work, and worship largely with people we did not know growing up. They did not witness our passages through the stages of childhood, adolescence and adulthood. We have only a tenuous hold on the larger contexts of community and the Sacred of which our personal and collective relationships are a part. We face having to become more conscious in sustaining our intimate relationships such as marriage even while the structures and support of religious and community institutions weaken.

The very institution of marriage has evolved from being primarily a social arrangement with emotional components to becoming as much an emotional arrangement as a social covenant. The role of marriage and the family is now increasingly being evaluated by members in terms of emotional support and psychological impact on personal development and well-being. Even the term "dysfunctional" used by psychologists and family therapists refers to the interpersonal dynamics that affect the intrapersonal functioning of family members who are often identified as victims of these dysfunctional patterns. Less and less is a family regarded as a building block of a community and a society but more as an environment where needs are met and personal development unfolds. One of the effects of this shift in perspective has been the attention to feelings of intimacy, states of being intimate, the process of intimate bonding, and the nature and strength of intimate connections.

We are all pioneers in the wilderness of intimacy. Each of us is called upon to mature beyond the superficial images of relating that pervade our media and the simplistic rules of public moralists. Forging the bonds of enduring relationships has become a skill and task that must be consciously cultivated rather than one that was integrated into normal social development in traditional societies. With changes in the work we do, mobility patterns, residential communities, family structures, and gender roles, as well as the great number of personal opportunities and choices, our quest for a deeper kind of relatedness requires exploring and cultivating new levels of intimacy if we are to find authentic belonging, love, and sacred connection, personally and collectively.

Goodness as Gathering

The word *good* has the same root—*gê*—as the words *gather* and *together*. One meaning of *goodness* concerns the sense of *fit* in terms of feeling part of a more inclusive and embracing whole. The experience of connectedness and home that is part of the sacred nature of intimacy derives from a vision of relationships that sees both self and other as somehow fitting into a larger whole, linked to a larger dynamic of life itself.

Fundamental to our nature is the sense of connectedness. Even when we feel that the sense of connection has been lost or wounded, the yearning for union with others and larger realities is itself an expression of this nature. This dynamic of yearning and connection underlies the intimacy to be found in romantic relationships, teams, art, and religion. When connection is not experienced, we feel alienation and loneliness, a sense that something is not quite right. We feel separate from others, torn apart internally, and disjointed in life.

Through embracing intimacy we heal those fractures bringing us into a sense of fit with each other, the world, life, and the Sacred. We unite head and heart, body and mind, self and other. We enact our two-sidedness, recognizing that at root we include many feelings and thoughts but are essentially indivisible.

Spiritual Nature of Intimacy

This sense of inclusive wholeness reveals the spiritual nature of intimacy. Spirituality points *beyond*: beyond the superficial, beyond the ordinary, beyond possessions, beyond feelings, beyond thoughts, beyond expectations and beyond self-concern. The spiritual can be the highest level of development in mastery of a life work, namely beyond what is taught. It can refer to experiences that are beyond the everyday. To live a spiritual life is to be inspired by and embody the qualities of the sacred that are beyond a life centered in material concerns and reality and yet is not divorced from physical reality. It is to be informed by a sacred way of seeing, feeling, being and acting. Spirituality involves both the affirmation of what is as well as what is beyond—what we can know and what is unknown and beyond our comprehension.

Spirituality transcends the ordinary and yet, paradoxically, it can be found in the ordinary. It places *what is* and *beyond* together. It is the extraordinary nature of all that is ordinary. It is also true that by attending to *what is*, the *beyond* can be touched.

The gateway of the spiritual opens us to the true abundance, to the boundless treasures of the sacred. Spiritual qualities are enlarged as they are shared, rather than diminished as would be the case in the material world. It is in this sacred space of intimacy that everyone can experience wealth.

As we cope with crafting a life of meaning, beauty, and love from the material of our modern world, we seek to overcome the ways life, relationships, and the sacred have become somewhat alien to us. We do not want to simply be "doing time" with life, surviving relationships, and cut off from real connection to the sacred. The heart posture of love and the experiential bond of intimacy have enormous power for physical, emotional, social and spiritual healing and awakening.

Buddhism and "Life is Not a Problem"

Buddhist practice is not a self-help program to solve the problem of our life. The practices may impact us but it is not basically a problem-solving approach. In fact it is the opposite. Buddhism suggests that life, even suffering, is not a problem. Life simply is. Challenges simply are. Buddhism is a path for opening the precious gift of life and all that that involves. It encourages us to recognize our basic wisdom, loving, and radiant nature, to open the precious gift of life, and to cultivate the loving qualities of being so that we are a magnificent contributing presence in the world.

In some Buddhist mythology, Maitreya, the emerging or coming Buddha, will follow the age of wisdom and intellectual achievements by bringing forth an expanded and intensified intuitive, intimate consciousness, in which the sense of the essential unity of all life will support the active love of fellow beings. This intimate sense of all life and its consequent active love will manifest in the practical integration and application of wisdom. This integration of wisdom, love, and action combines the warmth of caring with the clarity of inner vision and the creation of collective benefit and beauty. Maitreya embodies an all-embracing wisdom that is spontaneous, connective, and lovingly engaged.

I invite you to read this book as a meditation and opportunity for reflection. I invite you to experience recognition, sense the aliveness of your presence and your intimacy with the subject in that moment. This book invites you to create your own experiential tapestry. By absorbing each section, image by image and feeling by feeling, you enter the wondrous world of the heart that integrates mind, body, and the sacred.

As we begin our journey, imagine that we are placing the magical cloak of intimacy around our very soul giving us a sense of excitement, warmth, and deep love. Let us invoke the sacred that is found in and beyond the people and things of our lives. Let us become awake to the commitment our soul wants to make to participating in and contributing to a larger collective consciousness, to belonging in the home of relationships, communities, and life, to realizing the Divine (buddha nature) of all life, and to living in alignment with the truth and requirements of sacred meaning and love.

> A king's son became ill from sadness and depression. The king brought many doctors to court, but none of them was able to cure the prince. Then a doctor arrived from an unknown land. After examining the boy, he announced that he would be cured when he wore the shirt of a happy person.
>
> Court investigators were sent throughout the realm to wealthy people, whom they thought must surely be happy. But they were told by each wealthy person that, because of their many worries and anxieties about their possessions, they were not happy. As the investigators scoured the country, they were about to give up hope when they were told of a shepherd who was truly happy. When they approached him, on behalf of the king and the prince, to ask for his shirt, they felt the radiance of his joy and noticed that he had no shirt.

The story teaches that possessions are merely superficial ornaments, that moods can be difficult and persistent habits, and that reclaiming our real joy comes from tending the flock of our experiences and relationships with a natural radiant, openness.

2.

The Intimate Buddha

The sacred themes of love, connection, compassion, presence, service and wisdom can be found in all spiritual traditions. The figure of Buddha, like Jesus, Mohammed, and Solomon, represents the integration of these themes in the embodiment of an individual who made a personal journey into the Sacred and transmitted teachings from that consciousness in ways that sought to transform not only the individual lives of followers, but the organization and values of societies and cultures. While intimacy has not received much attention as a prominent feature of those teachings, it is critical to the understanding, practice, and realization of spiritual development and maturity and to the development of a mature culture and an integrally functioning society.

This book is not about Buddhism as a religion or spiritual system, but is profoundly inspired by my own experience as a Buddhist practitioner and what I have come to know as the essence of both Buddhist teachings and the principles of other sacred traditions. Buddhism is a simple yet profound approach to life that emphasizes clarity of mind, openness of heart, the direct intimate experience of life itself, and dedicated service to all sentient beings. The art that this book addresses is meant to uncover the core of intimacy and the essence of the practices that enhance this loving aliveness beyond personal history and conceptual understanding.

Buddhism, while having rituals for the blessing of many kinds of human relationships, has not given much attention to intimacy, to emotional development and to marriage. In particular the Buddhism that has influenced Westerners has come from monastic life where individual meditative practice and the life of celibate monks as a community have shaped many of the teachings that were introduced. There have been instances of teachings that treat emotions and intimate bonds simply as examples of weakness, distraction, and delusion. There has been an attitude that the complete way to enlightenment and spiritual realization can only be attained by those who have given themselves entirely to the life of meditative practice.

Triune Buddhist Principles

There is a growing movement in the West, including among Buddhist teachers from Asia, to change some of the emphasis to address the potential of an authentic lay path to spiritual development that includes the dynamics and challenges of marriage, family, and work.

Mark Epstein, author of *Thoughts without a Thinker*, points out: "Like everything else in Buddhist tradition, the purpose of love and marriage is to be a vehicle for awakening." He goes on to say: "Buddhism is about investigating all the different self-experiences with the ultimate goal of knowing true reality, knowing self and other—and in an intense emotional relationship like marriage the experience of the self is stretched.... When the self and the other get intermingled, it challenges our sense that our identity is fixed, and when we get hurt, it makes the illusion of the self very visible. We can have all of these experiences of the self because love and marriage are the intermingling of emptiness and bliss."[iii]

Much of the Buddhism that has made its way into the non-

Asian culture of the West has been the philosophy and practice that is derived from monastic Buddhism. At the same time, the meditative practice for laity in everyday life is the same as for the monk sitting on a cushion, namely to open completely, host the range of thoughts and feelings, letting them arise, pass through, and disappear, witness this entire process, engage the moment with presence, aliveness, and a loving heart, and transform the energies of everyday life into wisdom qualities for the benefit of all living beings. The principles that make up Buddhist approaches to life and the development of states of consciousness illuminate ways to be open and present with each other and support the individual and collective growth that is possible in living together in relationship. I have written this book so that the ideas and suggestions can be useful for people in any spiritual tradition as well as those who practice none.

The act of integrating Buddhism into Western and modern culture and times is a creative process that leads to a distillation of the essence principles and the refinement of practices. As Lama Govinda said, "If Buddhism is to take root in the West, we must play our part in the further development of the *Dharma*, thus infusing it with fresh blood and life. The doctrine of the Buddha is not a belief based religion but one of experience and recognition—an experience which must be born anew in each individual."[iv]

In Tibetan Buddhism, the qualities of a Buddha are often depicted in terms of three enlightened beings—Manjushri manifesting wisdom, Avalokiteshvara manifesting all-encompassing compassion, and Vajrapani manifesting the all-accomplishing power to create benefit. These three symbolize the triune principles of the Buddha's nature in terms of virtues. A virtue is a path to sacred realization, and wisdom, compassion and creating benefit are the aspects of profound spiritual development.

Similar triune principles are found in other traditions as

well. For example in Hinduism, the triunity of goddesses include Sarasvati representing wisdom, Lakshmi representing love, and Parvati representing the energy of creation, which includes the full process of creation from generation, sustaining, to dissolution. We find similar trinitarian perspectives in other traditions, including Christianity and Islam.

Of the qualities of wisdom, love/compassion, and creation/service of the triune Buddha, I refer to the second of these as the "intimate Buddha", the Buddha whose love and compassion reach out to all beings. This view of the Buddha, far from seeking to be free from emotions of love and caring, suggests an open, full engagement with others. As Lama Govinda has said, "I personally would rather take upon myself the suffering arising from loving others, than to be incapable of love. For it is only from this basic attitude that we can develop the capacity for compassion and sympathy with other beings."[v] "Not to allow love in order to avoid suffering is nothing but an extreme form of selfishness that is no better than the selfishness of possessiveness. To avoid suffering by not loving is a flight into indifference, which may be a stoic ideal but not a Buddhist one."[vi]

The Bodhisattva ideal teaches us to accept all suffering out of a heart posture of love. "The pain that we take upon ourselves for the sake of others ennobles us, makes us deeper and lifts us out of our isolation. That is the suffering out of which great character grows."[vii] "Our good intent may be universal and all-embracing, but our *love* can only find expression in a *personal* relationship."[viii] Lama Govinda continues by cautioning "...when people speak so much about universal love, then I fear they have made a wonderful *concept* for themselves that enables then not to love. Love always presupposes a personal relationship."[ix]

The key to sacred love is that it encompasses authenticity, openness, fullness of presence, and transcendent caring rather than superficial possessiveness that results in imprisoning attachment. At the same time, even possessive love, as Lama Govinda points out, can evoke and develop "…the capacity for genuine, freely-given love." "It can be the seed from which true love and true sympathy burgeons and bears fruit."[x]

Buddhism cultivates qualities of the human heart and provides a program to transform our superficial, reactive habits and attitudes so that we not only overcome our own suffering but also help relieve the suffering of others and contribute to creating a world of sacred belonging, happiness, and loving connection. In this book, I attempt to offer a more integrated and holistic way of understanding intimacy as a sacred phenomenon as well as a dynamic of relationships.

This book points the way to living intimately with life, moment to moment, even while you enjoy great pleasure or endure pain, or whether you are longing for belonging or dissolving in gratitude for the gift of beauty. Every moment is an expression of the loving embrace of a sacred, radiant presence, what some call the Divine, others the Tao, and Buddhists refer to the "suchness" that is an aspect of Buddha nature.

The Buddha

The Buddha was a prince who lived about 2500 years ago in the kingdom of the Sakyas in what is now southern Nepal and northern India. His name was Siddhartha Gautama. He was married at age sixteen to a beautiful princess and lived an opulent life of comfort. His family tried to protect him from the reality of sickness, aging, and death, trapping him in a cage of pleasure, material ease and superficiality.

When he was twenty-nine, shortly after the birth of his first son, he got his first glimpses of the suffering of ordinary people and he left the palace to become an ascetic, living in simplicity, extreme poverty and doing spiritual practices to find a solution to the problem of human suffering. He wandered for six years, meeting famous religious teachers, studying their teachings, and engaging in very rigorous spiritual practices.

Often the extremity of his practice made him ill and delusional and he failed to find the answers he sought. Abandoning the traditional paths of the ascetic, he, at the age of thirty-five, sat for forty-nine days under the Tree of Wisdom, the Bodhi tree. He saw that there is only one reality, that it is absolutely open and dynamically forming in every moment, and that we all have the same design, are made of the same materials, participate in the same awareness, and are all interconnected.

Buddha was not a Buddhist, for the term Buddha means "enlightened one or one who is unconditionally awake" and was given to Siddhartha by his followers. For the next forty-five years he taught anyone who sought his wisdom without regard to caste or class.

He taught people to become free of misconceptions and reactive habits so they could discover and live from their inner radiance resting in the open nature of pure awareness. He spoke of the paradoxically radiant and open nature of the essence at the heart of our being from which love, compassion, serenity and sacred heart postures arise. He pointed to methods that would free us from our core fears, such as the fear of death and of not being worthy, into a clarity from which our natural sense of presence would flow and our engagement with the world and each other would be authentic, alive, and unconditionally embracing.

Buddha suggested a way of being, a way of relating, and a way of acting in the world. In the Buddhist frame we see the world as a whole, as interdependent, interconnected, and continually changing. From this perspective we are less concerned about what things appear to be and more attentive to the processes, potentialities, and relationships of what is. We, and everyone and everything else, are both features of reality and parts of an integrated, interrelated and interactive whole system.

The One and the Many

Buddhism cultivates the direct experience of oneness through the recognition of the undivided nature of mind and the freedom, openness, presence, and inclusive harmony that arises from that recognition. Many traditions refer to a mystical union with God and although this represents a different expression, this union with the sacred nature of being is common to all spiritual work.

Paradoxically, the sense of oneness also illuminates the richness of diversity and a profound appreciation of the varied features that make up reality. The One and the Many are inseparable and the affirmation and engagement in one invokes the other. When we appreciate and take joy in the particulars of our relationship, we can enhance that delight by experiencing the fleeting uniqueness of the moment as an expression of the universal sacred.

As Ellen and Charles Birx explain in their book *Waking Up Together*, "…in Zen we say, 'Not one, not two.' 'Not one' means that we cannot ignore differences among individuals. Each of us is unique and that is what gives life its texture and richness. 'Not two' acknowledges the unity of everything in its essential nature. The experience of unity expands our awareness and capacity for love."[xi]

Unity and distinction are perceived and lived simultaneously in a conscious relationship. This happens moment-to-moment as we integrate the personal with the collective, the individual with the One, the particular with the whole. Our experience of the whole enriches our sense of our relative differences and deepens our gratitude for both the relationship and our partner.

Maintaining an Inquiring and Gentle Heart

Buddhism is more of a philosophy for living and a daily practice rather than a set of dogmatic beliefs. Buddhism does not emphasize the acquisition of external beliefs, but rather is about provoking inner wisdom. It is about being awake, free from self-deception, fears, and longings and generating compassion and loving kindness throughout our lives and relationships. Our deep, sacred or divine nature, our luminous, open essence, is called our buddha nature. The essence of all being is considered buddha nature.

In Buddhist wisdom, seeing the world as having Buddha nature and as an interactive, integrated whole, incorporates and embraces all positions and points of view. Buddhism encourages us to relate to the ways things are and the larger contexts in which life is unfolding rather than clinging to our smaller, fixed views.

The Buddha instructed his followers not to accept the authority of his teachings based on reverence for him or because someone told them to believe but to test the teachings in experience, in personal experimentation, and in reason. An inquisitive stance in relation to the teachings is an essential tenet of the experiential approach of Buddhism.

Buddha Nature and Buddha Genes

Trungpa Rinpoche affirmed this point in his teachings. "The heart of the Buddha is a very open heart. That heart would like to explore the phenomenal world; it is open to relating to others. That heart contains tremendous strength and confidence in itself, which is called fearlessness. That heart is also extremely inquisitive, which at this point is synonymous with *prajna* (discerning wisdom). It is expansive and sees in all directions. And that heart contains certain basic qualities, which we could call our true *basic genes*—our buddha-genes.... These buddha-genes have two characteristics. First they are able to see through...the reality of the phenomenal world.... Second, these genes also contain gentleness; they are ever so loving, which goes beyond just being kind.... The buddha-genes are also full of a sense of humor and delight, which is referred to as *great joy*."[xii]

One of the most important teachings of Buddhism says that there is a fundamental difference between the way we think about the world, our own existence, and our relationships and the way things actually are. The point is made that our everyday experience tends to relate to things, others, and ourselves as if we are all entities with an independent, definable, self-enclosed, discrete and enduring existence. We believe that we have certain essential characteristics that define who we are and that our physical, mental and emotional processes constitute a separable personality whose very existence has an intrinsically independent existence.

Yet if we examine deeply any of our self-concepts, we find that they are simply assumptions and do not correspond with physical reality. All things, events, and relationships, whether material or conceptual, lack any independent, inherent existence. For anything to have the qualities of inherent existence, they would need to be complete unto themselves and therefore entirely self-contained, unrelated to or influenced by any other phenomena. But we know this is not the case.

Emptiness

We realize that everything is relative and that they do not possess an immutable essence or intrinsic characteristics. Buddhist writings refer to this fact as demonstrating the "emptiness" or *shunyata* of the phenomena in that they are empty of inherent existence. Buddhist teachers suggest that the failure to remain conscious of the absence of intrinsicness leads us into acting as if what we like is inherently likable and what we dislike is dislikable. This leads to misguided attachments and repulsions, and it is these reactions that set the foundations for suffering, superficiality, narcissism, and alienation in the world.

The emptiness that is spoken of in Buddhism has many meanings. It refers to the open nature of all being. Emptiness points to the absence of inherent existence of all things and thus to impermanence. Emptiness indicates the vastness of reality that is inclusive. Emptiness suggests the Essence nature of being that is beyond anything and yet immanent in all things. Emptiness hints at mystery.

The Buddha is not considered a separate, remote deity in some heavenly place, but represents in human form the presence, openness, love and dynamic of aliveness that resides and moves inside each of us, every one of us. Our deepest longings for love, belonging, value, authenticity and freedom motivate us to find and manifest this core of what we are. These are the fundamental qualities of our being and of the world we live in. This is the truth of life and the sacred nature of our being.

3.

FACETS OF INTIMACY

Jesus said to them, "When you make the two one, and when you make the inside like the outside, and the outside like the inside, and the upper like the lower, and when you make male and female into a single one, then you will enter the kingdom."

THE GOSPEL OF THOMAS

Intimacy is what happens when we affirm and connect to life in the moment. Meeting life with the sense of presence, openness and love makes us joyfully, painfully, lovingly, erotically, curiously, and knowingly intimate. Intimacy is direct, subtle, simple, complex, desirable, frightening, explicit, everyday and sacred.

Intimare and Intimus

We are intimate when we experience closeness, a sense of familiarity or knowing with what is innermost and essential. The word "intimate" derives from the Latin word "intimare," *to make familiar with—to make known* and "intimus," *innermost*. In our experience, it arises when we sense an emotional connection, a kind of bonding or communion, a sense of knowing and possibly being known, and a feeling that a deep and sacred part of our being is engaged. Through intimacy the core of our being is touched or affected in some way. We can be intimate with a lover, a child, a friend, a partner, with ourselves, with nature and the world around us, and with the Sacred. Each person experiences intimacy in his or her own way. All intimacy gives us a sense of belonging, of home. Intimacy creates a sense of home.

The promise of intimacy is found in all arenas of life. For example, in working with a group of colleagues to finish research projects when I was a professor at the university, we developed such teamwork that we could collectively arrive at a vision of what we were writing and of the tasks involved and then work separately in an integrated way so that the individual contributions fit readily in a whole. We all sensed being intimately connected to each other and mutually dedicated to accomplishing our goal. The bonding from those relationships was close and endured for years even as job circumstances changed for various team members.

Experience with Teachers

In studying with my spiritual teachers, a profound closeness and knowing has developed that transcends time and space. I sense that we meet in a profoundly sacred heart space that involves the essence of my very being and creates bonds between us that embody love and compassion and a mutual dedication to not only personal spiritual growth, but also service to the world. As both a student and teacher, I have sensed that depth and breadth of connection and love that develops not only between teachers and students but also among spiritual practitioners and members of a religious community. The intimacy is not confined to human relationships; rather it extends to nature and to the entire domain of the Sacred, to the Divine.

The collective and sacred dynamics of intimacy occur in long term relationships, in ongoing social settings, and in spontaneous situations where people come together for a common purpose.

A few years ago, my wife and I and more than a dozen of Julie's closest friends, gathered around her bed in the small intensive care room for her final hours. This community of friends came together to weep, laugh, share, sing and support Julie and each other. With the blessings of the hospital staff, we spontaneously created an emotional and sacred send-off for our friend who was dying. The warmth in the room contrasted with the wintry weather that each of us had come through to be present to give our parting gifts to her during her final hours of life.

During these hours we shared stories and feelings with Julie and each other. We made music and sang. Each of us, having followed our own spiritual paths, were conscious of the momentousness of death, of the reminder of our own mortality, of bearing witness to Julie's passing, of the impending loss of a dear friend whom we had cared for during her many months of illness, and of the sacredness of this transition. We created bonds of intimacy as we spoke, listened, passed around food, collectively massaged her body, cried, laughed, and interacted with the hospital staff to enlist their support.

Elements of Intimacy

To be intimate with another person and with life itself means to be fully present, engaged, vibrantly alive, and at home in relationships. In the experience of intimacy, three essential elements are always at play: the closeness of connection, being at home, and caring.

When we are fully present, sensing in our body and our being the aliveness of the moment, we are intimate with life and there is an erotic quality to our experience of connection. This erotic quality is the way we connect to life, ourselves, and each other—by making people and things meaningful, significant, and valuable thereby transforming the raw material of experience into the beauty of loving relationship. We have the capacity to move beyond the simple feelings of happiness, ecstasy and love to the embodiment of these qualities as ways of being. We can actively create an environment for each other that manifests love. To embody love and be intimate with all of life as well as each other opens our hearts, inflames our soul with sacred passion, and infuses our personal and collective presence with joy and compassion.

The essence of all the qualities we want to talk about in this book such as intimacy, love, home, sacredness, collectiveness, beauty, and spirituality are all intangible and ineffable and thus, difficult to put into words. It is like trying to describe the fragrance of a rose. We all know what it is like but cannot find any words that accurately describe it. At best we can point to it using metaphors and stories that can evoke our own experience.

These qualities exist even though they cannot be seen directly or described objectively. In fact we could say that we do not define them, but that they can define us. Collective consciousness, spiritual qualities, and sacred ways of being cannot be intellectually packaged for it is their nature to be fluid, ungraspable, and immeasurable and yet experienced, knowable, and impactful.

On this journey to explore the geography of intimacy, we see that the act of becoming intimate with a heart posture of love transforms everyday reality into the experienced reality of a collective *we* creating a fundamental connection to life, to each other, and to the sacred.

The intimacy we are talking about here is not essentially about sexual or physical interactions and the love is not essentially about romantic love. Sexual intimacy and romantic love are really part of a much larger and more sacred domain of intimacy. We must release our thinking and feelings about intimacy from being imprisoned in the confines of romance and sexuality.

Intimacy takes root whenever we experience meaningful

emotional connection, bonding and communion, a sense of knowing and being known, and a sense of sacred engagement. Authentic intimacy touches us in our very core in some way. Intimacy arises with lovers, children, friends, partners, ourselves, the natural world, and the Sacred. All intimacy creates a home in the relationship, giving rise to a sense of belonging.

Intimacy as personal and mutual experience is the presence and connection in the moment. From the personal point of view it is the experience of connection, bonding, being the shape of the moment, becoming the shape of the flow of the moment, and the openness of awareness, the radiance of the energy, and the union of the personal and the collective.

From the collective point of view it is the integration, interconnection and interbeing of all forms from the personal to the collective to the universal. It is the integration of all dimensions of being at both the personal and collective levels.

From Awakening to the Intimacy of *We*

Alan Watts stated that "We do not need a new religion of a new bible..." but "…a new experience—a new feeling of what it is to be 'I'."[xiii] I suggest we also need a new experience and feeling of what it is to be "we."

As we are awakened through a spiritual practice, a shock such as the death of someone close, or simply the experience of being in love, we become more present. Our presence leads to more wholehearted engagement in life and an experience of connection. As the sense of connection deepens, we open to intimacy—to deeper knowing and being known and to the sense of home. As the sense of belonging strengthens, so do bonds that mutually embrace us. From this bonding a mutual sense of *we* emerges as does a collective consciousness that becomes a felt knowing in the individuals that make up the *we*.

With the development of *we*, our personal universe opens into belonging to a larger social universe. The *we* of a couple, of teams, of work groups, of churches, synagogues, and mosques, of friendships, and of many group affiliations, embeds us in numerous social universes. As our participation and commitment grow and our connections deepen, we can sense a larger collective consciousness operating. We are not only identified with the larger community, but its collective sensibilities begin to be expressed through us. We become a location where the larger body of the community is manifested and acts.

This does not mean we lose our individuality, but that as a member, we are integrated into a larger whole. We are simultaneously distinct, a part of a larger whole, and a particular location where the whole is expressed. This is similar to our physical body where our right hand is distinct from our left foot and they function differently and even separately but they are integrated into one body and carry the genetic information of the entire body.

This sense of mutuality and collective consciousness applies not only to relationships between people but also to our communion with nature and with the Sacred. Intimacy with nature leads to alignment with the dynamics of the elemental qualities that make up life and an interactive and mutual relationship with animals, trees, and plants. In sacred communion, we experience a spiritual presence arising within our heart and mind and know that our life is being crafted by the loving reach of our profound intimacy with the Sacred.

Intimacy calls on our imagination, our capacity to connect, our ability to identify *as*, and our impulse to love, open and be free. It is a manifestation of our human nature and the nature of the Sacred. Buddhism is also about the human design and our potential for living fully, tapping our deeper wisdom, discovering our sacred nature and that of all being, and manifesting that in our lives, relationships, work, and connection to the greater visible and invisible world beyond us.

Intimacy both takes us out of ourselves and into ourselves

more completely and deeply. Intimacy of all kinds puts us on the inside of our experience, engages us in loving connection, opens us beyond the confines of our minds and bodies, engenders a sense of praise and gratitude, involves surrender and service to the loving connection, and evokes from our depths a dedication to aliveness and giving our gift as a gesture of our love and a manifestation of our mission.

In the most intimate moments, we transcend ourselves, opening beyond our own body, our own thoughts, our own feelings. We enter the space and flow of something much larger than personal. We are infused with a sense of the beyond without the thought of beyond.

One of the great paradoxes of intimacy in all forms is that it requires us to be fully and authentically ourselves while simultaneously giving of ourselves wholeheartedly and releasing any self-centeredness. We must live in the middle of this paradox, finding a way to remain present with the demands of both elements. Being genuine requires a deep intimacy with ourselves. Being connected with another person demands that we become intimate with them. Living in the middle of these intimacies places us on the edge of the unknown, a growing edge where familiar habits can be left behind and new possibilities arise.

Intimacy puts us on the edge of the frontiers of our lives. Intimacy offers us the freedom to completely and directly experience everything with all the heat, light, challenge, and beauty of aliveness. Intimacy mobilizes, manages, and directs energy in close relationships. In the process it brings each person into the present moment in each other's presence and into the reality of what is true now.

Intimacy is a home with a welcoming open door. Intimacy involves the constant undoing of one moment into the other, of rigidity into openness, of what has solidified into fluidity. It immerses us in the flow of life energy, and we are carried away by its insistent current.

Through intimacy we establish roots. A tree without roots cannot survive or grow because it cannot absorb essential nourishment. The same is true of people in isolation who have no sense of connection to others and to life. As we grow from the seed of our nature, using intimacy to root in the soil of our life, we sense both the relationship of the Sacred to the everyday and our connection to each other.

Intimacy is more than a worldly dynamic. It is multidimensional and works at several different levels simultaneously. The outer dimension is its socially recognized form, such as marriage, a team, or a friendship. These are all sacred in the sense that they are recognized by and contribute to the well being of the larger community through time. For families, this includes creating a home that not only supports and contains the activities of the family but enriches others who come to visit. This outer hosting plays a vital role in weaving the fabric of community.

The inner dimension of intimacy includes the feelings and heart postures we experience as a result of being together. It is like a garden that must be tended. It is supported by both the outer circumstances of being part of a community and by the quality of attention and energy that is brought to daily activities and connections. When a garden is left uncared for, it deteriorates from neglect. So too does the inner quality of intimacy.

The alchemical dimension is the transformation that occurs within us, within the relationship and in the world as we turn the lead of everyday experience into the gold of benefit, beauty and an environment of love.

Engagement in Relationships as a Spiritual Path

There are many paths to spiritual realization. Some involve renunciation of the world as a member of monastic life. Others point to the life of a hermit or individual yogi. A few see art as a rigorous spiritual discipline. And still others encourage a life of selfless service. The path explored in this book is one of radical engagement in life and relationships. It encourages involvement and bonding beyond the reactive and unconscious attachments of ordinary life such that we transform the materials of the world in the creation of a sacred collective consciousness that will guide our communities to improve the wellbeing of the world and its evolution into the embodiment of sacred wisdom.

The radical themes developed here—intimate engagement in relationships and participation in the evolution of a collective sacred consciousness—are extensions of the notion of the Bodhisattva in Buddhism whose compassion is endless and whose life is dedicated to the enlightenment and happiness of all sentient beings in a world of harmony, peace, and love.

We participate in the universe of the sacred whether we are conscious of it or not. To become intimate and deepen any relationship activates spiritual qualities of self-transcendence, love and generosity. When we remain unconscious, these qualities tend to remain superficial and are often overwhelmed by the challenges of life and of a dynamic relationship. We then fall back on a repertoire of emotional reactions such as fear, anger, and sadness. These reactions often lead to distress, withdrawal, rigidity, and even the loss of connection.

By becoming more conscious we can actively strengthen intimate bonds and use the challenges to deepen connection. By sanctifying relationships we create a force that not only withstands the assaults of our narcissistic, isolating, consumer culture, but cultivates the seeds of wisdom and energizes a collective heart that longs for loving communion with each other and with the sacred. As this sacred community emerges from our efforts, it reshapes and enlarges the temple of our hearts. Each of us realizes that we are a manifestation of a loving divine host in our collective sacred home.

Connecting to the Sacred

By whatever name or label, the qualities, attitudes, and experiences of self-transcendence, presence, love, caring, home, compassion, celebration, clarity, and dedication are spiritual and are central themes in all sacred traditions. In Buddhism these represent the qualities that arise as we recognize the nature of life and of mind through meditation. In Tibetan Buddhism as in Hinduism, qualities of sacred wisdom and power are represented by deities. In Taoism they flow from the cultivation of subtle life energies and the alignment with the way of all being, the Tao. In the traditions of Judaism, Christianity, and Islam, these sacred qualities are incorporated and represented as the divine nature of God.

The superficial and the sacred are two different heart postures, two different ways of perceiving and relating to life, deriving from two different dimensions of awareness. In superficial consciousness we are preoccupied with the surface of the everyday world operating from habitual patterns of thinking, feeling, and behaving. To be trapped in the superficial is to live as if the only things that matter are what we can see, think, and feel as a result of our participation in the material world. The Sacred includes heart postures that are associated with spiritual qualities and powers and is consciously dedicated to a spiritual purpose, orientation, and relationship.

When a new heart posture is taking hold within us, we have to remember to go slowly and be patient with the step-by-step, moment-to-moment, and challenging nature of self-transformation, because we can never predict from our previous points of view the true course of our journey. Yet, once we make the commitment to our own freedom from our reactive habits and feelings and to maturing into a new way of being, our lives are filled with the richness of experience and the vitality of being increasingly present and actively engaged.

The path of intimacy, while including feelings of pain, sadness, fear, and anger, is fundamentally happy. While it takes work, it is not burdensome. It is not heavy; rather, it is enlivening and enlightening. The story of the jewelry merchant and a sales representative of tools refers to this sacred view.

> A jewelry merchant and a tool rep happened to check into the same hotel at the same time. The jeweler had a small suitcase containing his diamonds, rubies, pearls and other jewels. The sales rep had a big, heavy case containing hammers, drills, and other kinds of work tools.
>
> The jeweler asked the porter to take his case to his room while he checked in. The porter came back down to the front desk shortly afterward and put out his hand for a tip. The merchant gave him something. The porter looked at the gratuity, coughed, shrugged, and made it clear that he thought he should be given more. He mumbled that the suitcase was "so heavy" that it was difficult to "drag up the stairs and to the room."
>
> The jeweler said to him in alarm, "If you took a heavy case, you've made a mistake! My case is very light!"

Participating in the practices of sacred intimacy may be intense but they are lightened by the energy of joy and the connectedness of love.

One of our tasks in life revolves around building a sacred home of the world with the foundation of love, the tools of consciousness, the beams of encouragement, celebration, and service, the walls of Compassion, an open roof, and the doors of presence using the blueprint of wisdom. The foundation of love is a mix of significant meanings, deeply felt connections, generous support, and profound sense of interconnection. Our tools of consciousness include attention, intentions, organizing and aligning our energies, an awakened, refined, and disciplined imagination, intimate witnessing, and the process of learning from every experience. Our beams are made strong through enthusiastic encouragement, gratitude, celebration of all the gifts of life and the Sacred, and service to each other, nature and the happiness of all others. The walls of compassion are where we connect to the full human condition and the humanity of every individual and all living beings. Our roof is open to give us a continuous view of and to bathe in the radiance of Essence. Our doorways of presence are where we meet and are met by each other and the world. The blueprint of wisdom trains us in clarity, discriminating wisdom that distinguishes and unifies simultaneously, and integrates the Sacred into our way of being and knowing.

4.

The Sacred Nature of Intimacy

Oh, what a catastrophe, what maiming of love when it was made a personal, merely personal feeling, taken away from the rising and the setting of the sun, cut off from the magic connection of the solstice and equinox! This is what is the matter with us, we are bleeding at the roots, because we are cut off from the earth and sun and stars, and love is a grinning mockery, because, poor blossom, we plucked it from its stem on the tree of Life, and expected it to keep on blooming in our civilized vase on the table.

D.H. LAWRENCE [xiv]

Intimacy as a Sacred Path

Intimacy as a sacred path of consciousness development involves opening more completely to the fullness of our being and connecting to the larger qualities and energies moving within us, in our relationships, and in the larger world of life itself. Intimacy has sacred power, not because we sometimes get glimpses of bliss when we are high on romantic love, but because we relax into a connection that bridges self and other and we take on a more inclusive and self-transcendent heart posture. Intimacy is sacred because it moves us to grow into our great possibilities, using the materials of our reactions as fertile ground from which to grow awareness, love, compassion and dedication to the larger stories of life.

We bring a sacred vision of intimacy into everyday life only by respecting and attending to the details of making our relationships work. The Sacred, in all its greatness and glory, is enacted in the cycles and actions of ordinary life. With sacred vision we honor the rich quality of ordinary things and participate wholeheartedly in ordinary actions, such as walking to the store, cleaning the sink, and greeting our partner.

In sacred intimacy we are not simply friends, lovers, and coworkers. We become spiritual consorts who play an energizing and encouraging role in each other's spiritual development. We seek to awaken and initiate each other into the deeper nature and full magnificence of our sacred being and to produce value, benefit and beauty in the world.

Romantic Love

Passion, particularly the passion of love, has inspired people into action and connection since the dawn of our species. Sometimes it produces moments of divine grace and other times it sweeps us up in torrents of fears and longings that confuse and disorient us, often leaving us out of touch with the other person and behaving in hurtful ways.

A moment of beauty can penetrate to our core and evoke a body-wrenching ache that awakens our desire to sustain that glimpse of connection. When we encounter this with another person, we have little idea where this intensity of feeling comes from or where it will lead or where it fits into the life we have known until the moment before. We become infatuated as much with the aliveness and energy of this passion as we do with the person who stirred those feelings in us.

In our age we are also influenced by our cultural fantasy of romantic love that distorts the courtly love tradition that emerged in twelfth-century France in the poetry of the troubadours. This poetry saw the romantic feelings as a vehicle for connecting with the Divine. The courtly tradition removed the impulse for sacred connection from the domain of religion and placed it in the mundane world. Courtly love in its attention to the connection between a man and a woman still maintained a spiritual emphasis. In fact, its ideal was often expressed in stories of a knight and a lady who would fall in love although she was already married. They would not consummate their love through sexual union but would channel their passion into accomplishing tasks on behalf of their love that would spiritually purify them and lead to their own transformation.

By foregoing the sexual relationship in the mundane world, the knight and the lady would focus their attention on the pure intensity of the feeling and the quality of love within each of them. They would unite the two dimensions of the secular and the sacred. Through his devotion to a woman and her devotion to virtue, they would tap a powerful transformative energy that would be used for their own development and in service to the greater good of the community as represented by the king's court. The court of the king also represented the court of the King in Heaven and the service was both a secular and a sacred service.

This spiritual practice of romantic love took the human desire to connect and the insistent sexual urge for union and directed them into a deep devotion. This devotion provided the juice for accomplishing tasks that simultaneously refined the character of the devotee into a spiritual being, served to benefit the kingdom on earth, and brought the kingdom of heaven to earth through the example of spiritual virtue.

Over the centuries since the time of the troubadour tradition, the spiritual practice aspect of this romantic love has been dropped and the sense of sacred service has been lost. What remains is the sense that romantic love can somehow save us. We often mistake our beloved for the Beloved. Since we do not know how to relate to God, we make our lover our god instead of seeing our love itself as a manifestation of the Sacred and realizing the fullness and depth of love when that sacred dimension is present.

When we realize that love does not reside outside of us in the person of our lover and that possessing a lover is not the salvation from the storms within ourselves, we can begin to transform our neediness and our grasping, and realize the richness of love that flows naturally from the well of our own heart. Having discovered the treasure of our own being, we no longer depend on a lover to evoke love and learn to share with them more fully from the source of love that was always there.

Love

The Beloved is neither a person nor a place. It is an experience of deeper and deeper levels of being, and eventually of beingness itself—the boundarylessness of your own great nature expressed in its rapture and absolute vastness by the word "love."

STEPHEN AND ONDREA LEVINE[xv]

All our growth, service and connection is done out of love—love for ourselves, for other people, for life itself, and for the process of loving and relating. Love is an energy and a sense of connection that engages us in the sacred world. Loving ourselves, loving others, loving life, and loving the Divine are all ways we participate in the interconnectedness of all being and dance with Grace.

Love is the feeling of connection. Connection is the manifestation of love. Love is the expression of radiance. Radiance is the appearance of love. Love is the embrace of openness. Openness is the freedom of love.

The heart posture of love can penetrate the superficial and reveal the inner beauty and sacredness in other people. When we are the recipient of that kind of seeing, we, if we are paying attention, will feel seen. Seen, not in terms of how we feel and our likes and dislikes, but seen in relation to our core nature, our basic sanity and wisdom, and our deepest beauty.

When we are intimately seen in this sacred way, we experience being blessed. When we see in this way, we also experience being blessed. In this very act of seeing with the eyes of love there is simultaneous blessing and the distinction between giving and receiving dissolves as they merge in the blessing of love.

Rabbi Marc Gafni points out that the quote from Leviticus to "Love your neighbor as yourself..." leaves out three words from the passage. The "...complete verse is: 'Love your neighbor as yourself—I AM GOD.' To love your neighbor is to reveal, to disclose, their ultimate divinity."[xvi] When we see with the eyes of love, we are not only perceiving the divine nature of the other person, we can also relate to them as being the Beloved. As Gafni concludes, we identify their goodness, their sacredness, as the "true core of who" the person is.

Miracle of Love

The word *miracle* comes from the Latin *mirari* meaning to wonder at or be filled with wonder. The magic of love is that it opens us to the fullness of wonder in witnessing the miracle of the Beloved manifesting through the one we love.

The experience of wholeness that flows from profound love engenders the perception of the essential unity of all reality. With the eyes of Love, we perceive the Divine in everyone and everything. In intimate relationships, the roles of lover and beloved are mutually shared. When held in the context of the sacred, we realize that our beloved is a manifestation of and vehicle to the Beloved, the Sacred. As a lover we are, as Plato says, *éntheos*, "full of god." As beloved we act as a receiver of god's energy and as manifestation of god as Grace, opening to the fullness of love.

Soul as Lover

We have no reason to harbor any mistrust against our world, for it is not against us. If it has terrors, they are our terrors; if it has abysses, these abysses belong to us; if there are dangers, we must try to love them. And only if we arrange our lives in accordance with the principle which tells us that we must always trust in the difficult, what now appears to us as the most alien will become our most intimate and trusted experience. How could we forget those ancient myths that stand at the beginning of all races, the myths about dragons that at the last moment are transformed into princesses? Perhaps all the dragons in our lives are princesses who are only waiting to see us act, just once, with beauty and courage. Perhaps everything that frightens us is, in its deepest essence, something helpless that wants our love.

RAINER MARIA RILKE[xvii]

When we cultivate the heart posture of love and intimacy, we see with the eyes of beauty, transforming ordinary perception into a vision of the sacred. Living in the Heart Posture of Love, we perceive the Beloved in everything.

The realized sacred lover relentlessly uses the body, life, and the situations with others to transmit love and the sense of true intimacy. We often call these spiritually realized lovers saints, masters, *tsaddiks*, believers, *siddhas*, and bodhisattvas.

In modern life, we have made the province of love captive to romantic love and couple relationships. But love is part of the interconnected nature of all being and all life. The soul is a lover that manifests that love by making meaning and connecting us to the world, the people around us, and to the sacred. Only the expanse of the universe and all life can contain the potential we have as lovers. Our couple relationships are but a room in the home of the world. When we try to cram everything into that one room, they do not fit and many things feel out of place.

When we are intimate with our own soul as lover, we can begin to grow into the heart posture of love. Here love is a way of being, relating and perceiving the world. It can include the emotion of love but is not limited by it. There are at least two directions that emotions can take. They can be reactive, closed, and fragmenting or they can be active, connective, intimate and engaging. The Soul as lover uses the positive capacity of emotion to connect in an active way.

As we uncover and play with our deeper identity as a lover, we are challenged to align our thoughts, emotions, and actions to this loving depth and to have our living presence and everyday interactions keep pace with the emerging sense of being a lover. How do we bring this sense to our roles as mother, manager, attorney, or artist? How do we make all domains of our lives a spiritual practice of intimacy? What changes do we need to make in the way we live to include rituals that will bring forth our love and connection, will support the bonds of intimacy, and will create an environment of home?

In the East, it is customary to greet people by bringing our hands together at the heart and bowing slightly. This is a nonverbal way of saying "The divinity in me welcomes the divinity in you."

Making Meaning as Making Love

The process of turning experience into meaning and of assigning value to some things more than others is a fundamental alchemical cognitive phenomenon. The world simply presents itself to us and we transform some parts of it into a personal abode with our beams of meaning, windows of selective perception, inhabitants of relationships, and the treasures of values. We give form to the chaos of life through our structure of meanings and understandings, create gods to be followed and worshipped through our values, and generate bonds through our caring, affections, and ties to other people. In other words, we set time in motion by weaving a personal history out of these elements, a new and never before seen tapestry taking its place within the palace of life.

The story of Eros and Psyche describes mythologically the psychological and spiritual relationship between our capacity to love and connect represented by Eros and our life force and its capacity for learning and growth represented by Psyche. These lovers are brought together, separated, and reunited in much the same way we go through the process of developing as human beings. In the story, the guiding force for them throughout is the great mother Goddess of Love, Aphrodite.

The story of Eros and Psyche chronicles Psyche's journey as lover of the world, a maker of meaning. Meaning is what animates the invisible world for humans. Having access to the invisible world allows humans to explore, grow and realize potentials that would be impossible if we were confined to the limitations of material sensory experience. We become alive in a world of experiential, metaphoric, and conceptual meanings that give form to the sacred dimensions of life. Eros connects us and Psyche animates to create meaning.

Human beings survive and grow, not through instincts, but through being able to pattern information and make meaning by giving some information and experiences more significance than others. It is our feelings about something that gives us the power to make one thing more significant than another, to connect more with some people than others, and to choose directions for our actions. We are designed to use feelings to create importance so that we can protect ourselves, give direction to our actions, intellectually, emotionally, and spiritually grow, and to form intimate relationships.

Our aliveness seeks connection to everything that occurs in our lives. We want to understand. We want to establish a relationship with the people and things that surround us in the world. This is a kind of love. As we build on these connections, this is called learning. Loving and learning is the nature of our human aliveness. Each of us is a loving and learning being.

The sacred meaning then provides a platform from which we can create beauty and experience intimacy with the Divine in new and profound ways. When we look at ourselves in this way, we recognize ourselves to be lovers who can seek and connect to the force of love itself. We are the mothers of meaning, the invisible yet vital substance upon which our mental, emotional, and spiritual well-being depend.

Living Life Erotically and Intimately

"Eros…the great principle that connects us to things beyond our ego." [xviii]

Our aliveness intensifies through this marriage of Eros and Psyche in the making of meaning and the experience of connection. This is what it means to live erotically, to be fully alive and intimate in all aspects of our lives. Events are transformed into conscious experience of aliveness and meaning by the thrust of the erotic.

When we are fully present and alive in all kinds of situations, we fall in love many times a day. I have noticed during these times that I am moved by the smile on a child playing in the woods behind our house, by the tears of a student, by the song of the warbler in our yard, by the fluttering leaves of the Japanese maple, and by the stroke of the breeze on my cheeks. All of these evoke an intensity of presence, of aliveness, and of love. The erotic is a quality that arises from the spontaneous and open nature of our soul that resonates and naturally reaches out to the livingness that is outside of us.

Being fully present in engaged intimacy, we manifest the erotic marriage of the myth of Eros and Psyche. We feel the energy of excitement and behold the beauty of a friend. We delight in the fragrance of a flower, pulse with insistence of desire, and relax into the welcoming presence of the Sacred. Living intimately in this way, we wholeheartedly connect, we generate an environment through our presence that is open and welcoming to others and the world, and we make contributions and create beauty as part of our dance with life and each other. To be intimate and erotic, we are engaged heart to heart, live hand in hand, and work shoulder to shoulder with each other and with the sacred dimensions of experience.

Passion is the feeling of life wanting to connect with life; life inside us connecting with life outside.

WELWOOD[xix]

I can remember one spring morning early in April of 1977 when I was on my way to teach a class at the university. I had been a meditation practitioner for years. I was also going through a difficult emotional period being separated from my first wife and engaged in negotiations for an unwanted divorce. I had also recently resigned as director of a research institute because, after six and a half years of founding, building and maintaining the organization, I was burning out writing grant proposals, producing monographs, keeping people employed, managing the dynamics of a staff of thirty people, heading a teaching program, and teaching.

On that morning, the trees were just beginning to bud and the umbrella of sky was not yet obscured by a canopy of leaves. My eyes fixed on nothing in particular and yet a feeling of profound, ecstatic love spontaneously arose. This love was not attached to anyone or anything in particular and yet it connected me with everything, openly and unconditionally. My entire body vibrated with sensation and my heart, not residing inside my body at that moment, felt like it was a vast universe that embraced life itself.

In that moment, which lasted for days, I experienced being more present, alive and awake than I had ever been before. I was intimately at home with myself, the world around me, my family and life itself. Even as I went about the day teaching classes, meeting with students, walking along a river, and having dinner with my children, I rested in a core of vibrant stillness, encompassing silence, and embracing sense of love. I was inside a sacred way of being and my presence radiated that love to my children, my students and my friends.

When we are intimate in all domains of our lives, every activity becomes a way of making love—working, driving, walking, reading, writing, making music, drawing, arranging flowers, teaching, learning, engaging in sex, conversing with friends, worshipping, meditating, praying, doing service, taking political action, eating, and simply listening to birds singing. In the freshness of each moment we learn the secret of falling in love over and over again, not only with our partner but with life itself.

What would it mean to be intimate while cooking a meal? Our presence would meet the ingredients through our senses. We would use our imagination and creativity to decide, plan, and improvise in preparing the food. We imagine that each dish is infused with the sense of our caring and desire to nourish and delight.

For me, in the process of writing, my presence is meeting the presence of the subject as well as the computer or the pen and paper. I enter the world of the subject and its innermost teachings become my guide in navigating its landscape. My curiosity and my delight in the glimpses of understanding that come propel me further into that world. I am in touch with a great longing to dance with the inhabitants of that world and to be shaped by the encounter. I also sense how this world is connected to all the other worlds I know of and to many that

I can only guess. And finally, I am fully awake and ecstatic in the aliveness of the whole endeavor. In writing I experience the marriage of Eros and Psyche, the union of love with my life force. I am living and creating inside the Sacred.

Being Inside Changes All

Long ago in the province of Jiangxi, Zhu and his friend Meng entered a rather plain looking temple in which there were no meditation cells and the only inhabitant was an old, shabbily dressed priest. Spying the visitors, the old monk straightened his meager garment and greeted them with an offer to guide them in learning about the many statues of the immortals and the images of animals and people painted on the walls. The paintings were especially realistic and impressive.

On the eastern wall, among a group of fairies, stood a young woman with the loose hair of a maiden whose smile was particularly radiant as she was plucking flowers, and her cherry lips seemed to move. Even her eyes appeared to sparkle with moisture.

Zhu contemplated her a long time, unable to take his eyes off her. Suddenly everything around him except the picture vanished and he found himself floating in air as though he were riding a cloud. He passed through the wall into a place unlike any he had ever seen. Then he was in a crowd, listening to a teacher transmit the way of the Buddha. After a few moments he became aware of someone gently tugging on his sleeve. Turning, he saw it was the girl in the picture. She then walked off laughing. Zhu followed her to a small apartment. He hesitated to go in until she waved her bouquet of flowers in a gesture letting him know that he was welcome to enter. Inside, he was alone with her and instantly embraced her—without any resistance on her part.

They lived together for a number of days. Her sisters came by and, finding the lovers together, they laughed with a mix of joy and sibling teasing: "Dear sister, now that you'll soon be a mother, how is it that you still do your hair like a maiden?" They brought her hairpins and ornaments and helped her to tie her hair, as she sat blushing.

After they departed, Zhu decided that she looked as a matron even more beautiful than before. The crowning bun and ornamental pendants suited her face perfectly. He took her in his arms, caressed her, and inhaled the sweet fragrance of her being.

Interrupting their intimate embrace of love and happiness like eternity, there suddenly arose a clamor of shouts. A voice from outside seemed to be calling out, urgently asking if there was a human hidden in the house. The young woman told Zhu to hide under the bed and she disappeared out the back door. Zhu obeyed her instructions and hid under the bed, hardly daring to breathe. He stayed there for what seemed like hours. In this hidden space, his ears began to ring and his eyes burned with fire. His heart felt like it would burst. He could hardly bear it. Yet, he stayed still and waited for the return of the girl.

Meanwhile, Meng had noticed that his friend had disappeared. Wondering what could have happened, he asked the old priest where Zhu had gone. "He has gone to receive teachings on the way," replied the priest. "Where?" asked Meng. "Oh, not very far, in fact quite nearby." The old priest knocked on the wall and called, "Friend Zhu! How is it that you take so long?" At that moment the likeness of Zhu appeared on the wall, his head tilted in the posture of one who is listening. The priest continued, "Your friend is waiting for you." Zhu promptly descended from the wall and stood before them shaking and with his eyes wide open.

Meng was startled but asked him calmly what had happened. Zhu, still experiencing the seamlessness of his experience, could only think that while he lay hidden under the bed, he had heard a thunderous din and had rushed out to see what it was.

Returning once more to the realm of the temple, he turned to the picture and noticed that the young woman in the picture had taken on the coiffure of a married woman. Zhu, smiling with a mix of wonder and delight, looked at his friend and the priest. Meng gazed in amazement for he saw the difference as well. Zhu asked the old priest what it meant. "When we become intimate with something or someone we change and their appearances take their shape from the way they are seen, particularly with the eyes of the heart. What other explanation can I give you?"

The answer took up residence in Zhu even as he did not entirely understand. His friend remained somewhat anxious about not being able to make sense of it all. And so the two descended the steps of the temple and walked away.

The Beloved

The heart posture of love is the way we practice connective intimacy. In fact all the sacred heart postures of connection are ways of practicing and realizing intimacy with what the Western mystical traditions call "the Beloved." When we speak about the Beloved, we are really including the fact that the Sacred is love, lover and Beloved. All love is sacred. All acts of love are expressions of the Divine lover. All experiences of being loved are the Beloved receiving its sacred expression through us. Divine love is the infinite background to finite love. It is the supreme matrix within which all meaning, love and connection arise, are sustained, and eventually dissolve. Just as the eternal is experienced in the full presence of each moment, so eternal love can be known in the experience of particular love now.

Our soul is a lover of life as a way of embracing engagement with all reality, a lover of being as a way of opening to Essential intimacy, a lover of becoming, manifesting, creating beauty and having an impact as a way of expressing creative intimacy, and a lover of learning as a way of consciously knowing, growing and integrating all forms of intimacy into inclusive wisdom. When we embody the sense of love as a way of being, we experience happiness and freedom through that unreserved, unconditional love.

When we affirm all life with our presence, we are met with the presence of the world in a fully enlivening way. Our intimacy in the moment reveals the face of the Beloved that is always there but hidden behind the veils of our superficial distractions and reactions. Through experiences of profound intimacy, we come to know the nature and pervasiveness of sacred love.

Sacred intimacy encourages us to channel the often hidden dimensions of emotions toward the realization of the reality of unconditional, boundless, fully inclusive, and supremely satisfying love. This path of the heart emphasizes communion, connection, and devotion. In devotion we dissolve into Divine love, into the essence of love itself. From a spiritual point of view, when we fully realize and embody intimacy with the Beloved, we and the Beloved become one. Then our every thought, feeling and action expresses and manifests spontaneous sacred love. Our entire body and being are transformed into the radiance of pure, unconditional and unconditioned love.

The Divine as Beloved is clearly revealed in the marriage of two lovers. I have had the privilege to attend and perform a number of weddings and I am always struck with wonder at the sacred beauty of each event. A very special dynamic is happening in the wedding ceremony as the bride and groom stand together and the community is present. A sacred force enters the gathering at that time and our hearts are touched. It is not only the wedding couple who stand in awe. All of us who participate in and witness the ceremony weep at the beauty of the presence of the Beloved being enacted by the lovers who are being joined in a holy way. The Beloved Presence in each of us is released from the secret chambers of our heart to join the sacred circle of celebration of the marriage. The tears dissolve the veils of habit so the lover in our soul can shine through our eyes and radiate from our very being. In that moment we can also get a glimpse of the oneness of all being in the Beloved and the interconnectedness that flows from the collective experience of wonder.

Sacred intimacy takes form as an act of and expression of love. This form can be a special person, a creation of beauty, or the smile of an infant. When we love these forms, realizing that they are manifestations of a supreme form, we connect to the reality beyond form. Through loving in this world of people and things we also connect to the larger reality of the Sacred and the Oneness of all being. We find a home in the diversity of the world while simultaneously experiencing the embrace of the universal One.

Sense of Home

The longing to feel and be an intimate part of some whole, to experience belonging, is a desire to be simply "who we are, without reservation and condition." This sense of belonging is often called "home." Relaxing into the sacred nature of our own being, into the flow of life unfolding, and into the embrace of intimate, collective relationships brings us home. We sense being at home not only in ourselves but in the world in a profoundly spiritual way. This is not a personal abode but a shared home that encompasses both inner and outer worlds in a beautiful landscape that nourishes us and that we, in turn, support through our loving participation and contributions.

Belonging

Our bodies know that they belong; it is our minds that make our lives so homeless.

JOHN O'DONOHUE

In the experience of home, we dwell in the felt environment of belonging. "Belonging" brings together two fundamental qualities of human experience: being and longing. In a sense we live with the longing of our being and we face the challenge of being with our longing. When we realize our essential belonging, we sense the living, passionate presence of our soul. Belonging is at the heart of connection and provides the warmth of intimacy. Belonging is the glue that binds each of us to the sacred, to life, to each other, and as a community.

The fragmentation and dislocation of modern life can make us feel like outsiders, exiled from the intimacy of true connection to our own authentic being, alienated from each other and Creation itself. Our longing draws us toward belonging. We long to come in from the cold of individual separation and be at home again in the embrace of a larger belonging. Through belonging, we transcend our tendency for self-concern and the obsession that flows from loneliness, finding the joy and power of connection. Belonging confirms in us a sureness of heart that can endure and even grow from the pressures and confusions of life.

During the initial phases of our journey, the experience of divine love, human love, and even the sense of love comes and goes. It is not a constant presence. Yet the memory of loving connection can take root in our being. Then it provides a context and inspiration for our potential as lovers and how we can connect to new situations and people. The possibility of intimacy and love becomes an environment of belonging for other experiences as we maintain our inner sense of home.

Home and Love

Eden is that old-fashioned house
We dwell in every day
Without suspecting our abode until we drive away.

EMILY DICKENSON

The Zohar teaches that every erotic inside experience is a Shechina *experience of the Holy of Holies. It occurs when we become one with the way, when we have moved from the outside to the inside. It is in this sense that the Temple is called in Hebrew the* bayit, *which means, quite simply, 'home.' The holiest place in the world—is home. Eros is about coming home.*

MARC GAFNI [xx]

Intimacy may not increase our pleasure but it will make us feel at home—in being, in the sacred, in life, and in the world. Intimacy always brings us home, whether this is through a deep intimacy with ourselves and our own nature through meditative solitude, through being fully intimate with a lover, or through wholehearted, celebrative intimacy with the Divine, the Sacred.

We experience a sense of home partly through relaxing into ourselves and each other through a mutual acceptance. We find a place to fit where we accept ourselves, each other, and the reality that relationships do not measure up to ideals but can be informed by them to move in the right direction. The sense of home in relationship engenders a sense of *gratitude*: being thankful for what we *do* have instead of what we *do not* have. We relate to life and each other more with a sense of *praise*. We come to value difference, let go of resentment, release regrets, to forgive transgressions and wounds, to care, and to place another ahead of ourselves.

In Buddhism great emphasis is placed on the cultivation of gratitude—gratitude for this precious life, for the opportunities afforded in life, for wisdom teachings, for the multitude of ways that life is supported, for the blessings of spiritual teachers and masters, and for the possibility of being a beneficial presence and making contributions in the world. Gratitude takes us beyond ourselves into the world of connection and support.

Gratitude is not simply some warm and fuzzy feeling that

passes quickly. It is a heart posture that allows us to see and experience how gifted we each are by the blessings of life and even its painful challenges.

While on the surface, intimacy appears deeply personal, when we get to the core we realize that we are involved in a universal and sacred connection. Within the personal home of love we find the greater home of the Sacred. This is a home that is portable, like the god of the nomadic Hebrews that was and is always present. Even when we feel lost, we can always come home again by simply being present in the here and now.

In our spiritual journey, just as the mind can fall open to pure or naked awareness, so the heart can fall open to the pure connection of communion and interbeing. In spiritual work we reach a point where we can grow no further unless we acknowledge our interconnection to others. The way is only opened by love and compassion.

Gratitude

The spiritual definition of theft *is taking without being willing to grant the gift of receiving. We seek gratification of all forms without wanting to give of our souls in return.*

MARC GAFNI [xxi]

To receive a gift well makes us a giver to those who give to us. Gratitude opens the heart of love and radiates the power of that love to the giver.

Gratitude itself can become a heart posture so that we relate to everything as a blessing. Rather than wait for some final satisfaction in order to feel grateful, we hold the sense of being blessed by all the little things we are given. We feel spiritually alive in the satisfaction of the moment. In this way our gratitude generates fulfillment and fills the universe with the blessing of our love.

In a sense, life itself is a sacred gift that we need to open and make the best possible use of. Using it well is a form of gratitude. Our sense of love is part of the gift of God's love and our gratitude for this gift connects our love to the larger Sacred Love. The beauty of our gratitude and our love is our gift to the Sacred.

5.

A Home in the Heart

Loving and Giving

Intimacy involves participating with others in ways that we naturally give of ourselves. Whether we are giving pleasure in sexual intimacy, giving from our heart in sharing, giving our gifts to the community or giving of our loving nature in creating a welcoming, supportive environment for those we live with, the desire and pleasure of giving flows from our heart posture of love.

Being a lover means that we invest our attention, caring, and energy in not only our romantic and family relationships, but in our relationships with friends, coworkers, and even strangers. From the heart posture of love we treat the stranger as our guest. We welcome him or her with the care and generosity of spirit of a gracious host. Our love is a way of being, of perceiving, and of relating to life, in other words a heart posture. The more we give, the stronger this posture of the heart becomes and the closer our connection to all life.

To have love as a ground of being does not always involve the feeling of love in every situation. It is more like the background atmosphere of our being that hosts all the other feelings that arise, including our upsets, disappointments, frustrations and dislikes. Our heart posture of love is not conditional upon the passing feelings of the moment and yet it does affect how those feelings are experienced and expressed. From the conscious ground of love, we no longer get hijacked by the feelings and reactions or, if we do, we rapidly recover our deeper sense of our loving nature and our fundamental connection to those with whom we may be upset.

Love and Space

Intimacy takes us beyond space and time. The sense of connection can be present whether our lover, friend, child, parent or coworker sits next to us or is traveling in another country. One of the wonders of intimacy is that we may, at times, feel closer to someone when we are not physically together. Our thoughts, feelings, and love give them a central place in our heart and we sense the degree to which they are an integral part of our being. We experience the aliveness of our connection to them.

We may not have seen a close friend for years, yet, when we get together again, it may seem like no time has passed and that the bond feels alive and real.

The same is true of our relationship with the Beloved. We may spend long periods being distracted and distressed, but when we can remember our basic nature and the fundamental connection we have to the Sacred, we instantly come home. In this home of love, the present moment fills our consciousness and where we are includes all that is.

Rabbi Gafni relates the teaching of a wise Jewish master from Babylonian times who said: "*It is written that God withdraws his presence from the world to dwell in the empty space between the cherubs in the Temple. But how could this be? Is it not also written that all of heaven, indeed all the space in the cosmos, is not enough to contain divinity? 'Ahh,' says Master Yusi. 'It is to be likened to lovers. When they quarrel, even a palatial home is not enough for their needs, but when they love, they can make their bed even on the edge of a sword.*" (Italics are Gafni's) [xxii]

The Risk of Loving

Love opens us to both the outer world of other people and their unpredictable behaviors and feelings and the inner world of our tender wounds, fears, longings, and sensitivities. There is no protection from being hurt in a fully intimate relationship. Wounds will happen, most of the time inadvertently and unintentionally. These wounds challenge us to grow, to incorporate their healing into the relationship, and to find ways to deepen the bonds when they occur.

It is said that our heart must break for it to open and when it opens, we grow. When our heart "breaks open," the bands and shells around the core of our being crack and expose the part of our nature that is profoundly affected by experience. When we are open in this receptive way, we sense the living presence of the world and each other.

This does not mean we should subject ourselves to patterns of physical, verbal, or sexual abuse. Dealing with these challenges involves confronting such behavior and removing ourselves from harm's way if patterns are not changed.

It is important to make a distinction between a generally healthy and supportive relationship and one that is basically unhealthy and unworkable. In an unworkable relationship, your home environment is extremely unpredictable, unsupportive, ravages your sense of well-being and stifles spontaneity and expression of loving and joyful feelings. The relationship deadens rather than enlivens you and/or your partner.

The reasons for unworkable relationships are usually complex and, even where fighting and addiction are involved, often include a distressing dynamic between both people. It is not a matter of assigning fault so much as seeing that whatever you are doing does not work and is hurtful. You may be simply mismatched and need to end the relationship rather than remain locked in an unwinnable struggle.

The key perspective here involves never seeing ourselves as victims. Rather we come from the desire to maintain the integrity of the well-being of ourselves, others, and the path of growth. We do not placate destructive situations in the hope that others will love us. We remain committed to what is going to create benefit, beauty, and love on a foundation of basic sanity and wisdom.

Even opening to the possibility of a healthy relationship involves taking risks. While we may not see it so clearly, not choosing a love relationship is also risky. Not engaging in love relationships often leaves that part of our being that has been awakened restless, dissatisfied, and disappointed. If by choice or circumstance, we do not pursue the intimacy of love, it is vital to be conscious of the wound of unengaged love and to experience and channel the energy of those feelings into loving life and the world in all its joyful and painful aspects.

In long term intimate relationships, the vitality is maintained by periodically sharing our vulnerabilities with real honesty, taking an inventory, asking for help, being willing to be dependent, allowing ourselves to be shaped by the course the relationship takes, and being willing to serve our partner and the relationship. The sense of hazard plays an enlivening role in the growth of each of us personally and in our relationships.

There is no shelter in a relationship unless there are doors and windows through which fresh and unknown forces can enter. These edgy, sometimes chilly, and often refreshing winds of change and movement keep us more fully alive. Otherwise, without the openness, the relationship becomes a death chamber slowly depleting the oxygen as we struggle to live on the remaining air until finally there is no more. Something inside us becomes dormant, as if dead.

When intimacy flows from the heart posture of love, we openly offer ourselves to the wonders and challenges of relationships without the fear that we are being or could be diminished. The very vitality of the moment nourishes and enhances our soul.

Love both binds and frees. It releases us from the straight-jacket of reaction, free to follow the calling of an authentic bond. The spiritual practice of love is about creating the conditions for an authentic freedom, experienced at the very core of our being, through our engagement with life and others in intimate bonding.

Hero's Journey of Lover

Each of us must make a journey, a hero's quest. This is a journey without a specific destination and yet it takes us home, reveals our deeper nature, cultivates wisdom, and provides opportunities for us to realize our full potential for bringing our special gifts to the world. In this quest, as we move, however awkwardly and slowly, we are being refined and shaped by the divine carver to highlight the features of our true beauty. As we face the many challenges of growth, we are transformed by the fires of dedicated desire and hard experience into a powerful instrument of Divine Love and generosity.

Intimate relationships provide a home base for each of us to pursue our quest, to make our particular journey. As partners, parents, and friends, when we let go of our agendas for each other, we open to fully supporting their growth in bringing their unique gifts to the world, not simply to us.

Intimate relationships also provide a home in another, more profound way. As we bond and come to know each other, we create the conditions for being inside each other's world, knowing what it is like to inhabit that way of being, and sensing the deeper levels of wisdom nature that can be revealed and realized. From this communion, we experience and come to embody a deep sense of our essential unity, beyond identities, issues, support, and ideas of us. We are love. We are the Beloved Sacred manifesting through us.

6.

Five Sacred Intimacies

Trungpa Rinpoche taught that all reality was sacred when we have developed sacred outlook. From a Buddhist view we see the world as a sacred realm, as a "mandala of enlightened mind." In this mandala, we can see five styles of energy and ways of relating, also called *buddha families*: *ratna*, *padma*, *vajra*, *karma* and *buddha*. One or more of these can be used to describe a person's intrinsic perspective or stance in the world, their heart posture. The dynamics of each family can have either a reactive superficial or an enlightened sacred expression (its wisdom quality) in the thinking, actions, and ambiance of each person, depending on their consciousness.

Buddha Families

The dynamic quality of *ratna* is presence and its sacred expression is the richness of all experiences and reality incorporated in the wisdom of equanimity.

In the *padma* family, there is an intensification of presence in the passion of connection and its sacred expression is an appreciation of everything in its own distinct way and everyone in their own uniqueness that leads to the warmth of connection and compassion.

The quality of *vajra* is clarity and its sacred expression is the mirror-like wisdom of insight. This quality brings together all the elements of paradox and complexity in the penetrating clarity of its insight and the union of its embrace.

The *karma* family is associated with action and the dynamic of constant change. Its sacred nature is the process of creation and the wisdom of beneficial action.

The five buddha families and the wisdoms they represent are each present in the others. Which quality is predominant depends on the perspectives and circumstances that characterize a particular situation or focus of our attention. The five families are eternal prototypes, spiritual proto-images, the ever-present formative principles and configurations of the immanent qualities in every living being, just as the flower is immanent in the seed.

The dynamic quality of the buddha family is spaciousness and its sacred expression is the wisdom that hosts everything even as it is beyond everything, is all inclusive, and is immanent. It is the Essence nature of all being and all experience.

Sacred Intimacies

My experience over the years of practice with these buddha families has been that five types of intimacy emerge that roughly correspond to these sacred buddha views and principles. These are engaged intimacy, connective intimacy, insightful intimacy, creative intimacy and Essential intimacy.

Each of these intimacies is cultivated by a posture of the heart. Engaged intimacy is sustained by the heart posture of presence. The heart postures of love, caring, and compassion illuminate connective intimacy. Our heart posture of clarity and dedication to continual growth manifests the insightful intimacy of wholeness. Creative intimacy emerges from the heart posture of celebration and always creating benefit and beauty in our minds, words, and deeds—always generating beneficial karma. When we realize the empty and immanent nature of Essence, our Essential intimacy engenders a heart posture of openness and wonder at the vast mystery of life.

Engaged Intimacy

Engaged intimacy affirms *what is* through the fullness of presence. Our presence meets and dances with the presence of others and the world. We experience the reality of all *that is*, with all its richness, and are included and engaged in that reality in the moment.

The word *presence* suggests a state of being present here and now in a way that engages our attention. It is perceptible as immediate and real. The Indo-European root of the word *present* is *es* meaning *to be* and the derivatives of this root include *yes*, *essence* and *entity*. Another derivative of this root in Sanskrit is the word *bodhisattva*, one whose essence is enlightenment, which we will discuss later in the book.

With the heart posture of presence in engaged intimacy, we see everything just as it is and we are just as we are as another living presence. The fullness of our presence can include and host everything *that is* and all that is arising. Our awareness is open and fresh and we experience a sense of home in the fullness of the encounter of our presence and that of the other people and life. Our basic dignity manifests through our affirmation of life implicit in the act of presencing *now*.

The *presence* of engaged intimacy involves vibrant alertness. Alertness is the marriage of attention and aliveness. In fact, the alertness of presencing combines awareness, energy, and a sense of direct connection with the experience of *now*. When we are fully present, we feel an inner sense of sacred connection beyond ourselves simultaneously with the sensations in our body.

Our sensations are a vehicle to the intense aliveness of presence. We experience presence in our hands, our face, our cheeks, our feet and in all our cells. Presence is an attitude toward reality that involves an enriching engagement with life.

Presence empowers our landscape, our skills, and our activities with sacred vitality, making the world a temple where people, things, and settings have spiritual relevance.

Engaged intimacy places our aliveness on the edge. Presencing is the connectedness of that edge. Our sense of being in this moment-to-moment engagement includes the edge and all that is not edge. In this way we learn to see all things as complete in this very moment and to meet that completeness with our presence.

In the ancient Jewish tradition, the lower world of hell is called *sheol*, meaning the realm of diminishing presence. In Exodus (3:14), when Moses asks God to guide him in what to say about who has sent him on his mission, the answer is "Say unto the children of Israel, I AM has sent me unto you." In this frame, the Divine is pure presence.

In the same vein, our sacred maturity includes our ability to show up and be inclusive of everything we experience as manifestations of our aliveness. This carries us beyond our self concerns and into full throttle embrace of life, of others and the world. This includes all the complexity, ambiguity, conflicting feelings, competing desires, and paradox. We do not need to be clear about a right course of action. Rather, we want to be fully present with not knowing and let the energy of this unknown amplify our sense of presence and experience of aliveness.

When we are fully present in a relationship, there is a natural sense of sacred connection. When both of us are fully present in our relationship, this connection deepens the sense of being in a sacred relationship.

Connective Intimacy

Connective intimacy grows out of interconnections to all people, things and life. It is an expression of the intensification of presence as love and represents our relationship to others. The bonding that flows from connective intimacy creates for us and others a home in life and in the embracing world of the sacred.

Like facets of a jewel, each form of intimacy presents an aspect that can be distinguished yet is a feature of the whole as well as an essential ingredient in all the others. So engaged presence is critical for the experience of sacred connection and the soul embraces reality as a lover of life. The soul is also a lover of being and wonder as a way of opening to that which is beyond and immanent, a lover of beauty and creating benefit as a way of expressing creative intimacy and a lover of consciously growing into wisdom as insightful intimacy.

When we connect to life without reservation, we experience the happiness and freedom that flows from being totally in love. To mature we hold no illusions as we grow into the full meaning and possibilities of living beyond the superficiality of our fears, desires, and denials. We find the unconditional love within the conditioned reactions of our habits and the fickleness of romantic love. We open the gate of sacred connective intimacy through surrender, gratitude and praise.

The call of connection is everywhere all the time. Each of us hears the call with our heart but few pause to listen and fewer know how to listen. Our longing is the prelude in a love song of the Beloved inviting us to dance with the Sacred manifesting through and in our relationships. We may go through phases of a love relationship, for example, in which we fall in love as a solution to the problem of our loneliness, become confused when difficulties arise in the relationship, and mature in a deeper perspective of realizing that the Sacred is showing up as our partner. When we live with the heart posture of sacred love, we sense the love that suffuses every dimension of life. In the rapture of this love, the ordinary becomes golden and the everyday is eternally new.

The challenges of life for the soul as a lover, such as loss, betrayal, frustration, disappointment, and longing, can crack the heart open. The energy of these emotionally intense dynamics can be channeled into changing our reactive habits into wisdom when approached with the loving heart posture of love as a guide for connective intimacy. In love, the soul tries to wed every moment, every breath, every thought, and every feeling to a sacred sense of the Beloved. Developing this way of being takes enormous effort with determination and stamina.

Connective intimacy as it relates to relationships is a central theme in this book and its companion guide. In addition to being a personal experience, it is a collective experience of a couple, the basis for the development of both individual and collective capacities for intimate bonding, and the experiential glue for a wide variety of social systems from marriage and families, to social communities, to work groups and teams, to communities of spiritual practice and religious worship. It makes the connection between personal and mutual experience, between personal commitment and mutual responsibility, and between individual behavior and collective interaction. From the perspective of relationships, connective intimacy can be described in terms of three fundamental subtypes: heart to heart, hand in hand, and shoulder to shoulder. These will be discussed later in this book and in greater detail in its companion guide.

Insightful Intimacy

In insightful intimacy we experience the awakened presence of clarity that unites us with life through our awareness. We are freed from the prison of separation to experience union of subject and object, of self and other, and of all the elements of paradox and complexity.

The clarity of sacred insight is able to not only perceive our habitual patterns of reaction, but also to penetrate the superficial layers of the obvious to the subtle yet even clearer nature of experience and the dynamics of life. This clarity involves slowing the rapid pace of thoughts so we can redirect and consciously use attention. By relaxing beyond feelings of agitation and the tensions of conflicting emotions, we can view the perceptual filters that unwitnessed and intense emotions and moods insert into our consciousness.

For example, when our partner is annoyed by our tone of voice, we may feel frustrated and angry that they are not listening to the content of what we are trying to say. Our frustration and anger can further intensify our tone and an escalation of painful feelings can occur. We experience a tear in the fabric of our connectedness. Yet by witnessing our own statements and feelings and those of our partner, we can become aware of the how the dynamic is unfolding. We realize that our emotional charge is rooted in our caring—our caring for the relationship, our caring for being understood by our partner, our caring that the sense of sacred connection be honored.

When we settle into an open heart posture, the clarity of insightful intimacy integrates with the engaged intimacy of presence. Insightful intimacy brings us into direct connection with our basic wisdom nature and supports the cultivation of wisdom qualities as expressions of our aliveness.

Clarity begins with our self-sense. The self-sense is not the same as our identity that is made up of particular concepts about what we are. It is simply the pure sense of existing and being present. It is the sense that there is someone who reads this book, who remembers the fragrance of lilacs, who sees the vastness of the night sky through marble-sized eyes, who has thoughts and emotions, who can imagine worlds that do not physically exist and even travel to them, who can be present, and can simply "be" without having to be anywhere in particular. Sacred insight integrates awareness with our self-sense in ways that harmonize and align our awareness with our behavior.

Insightful intimacy is not a special knowledge so much as a way of relating to experience that is not mediated by concepts or beliefs. It is direct. In this way of perceiving, we experience our intimate witness that is fully engaged, always connected, and unconditionally open. The ultimate result of developing insightful intimacy is profound wisdom.

Creative Intimacy

Creative intimacy realizes the impermanent nature of life in the vital dynamic of change and constant becoming. In creative intimacy, we not only awaken to the lack of inherent existence (nothing exists by itself) and the reality of impermanence (nothing stays the same), but we understand that we are participants and contributors to what unfolds. The Buddhist concept of impermanence is not fundamentally a negative attribute. Rather, it suggests the natural process of arising, of fresh beginning, and of growth. We realize that our own lives are a process in which we can cultivate qualities that enhance our own change as growth. We become the vehicles for the creation of new karma, ideally in the forms of benefit and beauty.

All things come into being according to their design, what some call the intelligence of their kind. So an egg can hatch into a duck and grow according to the underlying intelligence that governs the ways and stages of duck development. The life of each particular duck blends the general intelligence of duckness with the specific characteristics and experiences of that duck. The duck manifests a pattern for duck and the uniqueness of its own unfolding. It is both the same and different. Its design transcends the life of a particular duck and is the same as other ducks and yet the particulars are conditional and changing.

In our lives, while the self-sense appears to persist, the conditions of life change. People we love die. We grow older and will die. Far from living in a static world, we are faced with constant motion and change. We are a part of this process of constant generation, growth and dissolution and death. When we work deeply with our own mortality, the constantly changing world around us, and the incessant flow of inner experience, we can enter the world of motion through dancing with the dynamic scheme of things. As we take the materials of our life and digest them through sacred imagination to create value and beauty, we participate in and contribute to the unfolding of life and experience intimacy with that sacred flow.

As we dance with life in creative intimacy, we also experience being danced. Life forces greater than ourselves work through us. We sense that we serve what is greater than ourselves. By offering ourselves through acts of celebration and service, we enrich the world of meaning and value for not only ourselves, but everybody.

Celebration, as a creative act, opens our heart with gratitude, love and praise. Authentic celebration unites our inner and outer worlds and intimately connects us to the creative forces that shape our personal life, our collective experience, and the cosmos. In the experience of this creative connection, we transcend the superficial and take flight on the wings of the sacred moment. We are swept up by a vortex of sight, sound, movement, and feeling into a realm of being that is continually appearing and disappearing, opening and closing, filling and emptying. We are transported beyond time even as we dance in time. Through prayers, meditations, dance, music, songs of love, joy, grief and praise, and simple listening to profound silence, we enter the world of ecstasy.

Celebration is a creative response to the wonder of sacred becoming and is fundamentally a form of praise. Praise is a creative act of connection. Praise is an act of reaching out and allowing our heart to be touched by both known and unknown wonders. To praise is to manifest creative intimacy as a lover. To love is to value wholeheartedly and to act on that love by praising through word or deed is to transform the superficial into the sublime.

Ritual is one way to bring the elements of celebration as

creative intimacy together. The word "ritual" comes from *ritus*, Latin meaning "to fit together." Ritual weaves the fragments of our lives, personally and collectively, into an intimate fabric of connection and meaning. As social interactions, rituals function to support communities as social systems. In many ritual settings, particularly those of initiation and graduation, the community acknowledges the development attainments of participants and validates social roles based those attainments. In other rituals, our authentic enactment of communal actions connects us and expresses our relationship to both the seen and the unseen worlds. Rituals serve to bring together collective and personal forms of participation as we perform our part again and again with the spontaneity of an open heart experiencing wonder in the moment.

The creation of beauty not only engages the creator but evokes for all who witness and participate a sacred awareness. Beauty opens a door into sacred aliveness.

In creative intimacy, we take sacred responsibility. Namely, we are responsible for creating value, benefit, and beauty from *what is*, no matter how it got that way. We engage in acts of generosity, support, and service to create a loving environment for others and insure justice. Our creative intimacy of service is informed by the sense of interconnectedness and sharing a collective fate. Beyond the feeling of shared fate is the knowledge of our shared eternal radiance as expressions of the sacred life force. This naturally leads us into compassion and the welcome obligation of serving those in need as a way of embracing them as members of our sacred family. Compassion shares our aliveness and creativity in building a more humane and sacred world.

Essential Intimacy

In Essential intimacy we surrender to and embrace the

fundamentally open, transcendent and immanent nature of all being. This relationship with Essence, even if we cannot conceive of the mystery of Essence—buddha nature, God—opens us beyond our ideas, our limiting beliefs and identities, and our tendency toward superficiality. It is inclusive and integrative in that it hosts all that is, is dynamic, free and poised, and its relating is wholehearted and unitive. Essential intimacy, like the dynamic of the buddha family, brings all the dimensions of our being and awareness together into a whole that embodies wisdom.

In the experience of Essential intimacy, we abide in pure, open awareness. In this dimension of awareness, there are no distinctions, nor characteristics, no self or not-self, and yet everything is included. In Essential intimacy, thoughts, feelings, and experiences arise and do not disturb the open embrace of awareness that is beyond all phenomena. We connect to all experience as the spontaneous arising of our fundamental nature that is inherently open and free.

In the mystical traditions, Essential intimacy is often found in the silence. Sacred silence is not the absence of noise. It is the listening of the heart to what is beyond all sound and in which all sound arises. Profound silence hosts all sounds.

In this experience, we merge with everything without reacting to anything. We open to the freshness of each moment, sensing no separation. We realize the Vedic wisdom "that which does the seeing, cannot be seen; that which does the hearing cannot be heard; and that which does the thinking, cannot be thought."

Essential intimacy combines the peace of being "at One" and the attitude of wonder with the miraculous of the hidden as well as the manifest in each moment.

SACRED INTIMACY	QUALITIES	HEART POSTURE
Engaged Intimacy	Fullness of Presence	Presence
	Richness of all that is	
	Vibrant Alertness	
	Personal presence meets the presence of others and the world in the process of presencing	
Connective Intimacy	Bonding to others and the world	Love
	Embracing reality as a lover of life	
	Sense of connection	
Insightful Intimacy	Clarity	Learning
	Witnessing	
	Discernment	
Creative Intimacy	Change	Celebration and Service
	Impermanent Nature of Life	
	Growth	
	Maturity	
	Responsibility means creating benefit and beauty	
	Creativity	
Essential Intimacy	Transcendent and Immanent	Openness and Wonder
	Silence and Spaciousness	
	Beyond	
	Being "at One"	

Relating to Embodiments of the Sacred

In the *vajrayana* or tantric traditions of Buddhism, the Buddha family principles provide a link between our superficial experience and the radiance of the sacred world. By working with the five types of intimacy we come to appreciate ourselves and the world as embodiments of sacredness. As sacred beings we recognize the sacred nature of life and dedicate ourselves to enhancing and enriching the happiness and freedom of all living beings.

Buddhism points to a way to awaken to what is right now and to be intimate with the reality of the present moment, now. The practice calls on each of us to relate to and realize what "is" in the midst of our impressions of what appears to be.

It is the art of being aware as an unconditional open presence and love, just as you are. It is about being intimate whether you are meditating, eating pasta, aerobic walking, making love or nursing a child. It is about realizing and manifesting your Buddha nature, your open, free, awakened and unitive nature as the light of intimate participation and contribution.

We can notice that each moment dissolves into an ever-present new moment. Each distinct moment dies to the next moment yet is not separate in the sense that open presence as a dynamic is always going on.

The Buddhist deity Manjushri wields a flaming sword that cuts through delusion and destroys the sense of separation. It is a sword that unifies and incorporates even as it makes distinctions. This is called discriminating wisdom. The sword of Manjushri kills the pretension of an inherently individual self even as it awakens us into life as a whole human being at one with oneself and the oneness of all life.

In the unity of all being and the nature of existence, our Essence nature is inseparable from the world of form, manifestation, and life. In Zen this is conveyed through many of the koans that are used to awaken people to full realization of the sacred. In one such koan, Zhaozhou is asked "What is the meaning of the patriarch's coming from the West?" The master replied, "The oak tree there in the garden." The question was really asking about the essence of Zen. The response pointed to a particular manifestation of Essence that is here now. Zhaozhou, not using abstract concepts, transmitted to the monk the unity of Essence and Presence, of the beyond and immanence in present manifestations.

Joy

The teachings of the Buddha have resonances in all the mystical traditions. For example, in Jewish mystic teaching, God's presence, the *Shechinah* ("indwelling"), is everywhere—immanent in everything. One of the main objectives for Jewish mystics is to transcend belief in order to experience, act, and embody *d'vekut*, a constant loving awareness of the Divine Presence. This takes us inside the sacred to a direct knowing of God. This awareness and love brings with it intense spiritual joy since the essence of God-awareness is bliss. Being on the inside of the sacred we participate in this Divine ecstasy and are sustained by its energy and embrace.

Joy and pleasure can be experienced on many levels from the superficial to the sacred. While we can enjoy the superficially sensual taste of a chocolate tart, this pleasure will be temporary and can create a hunger for more sweets until we become uneasy with the lingering hunger of not enough or the bloated feeling of too much. Yet if we delight in the taste as an expression of sacred joy and of the intimate closeness of the sacred, then our momentary pleasure opens a gateway into the fullness of presence and ever-present joy of eternal life. Eternal life, from a spiritual viewpoint, is not life extended into an infinite future, but the living moment that is beyond linear time.

One of the wild yogis in a Himalayan village was so poor that he often lived on plant roots he found in the forest. Despite his poverty, he was always joyful. Because of his lack of money, he wore a simple loincloth and nothing else.

One day, as he walked through the village with the dignity of a monarch and the radiant joy of love, a merchant asked him, "How can you be so happy? Aren't you ashamed to be so poor?"

"Why should I be ashamed?" he replied. "Did I steal happiness or poverty from anyone?"

Living as a Sacred Being

Getting a glimpse of our basic wisdom, loving nature is only a beginning. The harder part is living as this nature, this loving presence, being intimate with life and others moment to moment and serving all others through all the distracting and distressing appearances that others present to us. This is where the art comes in. Taking our insights deeper, expanding and strengthening our love, building the emotional, physical, and spiritual intimate bonds to the point where we embody the openness, radiance, and love that is our nature and that of all living beings. We live as an artful manifestation of buddha nature so that the tone of voice, the grace of our gestures, the openness of our posture, and the quality of our very presence are all beautiful expressions of the sacred. This requires years of practice in loving and in receiving and giving the sacred gifts of life.

We are the environment that other people experience and everything we do radiates out and affects everyone else. We are always a presence and our mission is to be a beneficial presence, giving the gifts of our aliveness to others and the world. We have a choice to be a loving presence radiating a field of welcome or to transmit the qualities and energies of fear and neediness. We manifest the heart posture of our being through the way we stand, the rhythms of our breathing, the clarity of our gaze and the words we speak. Our presence and action can support or diminish a loving environment for other hearts and minds.

We are all called upon to live as if we are a gift and every moment is an opportunity to radiate open love. Our shared gifts create an atmosphere of intimacy and our withholdings separate us. As part of the Buddhist path, we are invited to become a *Bodhisattva*. A Bodhisattva is one who is awake, open, and intimately connected from the deepest, wise dimensions of the heart.

Are you giving what you most deeply desire to contribute to those you love and to the world? Are you sharing the gift nature of your life or the contraction of your refusal to live in sacred openness and presence? Do you put conditions on when and how you are willing to be present and love? Do you insist that you will only experience love and caring when your pain is gone, someone loves you, you have financial security, and are successful? Do you fluctuate between gratitude for the gifts of Grace and the groans and growls of dissatisfaction?

Holding back our gifts by waiting until we find the right person, make enough money, or are secure and comfortable, creates inner tension and dis-ease. We limit ourselves and our intimacy with life when we do not live every moment as the most important one now. Suffering is holding back our gifts, denying our true sacred nature, and refusing to outgrow our reactive habits. The sense of ease, of serenity, of belonging, of loving, and of intimacy happens only through our sense of presence now and openness to the next moment.

One of the highest spiritual ideals in Buddhism is to develop compassion for all sentient beings and to work for their well-being and happiness. As the Dalai Lama states: "Although Buddhism has come to evolve as a religion with a characteristic body of scriptures and rituals, strictly speaking, in Buddhism scriptural authority cannot outweigh an understanding based on reason and experience."[xxiii]

In Buddhism nothing of profound value can be gained from gathering information on the teachings of Buddha but must come from direct experience. And the same is true in the area of intimacy. We cannot get what we deeply desire from simply reading a book but must develop insight and capacity from experience.

Relationships themselves are a form of practice in which we need to grow and change, meeting the challenges of our reactivity to each other as well as the possibility of growing together. The deep intimacy of a good relationship brings forth the profound loving nature of our being that is beyond our likes and dislikes, our disagreements, our desires, our past and our future. We experience each other in an embracing, encouraging, and open way that is unconditionally engaged with the reality of what is. This is wholehearted relating.

This wholeheartedness sees the entire relationship and the larger world in each small act. Just as our eyes as small as marbles can perceive an entire mountain or even the vastness of our galaxy, so small acts of kindness and love can be invested with and convey the enormity of boundless love.

7.

Emotions and Connective Intimacy

The more you understand yourself and your emotions, the more you necessarily love God.

BARUCH SPINOZA

Emotions are the way we connect. The range of feelings represents our relational capacity as well as a fire of life. The emotions are the activity of relating, involving perception, recognition, meaning, expression and connection. The activity of the emotional is how we know something is true, how we connect to our own physical and psychological states, how we relate to others, how we relate to the world, to life and to the Sacred.

I am using the term emotion in the broadest sense to include all basic feeling states. These include more than the standard list of emotions such as anger, fear, love, sadness, joy, and anxiety. Feelings such as pleasure, pain, desire, longing, wonder, inspiration, and determination are all part of the sensory system that not only perceives but establishes how we relate to what we perceive. Emotions move not only energy within us but move us as beings into relationship, sometimes toward and close, other times away and distant.

Emotions also reveal a sense of value through our caring. Caring not only creates significance in our world, it energizes us around those significant meanings. Some meanings evoke a great response and others elicit a hardly noticeable excitation.

The challenge we face with emotions is that much of the time we are swept away by them. They arise as if automatically in response to events, what somebody says, or something we see that affects us. When we are reactive, we not only experience the pain of our reactivity but we may develop fear about the way feelings take over and hijack our sense of ourselves and our well-being.

Confusion about Emotions

Our confusion around emotions often leads us in the reactive directions. We wait anxiously for a child who is late returning home from school. Upon her arrival, our relief at her presence can explode in a release of tension in the form of anger. At root even that anger is an expression of our connection and caring.

In times of loss we may be torn between going numb and extreme indulgence in intense feelings. The real challenge of developing a sense of the spirit, of a deeper, more profound sense of life, is learning how to be and live in the middle of strong feelings and pain without shutting down or being overwhelmed.

The confusion about emotions can be seen in some interpretations of spiritual teachings. Some people who see pain and suffering as unnecessary or unacceptable aspects of life approach meditation as a kind of escape capsule. They try to intensify their practice to the point where all sense of connection to the earth and life dissolves. They see meditation as a remedy to their illness or wound.

While I understand that various kinds of ecstatic states can be reached for a period of time in this way, there is the inescapable limitation of needing to stay outside the involvement in this world. It is an attempt to detach rather than to be both involved and unattached. In the escapist approach, emotions of all kinds are seen as afflictions, problematic, and distractions.

My own sense is that the embrace of all being involves the engagement in all dimensions of life for as long as we have a body. Everything is included and is realized as Divine.

Taking a spiritual approach to emotions does not mean that we eradicate the feelings. Buddhism is not about suppressing or repressing anything that is going on internally. Through becoming increasingly aware, we experience more of all the feelings of life, both our own and that of others. This strengthened awareness also helps us to deal with the emotions better by not amplifying them, dwelling on them or getting hijacked by them. We still feel excited, anxious, angry, fearful, happy and sad but we become more agile and free to be with the feelings, to express them when appropriate, to not descend into helplessness and hopelessness, and to stay connected to our deeper wisdom nature, to our partner, and to a greater sense of the Sacred.

One limitation of traditional Buddhist thought is that neither Sanskrit nor classical Tibetan has a word for what we call "emotion." This is not to say that Buddhists did not experience emotions but that in the philosophy there was no distinction between cognitive states and emotional states in the ways that Western thought distinguishes between thoughts and feelings, cognition and emotion, and between comprehension and apprehension.

Buddhism places emphasis on the types of affliction and the wholesome states of mind that we want to cultivate. There is less emphasis on solving problems and being "normal" in terms of the rest of the population and more importance placed on realizing our potential for spiritual development and maturity.

The afflictions, called *klesha*, are inner mental/emotional states and heart postures that distort reality and disturb us so that we lose self-control. We become unable to think, feel, and behave in ways that support our aspirations. These distorted states narrow our perspective to self-concern and self-preoccupation.

In an embracing approach to spirituality, we host all that arises and there is always arising. We host and are hosted. We are always directly connected. We resonate with the songs of the lark, tingle at the caress of the breeze, see the luminous and beautiful contours and colors of lake and mountains, inhale the fragrance of a lilac, and taste the tangy sweetness of an pomegranate. We are intimate with the world and meet all life with unrestrained presence and love. We luxuriate in the joyous embrace between ourselves and life and generate a radiant field of presence.

Spiritual Value of Emotional Engagement

When we emotionally and spiritually engage in the world moment to moment we taste the deliciousness of living life beyond the safety of our habits and reactions. We feed ourselves, our community, and the larger world by the beauty of our tears, our celebrations, our whole-hearted quest to create value. When we express not only the feeling but the larger sense of life, we are participating in the making of a world that encourages, supports, and expands life through time.

The caves of emotion hide treasured meaning and warehouse dazzling images of fears, griefs, angers, of times past, hopes fulfilled and unfilled, and longings waiting to be realized. Rather than live in the dungeon of archaic fears, angers, and crippling grief, we want to build a temple of aliveness, wisdom, freedom, connection, and beauty and take residence there. We welcome everyone and everything to be our honored guest. The path for doing this involves plumbing the depths of these caves and bringing the demons and jewels to the surface of consciousness. There we can work and transform them into the material for spiritual growth, for sharing in relationship, and for creating benefit and beauty in the world. All this creates value from what had been distressing and oppressive.

It is our emotions that open us to the possibilities of larger participation and contribution, even as they threaten to sweep us away with their power. When emotions are in service of wisdom and relationship, not habitual reaction, self-preoccupation and expression, then they bridge our soul and our body/mind.

When we manifest the love and compassion of an open heart and align ourselves in all dimensions of being—from our most material functioning, to our sense of self and connectedness, to the wisdom qualities and energies of the soul dimension, to pure being and Essence—we connect to the source of all that is and evoke our basic wisdom nature that can guide us in the exercise of our true growth and freedom. From this flows a fundamental confidence in being present and relating to all of life. Profound intimacy in a conscious relationship brings forth a mystical union of such intense bonding that we are united with all that is, embraced in the essential Oneness of pure being, pure awareness and pure love.

Compassion and love, informed by wisdom, open our hearts and bond us to life and each other. They profoundly engage the emotional in the service of the sacred. They have the capacity to override and retrain the body of habits or at least interrupt the reactive response. They affirm our interconnectedness, our interdependence, and our interbeing. They can lead to intensity of being and the cultivation of collective as well as individual energy and beauty.

Sacred Passion

We are caught in the dilemma that the intensity of passion brings us close to the sacred and if, uncontained and directed, will destroy us and those we love. We must not mistake intensity for authenticity because only intimacy combined with the clarity of our true nature and presence can bring about authentic relationship.

There is an aspect of the most clear and intense emotions that, beyond being connective, is alive, intelligent and unsettling. These clear and intense emotions move us and situations off stuck places and artificial foundations. Their underlying wisdom penetrates and dissolves pretension and unconscious habit. They are spontaneous and unconditioned. Encounters that flow from these emotions can result in a new, engaged, sacred dance together.

We all, and especially women, have this potential for emotional clarity, intelligence, and penetrating display of wisdom. However, this is often corrupted and rechannelled by our narcissistic and psychologizing culture into the reactive emotions, promoting extreme indulgences in hostile or sad feelings to the point of addiction and depression.

To be present with our emotions without indulging or deifying them and to penetrate through the surface feelings down to the wisdom underneath involves the sacred path of witnessing and working with them to create loving value. Sacred passion sees our true nature, our potential, and our beauty even in the midst of our reactions and distorted feelings that arise from fear, longing, overwhelm and hostility.

By channeling the energy of reaction into the pure sense of presence we open to the experience of the more inclusive heart posture of love. Then our emotions become less responses to the world and more manifestations and expressions of our basic wisdom nature. We become vehicles for the Sacred. All our emotional actions are the awakening and welcoming arms of the Beloved. Even wrath as a display of sacred passion, far from having a harmful intent, can be used as a wake up call meant to dislodge us from remaining stuck in frozen patterns of reactive habit.

Sacred passion fires the furnace of our heart into full

radiance, propelling us along the track of living a life infused with sacred meaning and unrelenting devotion to the Beloved. This passion provides the juice for commitment to the path and mobilization of all our energies in Divine service.

A Passionate Life

Love Song

I have made the lake my lover
caressing my skin as I stroke along her surface
and sink my head in her deep pool.
The ground is my lover,
holding me fast with the hug of gravity
as I relax on her firm mounded body.
The sky is my lover,
opening me completely
and delighting my eyes without limit.
Space is my lover,
Everything arising within it never disturbing its embrace.
The sun is my lover,
my passion and love
reflecting its brilliance and uncompromising fire.
I love and am loved by goddesses and gods,
and yet some would have me myself sell in the market,
You can't be serious!

MARTIN LOWENTHAL

The Holy Longing

Tell a wise person, or else keep silent,
Because the massman will mock it right away.
I praise what is truly alive,
What longs to be burned to death.
In the calm water of the love-nights,
Where you were begotten, where you have begotten,
A strange feeling comes over you
When you see the silent candle burning.
Now you are no longer caught
In the obsession with darkness,
And a desire for higher love-making
Sweeps you upward.
Distance does not make you falter,
Now, arriving in magic, flying,
And, finally, insane for the light,
You are the butterfly and you are gone.
And so long as you haven't experienced
This: to die and so to grow,
You are only a troubled guest
On the dark earth.

JOHANN WOLFGANG VON GOETHE [xxiv]

8.

Meeting in the Home of Presence

Presence

Hebrew mystics made the dazzling claim that the present moment manifestation is actually the name of God. Yah-weh—the God point. The Hebrew God name is an impossible grammatical construction because it is simultaneously past, present, and future, indicating the collapse of time into the present moment.

MARC GAFNI [xxv]

David Whyte points out that we are the only thing in the universe that can refuse to be itself, that can leave parts of ourselves out of our participation in life. When we do not pay attention and are not present, there is no one home to meet the world or greet other people as they knock on our door.

In order to be intimate with the sacred, we must open our hearts, our minds, our very being to let that sacred presence in and to realize that presence that has been inside all along. When we are fully present, totally engaged in what we are doing, intimate with who we are, incorporating our heart and imagination, we are inside the Sacred and manifest engaged intimacy through our heart posture of presence. We are so intimate with life at that moment the sense of boundaries between us and the Sacred dissolve and we are at home in the holy temple of the Divine, what in the mystical Kabbalah is meant by the Holy of Holies.

Every moment is alive, rich, intensely impactful, dynamic and instantly gone. It is replaced by another moment. And another. And another. Eternity is not an infinity of moments. Rather we enter eternity through intimacy with the moment. This moment of intimacy transcends time into the sacred beyond.

Everything we experience is a teaching about the nature of the Sacred as it is being revealed to us. Our open nature actively embraces the massive presence of the entire moment, taking the whole into our bodies and souls as a passionate lover, ecstatic with the vividness of living color, the freshness of wonder, and the bursts of radiant energy. Our exuberant radiant nature enters every moment with everything we have, relentlessly dedicating us to offering our gifts, penetrating and pervading the open moment with light, generosity, and rapture, and boundlessly sharing our essence.

When we attend mostly to our own thoughts and feelings, we live in a cocoon of superficiality and narcissism that imprisons our own presence in our head and body. We only think we are present. Everyone else can see and sense that we are not. To be present means to open to the presence of what is beyond us and always there.

The soul is nourished by lived experience and for experience to be real and vital we must be present in an intimate way with the flow of life moment to moment. Full presence in the moment puts us inside the Sacred as the nature of all that is. Through engaged intimacy we become fully alive and human.

Being fully present opens our hearts to receive the enormous gifts, emotionally and spiritually, that intimacy can bestow. Through the heart posture of love we marry the sense of presence, the clarity of awareness, the joy of celebration, and the openness of wonder with the impulse to intimately bond with the Sacred as Beloved, as lover, as parent, as child, as nature, and as the earth.

Intimacy calls upon us to marry the clarity of mind of presence with the embrace of the heart of love. Conscious relating asks that we stay present, open to life, and vulnerable to the sacred truth of each moment.

The world always greets us as if we are exactly where we are meant to be. The challenge for us involves living in the essential integrity of what is with presence and a sense of connection. To be present is to be intimate. To be present is to live in the middle, to be in the midst of all presences, feelings and contradictions.

Reverence

We are always in the presence of what is beyond us, whether that is another person, a group, or our physical surroundings. Even walking by ourselves in a woods or by a seashore, we are not alone. The naked beauty of the world is offering itself to us if we only open to allow our presence to meet the presence of exactly where we are.

Thus our relations include not only our loved ones, our family, and our community. Our relations include the trees, the animals of the forest, the plants, the grasses, the insects, the fish, and the creatures that live in the earth as well as those on the earth. Our relations include rocks, sand, and the wind.

Being environmentally friendly means showing up with our aliveness and presence and bringing a sense of reverence. Our reverence for other human beings, for nature, for life, and for the Sacred deepens our intimacy with life.

When we greet a lover, a friend, or a stranger, it is our presence that recognizes the sacred presence in the other. The true recognition and acknowledgment derives not from the information we have about each other and the impressions we have. It flows from the sense of being in the particular presence of the Sacred as manifested by the other.

To see and be seen in this way opens the ground of our being so that intimacy arises and heals the sense of alienation and loneliness that can weigh so heavily on our hearts. Fullness of presence with a sense of reverence leads to the experience of love which in turn supports sustaining the sense of presence.

All the way to heaven is heaven.
CATHERINE OF SIENA

The Present Moment

Each moment has its own perfect clarity, so long as we stay fresh for as long as that moment lasts. The keepers of the mysteries know that a moment later whatever has been there has morphed into something else and that only the freshness of open presence can relate to the transformation.

When we are present in every moment, each moment is fresh and new. We experience the fact that this moment has never happened before and will never happen again so we realize how precious it is. Being present, we use the *now* of time to enter into eternity, beyond time, experiencing Essential intimacy.

A moment refers to the world of awareness not the world of time. A moment can be long or short in time. Being present allows us to hold the moment without any conscious effort at holding. We simply are consciously present with the experience of now.

Thus, there are moments and there are moments. They can be small, fleeting and ego-centric or the moment can be huge, transcendent, and ecstatic. We begin by being present in the small moments and cultivate the capacity and qualities of the wondrously vast moment.

The Changing Present Moment

He who binds to himself a joy
does the winged life destroy;
But he who kisses the joy as it flies
Lives in eternity's sunrise.

WILLIAM BLAKE

To treat something in a fresh way, we want to be free of, or at least unattached to, preconceptions and to realize that each moment is full of energy, meaning and implications. In a relationship we need to cultivate a measure of surprise to bring out the richness of the wild as well as the vitality of all the predictable and necessary routines that are the foundation of the relationship as a home.

Intimacy is not static. The contents of our intimacy are always changing. Intimacy is like a river. The currents of the moment continually come and go, yet the river remains. And these currents are sometimes swift and sometimes leisurely. When we are present with the currents of intimacy, we are periodically and unpredictably changing. As in navigating a river, we must pay attention and be on the edge of the unknown, with the poise to respond to unexpected challenges. We, in a marriage for example, must be willing to endure and experience the river's periodic wildness, allowing it to bring forth the wildness in our own nature and the untamed possibilities of the relationship.

Connective intimacy also involves creative intimacy that requires our participation in the face of both comfort and challenges. In the face of our defeats, we must find the core of presence that can celebrate and love. The source of this core is unconditional, not determined by the successes or failures in life.

9.

Becoming Conscious and Maturing

This unconditional quality of love arises from that which is unconditioned in us and responds to that which is unconditioned in another—the heart, that is, our basic openness to reality. *This openness of the heart, which born tender, responsive, and eager to reach out and touch the larger life around us, is not something we have to manufacture. It simply* is.

JOHN WELWOOD[xxvi]

Rabbi Zusya said, "In the coming world, they will not ask me: 'Why were you not Moses?' They will ask me: 'Why were you not Zusya?' "

MARTIN BUBER[xxvii]

"Rather than being liberated from life, *we can be liberated* into *life."*

JOANNA MACY

To study Buddhism is to study the self. To study the self is to know the self. To know the self is to forget the self. And to forget the self is to become one with all the things of the world.

ZEN MASTER DOGEN[xxviii]

The dream of love and the world it promises has entranced us as a culture. This was definitely true for Jinny, a woman in her early forties who had been married and divorced twice and had had a series of disappointing relationships with what appeared to be the men of her dreams. Far from living the fairy tale ending of living happily ever after, she was confronting the reality of not being in a lasting love relationship, of not having a family and of needing to support herself. In all her relationships with men, she would desperately cling to them and placate what she thought were their wishes to such an extent that all they would see was her desperation, distress, and attempts to control them.

When she came to meditation, feeling alone and disillusioned, she wanted an escape from her heartache. As she learned to meditate, she began to fall apart and her dream of salvation through a lover dissolved. During a retreat, she descended into hopelessness for hours. She was becoming disillusioned with her old fantasies.

Gradually in the course of the retreat, as she realized that no one else could save her from loneliness or meet the requirements of her neediness or give her security in the face of life's changes, she relaxed and felt the aliveness of being in touch with certain realities of life. Instead of fighting them, she surrendered into simply being present and feeling the enormous energy of that experience of *now*. In this way she connected fully with herself and sensed her own sacred nature. Over the following months of practice, a deep confidence emerged and she approached new situations with interest and delight without burdensome old agendas.

Consciously Working with Reactive Habits

Buddhist thinking has given a primary place to the role of consciousness in determining whether we experience happiness or suffering and are able to transform reactive habits into heart postures that reflect our basic sanity and love. This enables us to develop wiser ways of being even as we experience the ups and downs of life and the traces of our personal histories.

The intimacy of the Buddhist way does not promise immortality (in fact it makes death an ally and a profound teacher), physical health, pleasure (all life involves pain from time to time), or emotional happiness. It does point the way to the eternal in the moment, the aliveness of engagement, and happiness as a ground of being that can include the feelings of sadness, joy, fear, delight, longing, and peace.

Our reactive habit body has its own momentum and can continue in the tendencies of even highly developed spiritual people. The profundity of our realization does not mean that our bodymind is not affected by past experiences and patterns and present habits, not to mention external situations. This simply is what is. We may change it to some extent but that is not an excuse for not being aware, awake and present right now with those patterns and everything else. Open to the experience of the moment, whatever it is, and offer your gifts of presence and love in the midst of it all.

The persistent pains and issues of self-worth and self-esteem are not necessarily going to be resolved by choosing to follow a path of our heart's integrity, dedication and service. While this is the only way to live out our soul's authentic journey, it does not necessarily change our genetic tendencies toward depression, our desire for the kind of love we thought we should have received in childhood, or our ability to financially succeed in the world. Rather we recognize our limitations and tendencies and do not get hijacked by them. We may even relate to them with a sense of equanimity. At the same time we can practice being open and a loving presence in this very moment and every moment, however problematic our lives and the world seem to be and to remain.

Capacity for Learning

At the same time, in the Buddhist tradition, it is understood that we have a capacity for learning and transforming our ways of thinking, feeling, behaving, and being throughout our lifetimes. Recently, modern neuroscience is gradually coming to a similar conclusion as it moves beyond older assumptions that our brains become somewhat fixed and unchangeable sometime after adolescence. Now some neuroscientists are talking about "brain plasticity" and pointing to the possibility of developing new neural networks throughout our life. Some studies that included experienced meditators found that they have more activity in the left frontal lobe, the part of the brain most associated with emotions such as happiness, joy and well-being.

The idea in Buddhism that we all have the natural capacity for learning, enlightenment and spiritual realization fits well with the findings in the neurosciences that we can learn throughout most of our lives. This suggests that, although it may not be easy, we can, through regular practice, train our minds to improve the capacities of our attention, will, tenacity, stamina, and ways of relating. Athletes and musicians demonstrate clearly the value that prolonged and regular practice can have on our habit body to be able to perform in extraordinary ways.

Conscious States Support Personal and Relational Development

Becoming more conscious not only develops states of awareness, it supports our personal growth. It also enables us to become more fully intimate, thereby strengthening our relationships. Intimate relationships of all kinds also serve to make us more conscious. There is always an element of fragility to life and relationships. We do not want to be consumed by that fact and live in fear and anxiety. Rather the sense of fragility can help keep us more conscious and alert, making our relationships more resilient.

Whether we are driven by *doing* to prove we are good enough, by *having* to prove we are worthy, or by *merging* into the dramas of love and loss, at heart we all long for the depth of sacred belonging as *home*, unconditional giving as *love*, and the serenity and clarity of profound *wisdom*. When we experience being a feature of reality without a separate self, we sense the unity of being and our connection with everything and everyone else. From this heart posture, we are challenged to embody and live this out in our partner relationships.

Every activity, every feeling, and every relationship in your life can be an offering in which you give yourself fully, opening as boundless love and sacred freedom. Make everything and everyone an opportunity for sharing the fullness of your heart and the depth of your soul. Do not reduce your work, your marriage, and your family to dramatic substitutes for the bliss that is at the heart of life and the core of the Sacred. And certainly do not burden your lover, your children, your career with the task of deluding you and placating your desire to hide from the truth and from real intimacy.

Meditation

Consciousness brings us into the present, makes us more intentional and can interrupt the patterns of our reactive behaviors. We can find many devices and practices to help us remain conscious, some that are traditional and others that are creative and uniquely our own. Among the practices that are very powerful, mindfulness meditation stands out as one of the most useful.

The purpose of meditation is to make us consciously aware and to bring us home to our authentic nature—being totally open, boundlessly radiant, and always presencing. The basis of meditation is experience, recognition and cultivation.

Meditation is a path of growth that initially involves relaxing the body and the mind, training the mind to stabilize attention, training the will, witnessing and hosting whatever arises, cultivating wisdom qualities, and training the bodymind to manifest those qualities in our intimate engagement with life.

When we meditate, we begin by consciously placing and maintaining our attention. The capacity for intentionally using attention is one of the precious gifts of life. Attention directs the mind and focuses the range of energies of our being. Attention is a beacon that reveals the nearest and farthest reaches of the inner world and brings the outer world into intimate relationship with us.

We can attend to things, thoughts, feelings, witnessing, and/or the sense of our own being. Our attention can be captive to the content of our mental commentary on what we think of this book, namely the surface dimension of awareness. Or we can intentionally place our attention in other dimensions of awareness such as the sensations in our hands, or sounds in the room, or the value of the suggestions, or the feelings we are having as we read, or in witnessing all those sensations, sounds, thoughts, and feelings.

In the experience of mindfulness we are consciously aware and present in the moment. Mindfulness keeps us present and allows us to see clearly things as they are. Mindfulness is the simultaneous practice of concentration, the ability to stabilize the mind in a state without distraction, and decentration, the ability to open attention to whatever is arising. It integrates insightful intimacy with being engaged through our sense of presence and our connectedness.

As our skill develops with mindfulness, we move from the sense of working hard at it to having it arise more naturally and finally it becomes a stable part of our lives. Initially we apply effort to attend consciously. With practice, our natural awake quality begins to emerge, but it tends to come and go and we move back and forth between effortful and natural mindfulness. Eventually, being naturally awake becomes stable and we can abide and operate from within that state.

In this progression we begin by intentionally placing our attention in a witness dimension of awareness, becoming aware of the surface thoughts, feelings and reactions. Since we normally become hijacked by these surface phenomena, it takes real effort to stay alert and notice what is happening. In time we develop a capacity for multiple attention so that we can both experience and witness, thereby remaining consciously present.

Intimate Witnessing

Intimate witnessing is the direct, immediate quality of being present in the moment. It is intimate and involved but unattached, making no judgments and bringing no commentary or agenda. Like a mirror that reflects all images without having the qualities of any image, so the intimate witness remains open without being disturbed by changes in our lives. This witnessing includes both insightful intimacy and Essential intimacy.

The witness we are discussing here is not the "numb observer" that is disassociated, remote, and experiences events as though they are happening to someone else. The numb observer is distant and unfeeling and withdraws the energy of aliveness from situations. Everything is reduced to information rather than energetic engagement and reciprocal flow.

This witness is also not to be confused with the reactive observer that judges, feels needy, is haunted by longing, feels diminished or defeated by painful experience, and/or wants to merge with pleasurable experiences.

To the intimate witness, all phenomena simply are and we experience both a connection with and detachment from all this. The attention of witnessing brings a sense of inclusion, of hosting, to our sense of presence. This intimate sense of presence and hosting in the moment is both transcending and transformative.

Applying Witnessing to Emotional Reactions

Our reactive stories about our partners are like the tar baby that Br'er Rabbit encounters in the Uncle Remus tale where the more our mind strikes out and struggles with it, the more stuck in our reactions we are. For example, I remember earlier in my marriage that after feeling disrespected during a fight, I would feel hurt and angry. My mind would swim with predator thoughts and painful associations. Each thought of how misunderstood I felt bred more thoughts of times I had felt that way with my wife. Each replay of a contemptuous statement from the argument enlisted an army of examples that deepened my distress and pushed me toward wondering about the very essence of our relationship. This vortex of thoughts and images amplified a small incident into a tornado and I would lose touch with the actual state of our marriage, which was fundamentally good, and the reality of what was happening.

Learning to intentionally take a break from this potential cyclone inside my head and the whirling feelings in my body, I now witness what I am doing and become more present with what actually is occurring. With practice, I can now notice all the commotion that was triggered and the fact that what is happening in the *now* is simply what is happening now, not all those other memories, fears, and pains. I simply experience the pain of the feeling at the time, become present with it, and witness it, not denying or amplifying it. Instead of being hijacked by it, I use it to become more conscious and deal with the issues that need to be addressed.

In this way I regain my balance and confidence and move beyond the sense of battle into a stance of learning. Having greater clarity, I am free to become more actively engaged rather than reactively attacking or withdrawn.

The mindfulness practice I use involves sitting in a posture of basic dignity, hosting everything that arises with a sense of presence, attending to the breath, witnessing whatever arises, particularly thoughts and feelings, and always returning to simple presence. This practice allows everything to be hosted in the space of our awareness as we continue to embrace it all with our presence. We intimately witness the way our stories about who we are, what has happened, what we are doing, and what will happen next and our feelings about all these capture our attention. We are simultaneously engaged in the experience of each moment and witnessing the content and process of what arises. Over time we will experience a more settled sense of our own being, a clear, open, flowing, and abiding sense of presence that hosts all our various experiences and states of mind.

Becoming Intimate with Experience

Through this kind of practice you can learn to be more present, affirming, and intimate with whatever is happening in your life. You can be with each moment just as it is without adding the baggage of beliefs, fears, hopes, judgments, and fantasies. This helps you connect with your basic sense of aliveness and well-being and develops a fundamental confidence in your own sacred nature, realizing that your partner shares that same sacred nature.

We may not like what we see in our witnessing about ourselves and what is happening in a relationship. As we examine failures, wounds, and frustrations, we may doubt that our capacity and that of our relationship can handle all of this and may be tempted to withdraw into denial or to flee the relationship. This is where we must have courage and determination to confront each piece, feel it, and work with it both personally and mutually. We experience our own rawness and share this rawness with our partner.

In this way we become *intimate* with our experience and cultivate our ability to be *present*. This also gives us an authentic ground from which to share with and connect to our partner.

Now we are coming from our heart. The word *courage* derives from the French word *coeur* which means "heart." This sharing takes courage for it is indeed a heart to heart connection in which we are willing to open, to touch and be touched in the core of our being.

Integrating meditation into our lives contributes to the well-being and durability of our intimate relationships. Beyond making us more present, the witnessing also gives us practical feedback on the conditions of our situation. We become clearer and can gain insight into our own patterns as well as the dynamics operating in the relationship. These insights open opportunities for change and improvement. We must not be satisfied with the comfort of insight alone. Insight is not enough. To see a bicycle is not the same as riding it. This takes skill and effort. In the case of intimate relationships, the skills and efforts around interaction and communication are essential.

Spiritual Friend

Having a spiritual friend can be very intimate and supportive in our growth. As spiritual friends we establish a special trust, offering each other a safe haven where we share about our spiritual journey and the challenges we face on our path. We can meditate, be silent and do rituals together. Our rituals connect to our inner world, to the sacred and to each other. We become more conscious and reflective as we mutually create a hallowed time and place.

Five Spiritual Powers

The Buddha taught that there are five spiritual powers that create the ground for inner balance, outer harmony, and authentic freedom. The first is faith (*saddha* in Pali) which points to a basic confidence in the possibility of a beneficial outcome of action and practice and arises from clarity about the nature of the present opportunity. The second power is making the effort, acting on the vision in the faith. This is the energetic component. The third spiritual faculty is consciousness, being alert and awake in our faith and effort and maintaining our attention in the moment and not being hijacked by reactive habits of thought and feeling. The fourth power is concentration which strengthens our efforts so we can persevere. Concentration carries us through the challenges we face on our path. The fifth faculty is simple wisdom to receive feedback and revise our efforts to become more skillful in the world and in manifesting the more profound wisdom qualities of compassion, love, and equanimity.

Direct Experience and Being Embodied

The word *experience* speaks to a unity of feeling, knowing, and living. *Experience* is beyond simply feeling in that it involves knowing, not only perceiving but also knowing about. *Experience* reaches out to taste honey and comes to know sweetness as well as lemon to know tartness. *Experience* knows about life not as an object to study but as a vibrant reality that can be embraced and that fully returns the embrace.

To experience intimacy we need to be embodied. This is true even in our relationship to the Sacred. In spiritual work what is needed is the sense of embodiment not a strong or weak ego. By following a religious path, we become increasingly present with nonverbal, energetic and sensory based experience. The body is a temple to God as Beloved and working with the body is essential to the full realization of connection and love. To be fully embodied is to live in a world of direct knowing in which we receive and integrate information kinesthetically and energetically.

In spirituality, relationships and personal growth, it is vital that our primary teacher be direct experience. Beyond theories and beliefs, there is the reality of direct experience. Direct experience is not mediated through ideas and theories.

As we have more direct experiences in life, our glimpses of intimacy are often powerful. Although we may not experience it all the time, those intimate direct experiences give us a taste that whets our appetite and draws us toward aliveness and the dedication to expand the place of intimacy in our hearts and its role in our lives.

Spiritual Practices for Cultivating Conscious Intimacy

> In the past, we may have made the primary mistake of distinguishing between the inner world of our mind and the world outside. These are not two separate worlds; they belong to the same reality. Notions of inside and outside are helpful in everyday life, but they can become an obstacle preventing us from seeing ultimate reality. If we are able to see deeply into our mind, we can simultaneously see deeply into the world. If we truly understand the world, we also will understand our mind. Buddhists call this "the unity of mind and world."
>
> THICH NHAT HANH

What does it mean to spiritually grow and mature? During childhood and adolescence we physically, mentally and emotionally grew. The changes we experienced were centered primarily around body capacities, mental skills and interests, and emotional preferences and connections. Growth in these domains as adults is more a process of elaboration, refinement, retraining and aging. In terms of the spiritual, our attention moves beyond the physical, mental and emotional to other dimensions of our being, to the sacred dimensions. We seek fulfillment, meaning and connection in ways that are not governed by the appearance and limitations of the body, or the tentativeness and blandness of understanding, or likes and dislikes. We mature by opening to the sacred nature of our own being and that of all life. We may initially think that we need to improve our body, perfect our mind, and balance our emotions in order to be spiritual.

These goals are worthy and useful but miss the point of what it means to spiritually mature and experience sacred intimacy. It does not matter whether we are ill and crippled. Being able to solve complex problems does not help and can in fact mislead us into treating spiritual development as a problem to be solved. Feeling anger, love, sadness, fear, and desire does not result in any particular spiritual realization as such and can tempt us to mistake intensity for authenticity and depth.

Spiritual work cultivates our attention and consciousness beyond the superficial appearances and feelings of life. It embraces the sacred depth that is hidden within the conditions of our physical, mental, and emotional life. It frees us from having our attention entirely hijacked by reactions, so that we can encompass the wider picture in each living moment and experience the depth of connection because we are fully present, open, clear, loving, and dedicated. We feel more openly and deeply as we experience the core of aliveness and intimacy in the moment. We move from moment to moment by openly relaxing into the flow of life, constantly becoming, even as we continue to act responsibly in creating beauty and benefit in the world.

Buddhism teaches us to live with paradox, namely to live with what appears contradictory and contrary to expectations. We hold two, three and even more apparently incompatible truths simultaneously. Buddhist teachings speak of emptiness is form and form is emptiness, and of light is darkness and darkness is light and how to live not-one and not-two simultaneously. The point in living with paradox is to embrace all aspects of ourselves, our partner, and life.

There is an ancient Chinese tale that is often told in Zen

teachings about Qian, a young girl whose father was devoted to her. Her mother and older sister had died, so her father loved Qian all the more. As a child, one of her closed friends was a boy named Zhou. As they grew up together and fell in love, they hoped that they would be married one day. However, when Qian came of age, her father arranged for her to marry another young man in the village.

When they found out, Qian and Zhou were devastated. Zhou felt so despondent that he could not imagine remaining in the village while Qian was wed to someone else. He decided to move to another village and begin a new life. He set out late one night down the river in a small boat. As he rowed downstream, he noticed someone running along the bank, waving at him. To his great surprise and joy, it was Qian who had followed him. Proclaiming their love for each other, they decided to travel to a distant land and make a life together.

In their new village, they were married, had two children and lived happily together as a family. One day Qian, realizing how deep a parent's love is, felt bad about having left her father so abruptly and longed to see him. She approach Zhou who admitted that he was feeling homesick as well and so they agreed to journey back home to see if reconciliation was possible.

So the family traveled in the small boat by the river to their hometown. When they arrived, Qian stayed in the boat by the river with the children while Zhou went to speak with her father to explain what had happened and ask for his forgiveness. When he got to the house, Qian's father opened the door and was surprised to see Zhou. As Zhou started to tell their story, her father became confused and said, "I don't know what you are talking about. Qian has been here with me. After you left the village, Qian became ill and has been bedridden all these years."

Zhou objected, saying, "That's impossible. She followed me, and we ran off together to a distant village. We are married and have two children! You are a grandfather. Qian

> is in excellent health and wants to see you again and ask your forgiveness for running away and marrying without your permission. If you don't believe me, come down to the boat and see for yourself."
>
> The father was reluctant so Zhou set off to bring Qian to her father's house. Meanwhile, her father went into the bedroom to tell the sick Qian what had happened. Without a word, she arose from bed and rushed toward the river to meet the approaching Qian. As they met they merged into one person.

Zen masters ask the question: "Qian and her soul are separated; which one is the true Qian?" When we are feeling fragmented and torn, we are not our authentic self, not our whole self. As we reflect, we can notice that we have many thoughts and conflicting feelings. We experience that we can host and experience them all without reflexively reacting, projecting onto others or repressing them in denial. We realize that we can have them without becoming them or being swept away by them.

Buddhism is not only about meditation and recognizing the nature of mind. It is also about experiencing presence in the world, in our body, and in our partner. It is about moving beyond our own particular body to the experience of the larger body of the physical world, including mountains, rivers, fire, wind, rain, and trees.

By incorporating a spiritual practice into our lives, whether this be through meditation, prayer, or ritual ceremonies, we become intimate with the essence of love beyond desire, caring, identification, and attraction. We get to a core way of being that includes the sense of connection, awe, and transcendence that cannot be thought or expressed. This way of being takes us completely beyond ourselves. It is both inner and outer without the sense of inside and outside, where we become a boundless atmosphere of loving-kindness.

10.

Caring as Conscious Work

Caring is an emotional way of making meaning and connecting. Care connects us to others and brings the sense of other into us, as a parent with an infant or a lover with a loved one. Caring and the ability to include the perspectives, pains, passions, and positions of others are crucial elements in conscious relating and developing the wisdom of virtue. Caring, like all forms of intimacy, moves our attention from our interior world to the exterior world of others.

Martin Buber calls this the *I* and *Thou* relationship in which the other fills the space of my awareness. There is a sense of collective awareness in which we are mutually engaged in the collective virtues of love, intimacy, friendship, compassion, empathy, communion, and loyalty.

This conscious relating is the basis for ethical action and the social use of virtues for both personal and collective development. Let us examine four domains of our lives that we want to make conscious and intimate through our caring:

- Conscious Relationships
- Conscious Speech
- Conscious Action
- Conscious Livelihood

Conscious Relationships

Being conscious in our relationships with each other is a challenge that both breaks us down and opens us up to the larger sense of connection and to being worked by life. In every relationship we are called upon to bridge our world and the world of others and to create meaning and beauty in the middle.

Our major barrier is the power of self-concern based in our reactive fears and longings. Our underlying reactive habit of fear not only addicts us to comfort as a relief but to urgency as a way of attempting to control what is inherently an uncontrollable life.

In becoming conscious, we want to be informed by a sense of the larger good that we participate in and are a small part of. We are humble in our sense of being grounded in the earth and our place in the larger story of life itself. We realize that we play a role in a community of effort, both human and non-human. Our existence is supported by the efforts of plants and animals as well as other people. Everything we receive is a gift so that we can make our contribution to the whole.

In a relationship, giving and receiving attention creates an environment of caring, presence, and connection. One of the guiding practices in Buddhism is that of giving and receiving. At a basic level, we give our presence and receive the presence of our partner. We open to each other with a sense of appreciation and of being blessed.

Just as in meditation we receive the gift of life just as it is, so in our relationship we receive the gift of our partner just as they are. Receiving in this way is a form of giving, a generosity of attention and engagement. This receiving by the giving of attention and caring takes us beyond ourselves into a collective home in the relationship.

While we want to give our time, attention and love out of a spirit of generosity, for a relationship to work, there must be a measure of mutuality. This does not mean keeping score, but it suggests that the quality of the relationship is improved by reciprocity and balance.

Giving and receiving are two sides of one coin. When receiving we are hosting the presence of our partner as an honored guest. In terms of Indo-European origins, the words "host" and "guest" have the same root in the word "*ghosti*." This wisdom of inseparability is also found in Buddhism where the host is our essential nature, Essence, and the guest is a particular manifestation of Essence. From the perspective of Essence which is both beyond and immanent in all things, when the host gives to the guest, the host gives to the host. When the guest receives from the host, the host receives from host. Host and guest actually host each other.

In conscious relationships we hold the sense of both personal and mutual good that derives from strengthening beneficial behaviors and weakening those that diminish ourselves and others. We release the grip of our need to control others. Restraining ourselves from taking over the entire space of a relationship in our attempts to shape other people to our values, our way of thinking, and our way of living, we must lose the innocence of our righteousness and be matured by the forces of vulnerability, difference, mystery, unpredictability and the unknown. We must enter an endless conversation and dance with the other.

Relationships, particularly intimate ones, are about breaking the heart open so it can hold more (not breaking down or apart into a helpless victim). This breaking open happens by the forces of love, beauty, disappointment, grief, and being fiercely challenged. All of these call upon us to connect intimately, directly, and wholeheartedly rather than contracting, withdrawing, and remaining apart from the larger stories being played out.

Conscious relationships involve maintaining the sense of

caring, love, respect, and honoring of each other as we mutually work to build and maintain a collective environment of home that supports us and others. Insight into our own reactive patterns needs to be coupled with the ability to share what is personally happening from our heart with trust and without pretension or reservation. In conscious relationships we realize that each of us is a mirror for the other in which we can see elements of ourselves and the consequences of our behaviors are reflected back to us. Conscious conversations and interactions also convey a sense of larger purpose, of dedication, and of teamwork.

Conscious Speech

Conscious speech brings attention to what is said, both verbally and non-verbally. What we say matters. Our communications are intended to direct the attention of others and, along with our presence, actions and work, create the environment for others. Kabbalah, the Jewish mystical tradition, teaches that what we say creates angels that go out into the world and have a life of their own. It is impossible to re-call an angel, so it is incumbent on us to be very conscious in what we say, for what we say is always contributing to the environment that all live in.

The idea of etiquette has as its central concern the environment that is created by our words, dress, and deeds. At minimum, etiquette creates mechanisms for the smooth interaction between people. At best, it becomes a vehicle within which people can reliably engage each other and meet in deeper ways that are authentic and wholehearted.

◆ Is this the environment you want to be making?

◆ Does what you say and the way you say it really reflect the world you want to live in and share with others?

◆ Does your communication contribute to the wisdom, caring, beauty, and better working of the world?

- Does it feed the sacred?
- Are you being conscious or simply reactive?
- Does your speech embody and carry a basic caring within which all other virtues of speech such as honesty, fidelity, love, and gentleness must operate?

Conscious speech requires that you notice how you show up in your communications.

- Are you usually the subject?
- Do you call attention to yourself or to others?
- Do you acknowledge all that is greater than you?
- Do your stories focus attention on you or do they carry the listener to worlds of wonder, wisdom, and growth?

Conscious speech includes conscious listening. When we speak, we are closing our attention around the words we want to say. When we listen, we open to the unknown of what is coming in. Conscious conversation is a dance of opening and receiving through listening and closing and sending through speaking as we articulate what we want to share. In time it is possible to train ourselves to remain open as we are speaking and to transmit even as we are listening.

Conscious listening involves not only the brain but also our entire being. We listen with all our channels of awareness, not only to words and meanings but also to the silence out of which the words arise.

Conscious Action

Conscious action not only transcends reaction, it cultivates beauty and benefit for others. It creates harmony and promotes creativity. Conscious action makes a difference in ways that are aligned with our deepest purposes and our sense of what is needed.

Generosity is one of the great action virtues emphasized in

all spiritual traditions. The most important gifts we can give are our attention, our caring, our time and our energy.

Conscious action is always informed by clarity and intention. It arises from our intimacy with what is so, engaged intimacy, and our awareness of the nature of Reality. As an active, creative participant in life, we are always making a contribution and our contributions are guided by our conscious intentions.

Wanting to reform the world without discovering your true self is like trying to cover the whole world with leather to avoid the pain of walking on stones and thorns. It is much simpler to wear shoes.

RAMANA MAHARSHI

Conscious Livelihood

Livelihood includes all the forms of work that we do as part of our society, whether in a job, raising children, caring for the ill, or maintaining a household. The operating principles for conscious livelihood are 1) not causing harm and 2) helping others with our minds, our hands, and our hearts. Conscious livelihood merges the practical contributions of work with the sacred heart posture of love and compassion. The opposite of conscious work is not play, but not investing ourselves in anything of value.

Often our employment situations are physically, intellectually, and/or emotionally challenging. We may get discouraged when we want to be inspired, offended when we want peace, diminished when we want to be encouraged, and exploited when we want to be respected. If we can release the grip of fear, insecurity, and the haunting self-concern of not being good enough, we can find ways to relax in the midst of pressure, to project confidence in the center of chaos, to be kind because that is what others need, and to be supportive in the face of competition. To be conscious in our jobs is to see the links between our accomplishments and the work of others, weaving a tapestry of colors and shapes that make a society function.

Managing in the World of Clocks, Living in the World of the Compass

To borrow from Stephen Covey, our challenge is often managing in the world of clocks, living in the world of the compass. In his book *First Things First*, Covey identifies two powerful symbols of our time—the clock and the compass. "The clock represents our commitments, appointments, schedules, goals, activities—what we do with, and how we manage our time. The compass represents our vision, values, principles, mission, conscience, direction—what we feel is important and how we lead our lives." [xxix]

Busy-ness is one of the most common complaints that I hear as a teacher concerning why people cannot practice or give time to the Sacred and to service. We all experience a wide—ever widening—gap between what's most important to us, what we most care about, and the way we spend our time. We have developed habits of activity and stimulation and a nagging fear of boredom. We thirst for doing as many things as possible, filling any sense of void.

Clearly, to be conscious in our work and contributions to the world we need to organize our time and energy to support what we value. In this we always start by working with what we have now. To practice virtues is to use time as a training tool for developing qualities, capacities, and skills. This changes our relationship to time from one of pressure to one of support for growth. Often the biggest obstacle to spiritual work is not giving ourselves the time necessary to do the work.

Dedication

A consciously intimate life is dedicated to creating benefit in the world through all our activities and connections. Our dedication to manifesting wisdom qualities is a way of making relationships matter, of honoring and enriching the connectedness that inherently exists and enlivening the universal principle of relating.

A fully intimate life relates to everything as a blessing. Blessing means to strengthen. Whatever strengthens us is a blessing. This includes what nourishes us, challenges us and teaches us wisdom (whether the teacher was wise or not does not matter.)

Our deep calling, our fire within, what Robert Graves referred to as our genius and Joseph Campbell called our bliss, inspires and informs our path of growth and contribution. It defines that domain of our heart that is committed to a mission. It reflects our desire to create a legacy that is beneficial. It grows out of our fundamental sense of being an intimate part of a larger story and our impulse to contribute.

We find our calling not from working it out but from uncovering our true intent. When we live with tremendous attention, the world calls us. The world sometimes whispers, sometimes shouts, what our mission is, what needs our contributions and participation.

Legacy is our contribution to the lives of others. Our world today is the legacy of those who have gone before us and our actions and the way we show up in the world now creates a legacy for those who will follow. In this way we become intimate with the future.

The qualities we want to make our legacy are discovered through our life experience and inquiry into the deeper nature of soul. This work requires a great faith. A faith that what is here in this moment can grow something that will flower and bear fruit. It comes from a deep place that we do not know. These seeds are always buried in the dark earth of our experience. By becoming intimate with these deeper domains of our soul, we tap the aliveness residing there. As we bring that to the surface, we find that our intimacy with each other and with life itself enlivens and becomes ever more radiant.

A Calling to Music

The story of Dave, a jazz musician who participated in one of my retreats on dedication, illustrates the need to renew our intimacy with our calling, even if it is not the way we make a living. Dave had been a modestly successful pianist on the regional jazz scene in his younger years in the mid 1970s and had two critically acclaimed albums of his tunes and playing. The music scene in those days was simultaneously exciting, stressful, financially unrewarding to musicians like Dave, and plagued with alcoholism and addiction. When confronted by his wife about the life style and the degeneration of their relationship, he decided to go to a rehab center and do a twelve step recovery program. He went back to school and became a psychologist, specializing in work with artists of all kinds. He continued to play informal gigs but music took a back seat to the demands of his family, job, and recovery work.

Now, twenty years later, still married with grown children and financially successful, he found that part of him had stopped growing. He could not identify the specific source of his dis-ease but he was haunted in ways that he called a "mid-life crisis." After doing a short but intensive inquiry into this as part of the retreat, he realized that his relationship to music had been frozen in time decades earlier and that one of his special gifts to the world—playing, composing, and recording—was not being given. Having a new sense of purpose in his life, after the retreat he began taking steps to put together a regular jazz group and to create a new album that reflected his current maturity and new-found passion. Without worrying about having to be financially successful, he found that the freedom to create also brought forth a deep musical integrity. He has now recorded a new album with another in the works. He feels ablaze with the joy of his music even as he integrates it with the rest of his life.

Wisdom of Silence

We can tell a lot about a relationship from the way we are silent together. When we are disconnected, bored, self-preoccupied, and/or unengaged, the silence is one of absence. We are not showing up together and the silence expresses the distance. The silence of intimacy is a silence of presence, a silence filled with aliveness, connection, and sharing. It is satisfying and there is no need to fill it with words. The words that are spoken simply arise within the silence to elaborate its beauty. They do not disturb it. In fact, in the deep levels of love and intimacy, sounds and silence are there simultaneously, with sound simply arising in the space of silence as we might dance in the space of a room.

To open to intimacy we must have the experience of silence where our ideas and our personal story do not intrude to provide a preconceived or well worn perspective. In this we are asked to be fresh as if with new eyes, ears, body and heart. We are awaking to a new, unknown day that holds the promise of the light of connection, the feel of love, and the joy of being at home.

Free to Be Wholehearted and Vulnerable

When we are openly intimate with the raw, unfinished edges of life, we become free—free to experience, free to love, free to grieve, free to dance wholeheartedly, free to unconditionally be ourselves, and free to be completely at home in the world.

We are then free to be vulnerable and it is vulnerability that further cements relationships, particularly intimate ones. It is in our vulnerability that we provide an opening for the supportive presence of others. Sometimes what is needed is simply their witnessing and caring, sometimes their active concern, sometimes actions of assistance, and sometimes their advice in solving some problem.

Our vulnerability and willingness to be present with and

share our distress magically transforms life in the moment into an experience of bonding and presence. When we experience and hold any feeling fully and openly, including feelings of emptiness, we experience becoming filled with the richness of Divine presence. We realize that every frustration of our desire to control life is an invitation to dance with the reality of what is.

Dancing with Life

To dance with the reality of what is requires that we learn to experience and contain our feelings and reactions sufficiently enough that insight arises and we are able to channel our energies into our own sense of presence. When we cannot hold all the energy, it is useful to find healthy ways to discharge some of the excess. The greater goal, however, is to build our capacity to embody and experience the fullness of our emotions and to use all of this to intensify our sense of presence and our connection to the presence of others.

When the passions of a relationship are set aflame, whether by desire or suffering or even reflection, a sacred force is at work. It is up to us to be mindful of its presence and become present ourselves to it, meeting it and dancing with it rather than being hijacked by it.

All barriers to presence arise from distractions and preoccupations with things that are external to the context of *Now* in the relationship. These distractions can range from mundane concerns about what someone thinks about us to turbulent feelings about past wounds. When having a meal with a partner, these can include concerns about schedule, unfinished business at work, past memories of issues, or future plans.

The challenge of being present involves mobilizing and directing the energies of our aliveness to what is happening now and meeting the presence of each other. We disappear from the present when our thoughts or feelings hijack our attention into other situations, past memories or future projections in such a way that we are living in the unreality of what these thoughts and feelings have created. Learning how to become present in the experience of the here and now helps us recognize the fears and preoccupations that distract and constrict us from the experience of *Now*.

Dancing with presence is often easiest when we have a sense of play. Play takes the edge of seriousness and consuming functionality out of activity in such a way that we can take delight in what we are doing, not simply focusing on the utilitarian end that we think it serves. Play in this sense is not frivolous. It contains the paradox of being wholeheartedly engaged without an oppressive burden of success and failure.

11.

Maturing Habits of the Heart

"What does that mean—tame," asks the Little Prince.

"It is an act too often neglected," says the Fox. "It means to establish ties. To me, you are still nothing more than a little boy who is just like a hundred thousand other little boys. And I have no need of you. And you, on your part, have no need of me. To you I am nothing more than a fox like a hundred thousand other foxes. But if you tame me, then we shall need each other. To me, you will be unique in all the world. To you, I shall be unique in all the world.... You have hair the color of gold. Think how wonderful that will be when you tame me! The grain, which is also golden, will bring me back the thought of you.... One only understands the things that one tames."

THE LITTLE PRINCE, ANTOINE DE SAINT-EXUPÉRY

For the mature person, the Tao begins in the relation between man and woman, and ends in the infinite vastness of the universe.

TZU-SU

In this exploration of the role of conscious development, I am suggesting that when conscious work is done in the context of intimate relationships, it can naturally support personal growth in terms of emotional, spiritual, intellectual, and social capacities and ways of understanding. The cultivation of states of consciousness that embody increasing levels of wisdom, when continuously applied to living in a family and workplace, has the potential to expand the capacity for consciousness and the ability to effectively and beneficially interact in relationships.

Conscious Development into Mature Intimacy

The work of a relationship and the development of intimacy must not be romantically idealized. Doing relationships well is the work of a lifetime, 24/7. We are engaged in a process of self-exposure, mutual exploration, insight, tension, healing, conflict, paradox, and growth. We can only do the best that we can, there is no way of doing it perfectly or "right." Intimacy happens and grows in the moments when we make ourselves available to each other with whatever clarity, care and love we have.

The development of intimacy moves us through many processes of personal connection, personal differentiation, personal integration, mutual connection, differentiation, and mutual integration. We need to call forth a thread of basic sanity to consciously grow the relationship from a simple connection to a complex home that includes joys, sorrows, shared meaning, differences, conflicts, mutual investment and communion.

Part of this basic sanity means that we must not confuse support and love with placating our partner for whatever they want and do. Having unconditional love does not preclude having standards and conditions for interactions and living situations. Unconditionally tolerating the destructive and painful behaviors of a spouse can have devastating consequences. The sacred *yes* we may have in our heart for the being of another is part of the sacred dimension and must *not* mean saying "yes" to everything no matter what it is.

For some of us the motivation to spiritually mature is our desire to lead a dedicated life that is free, that matters, that makes a difference, that creates beauty, that is aligned with a deep integrity, and that demonstrates the power of example. We seek to express the boundless radiance of the infinite sacred and to realize and embody supreme awareness.

Others of us yearn for love, for the connections that flow from sharing the great and small, always passionate dramas of life, and from making a home filled with beauty, caring, and nurturance. We want to dance the play of life's sacred energy as a way of making love and creating life, using all the senses as an expression of our divinely rich nature.

To personally mature on a path of sacred intimacy we need to first abandon our wishful thinking. Then we surrender exclusive self-concern, working for the benefit of others as well as ourselves. As part of this work, we are dedicated to the benefit of the relationship. We also realize that our intimate relationships support each of us bringing our gifts to the world. Finally we experience the relationship as a gateway to self-transcendence, communion, and rapture in the essential unity of all being.

This personal growth can emerge in many ways. Whether we are a part of a support group, engaged in therapy, members of a religious or spiritual community, meditate, or simply process our inner world with friends, the firm foundation for moving beyond our reactive fears, hopes, and denials is conscious experience that we can learn from. Conscious spiritual work retrains our heart postures based on wisdom and our systematic work to explore and experience the nature of life and reality.

In this growth we become increasingly willing to show the signature lines of our failings and our griefs. The contours of our grief, our joys, our wounds, and our passions are the outer display of the landscape of our mature beauty.

Maturity and Mastery

In our work to develop wisdom and the heart posture of love, we come to realize that maturity is even more important than mastery. In maturity we realize that being fully present and open as a lover means we dance with the circumstances of life and play in the field of Reality. We choose to swing with the rhythms of the moment at one time and to express our freedom by intentionally opposing circumstance at another time. We express our essential free nature to be present with the act of choosing. We realize that our growth is not linear, resembling more of a spiral that moves in the right direction. Mastery in terms of control and power are not what is fundamentally important, for a mature heart posture includes both mastery and being mastered.

As a mature lover, we readily dance with and in the midst of all that arises. The world and our relationships are our home for the ongoing practice of alchemy, of transformation of the ordinary into the extraordinary, of the lead of experience into the gold of wisdom. The world is our stage on which to act with clarity and love. Our simple actions reverberate with the immediacy and power of thunder as the forces of the Divine are channeled and expressed as naturally as the cry of a hawk and song of a bluebird.

Mature intimacy involves a sense of authentic home in the sacred nature of life. From this ground of being, we experience a true freedom—free from inhibiting fears, free of longings, and free to act in the world with love, compassion, and a dedication. We create benefit from a heart space of clarity and wisdom.

Virtue: Training Ourselves and Supporting Each Other

George Herbert Mead, an early twentieth-century philosopher and social psychologist, coined the term *significant other* to refer to the people who reflect back to us the impacts of what we say and do, demonstrating the social meanings of our actions. This helps us develop our ability to act beneficially with others, to act responsibly.

We are social animals and what we do affects others, even our simple presence. Nothing we do takes place in a vacuum, even when we think we are alone. As anthropologist Clifford Geertz noted, behavior is "more a wink than a blink." The blink and wink involve similar physical actions and they may appear alike but there is a world of difference. A blink is self-contained as an unintended and automatic movement of the eyelid to lubricate the eye. A wink on the other hand has a social purpose of conveying an intention to another and requires the presence and witnessing of another person. It takes two to make a wink and, if we always sense being connected beyond ourselves, all actions have the social quality of a wink.

Being present in all our aliveness means bringing forth more of who we are and making ourselves more available to whatever arises in life. The qualities of virtue, such as consciousness, courage, kindness, patience, generosity, humor, and gratitude, enable us to be fully present and intimate with what is. Consciousness, for instance, keeps us aware and intentional as we open to what is within and around us. Kindness and generosity extend the reach of our caring impulse to others, while humor helps us play with our situation and keeps us from making everything heavy and burdensome. Each quality of virtue helps to train us in working with engaged and connective intimacy. The more proficient we become with these qualities, the more we can embrace the whole of life in an intimate way.

Our actions and attitudes in our connections with each other and life either strengthen our wisdom qualities or weaken our integrity, either benefit or diminish the relationships and worlds that we are a part of. The degree to which we are conscious plays a primary role in shaping all our relationships. Being conscious in our communications, interactions, work, and relationships brings a quality of the sacred to each of these domains.

Virtue can guide, promote and sustain a conscious life, including a life of intimacy. Virtue can be defined as living within the guidance of spiritual principles. These spiritual principles all support a kind of self-transcendence. We transcend our reactive habit self. We train ourselves to transcend our limiting beliefs, self-images and attitudes. We transcend self-concern, entering the realm of a larger caring.

The basic principles of virtue are to be a beneficial presence and create benefit in the world. Virtue preserves or enhances what is good. It begins by not polluting or contaminating our lives, our relationships, and our environment—being a presence that is not harmful. Beyond that, it has to do with making the world better through our presence and our actions. The practice of certain qualities of virtue serves to retrain our body of habits so that our lives are increasingly an expression of our authentic and wisdom nature. Virtues ground us in the way we live life and interact with each other.

The word is derived from the Latin *virtus* meaning excellence, strength, courage. An old definition meant the embodiment of a supernatural power or influence of a divine being. Its more common usage is in terms of moral practice or action, moral excellence, and integrity of character. Socrates identified virtue with wisdom, which he conceived to be knowledge of the good, asserting that people act in terms of what they think or feel is good and that when true knowledge of good is arrived at, they will act accordingly. Plato identified four cardinal virtues of wisdom, courage, temperance, and justice. Aristotle thought of virtue as a habit that chooses excellence in conduct, primarily conceived as a middle way between excess and defect.

The Buddhist tradition, like all the spiritual traditions, emphasizes virtues to support the transformation of our reactive habit body into an embodiment of wisdom, or what many would call character. The development of character continues even after we have realized "enlightenment" and is the ongoing work of both formal spiritual practice and participation in everyday relationships. As Yamada Roshi says, "There is really no end to the practice of Zen. You cannot accomplish a perfect character in forty years. Practicing a million years is still insufficient."[xxx]

One of the core virtues is living with integrity. Integrity has many levels of meaning but at the core it concerns the alignment of our actions, our values, our heart postures, our interconnections with others, and our deepest wisdom nature. It does not mean being true to our reactive emotions that are distorted responses and projections that arise from confusion, fears, hopes, and feeling overwhelmed. It also does not mean the unwavering pursuit of what we want. Integrity involves clarity of mind, openness of heart, presence in the moment, and the equanimity of being at home in ourselves, with other people, and in the world.

Relationships are great settings for working on acting with integrity as we live true to not only ourselves, but also the integrity of our partner and of the relationship itself. Integrity involves honoring what is of real value and acting from that heart posture of honoring. This honoring also means that, no matter what our spiritual path is, we support our partner in pursuing their own spiritual path or even no path at all.

One of the great challenges in conscious intimacy is to access and manifest those qualities that we know exist in our soul but are usually obscured by our daily habits of mind and reaction. While our thoughts and emotions may seem real, the deep core of wisdom that is in our nature is the real source of our aliveness and more profound happiness.

Having a spiritual practice brings this wisdom vein of gold to the surface, makes it available to our conscious mind and manifests it through conscious actions and relationships. When we are spiritually mature, we are able to reveal and extract wisdom and peace from situations where others find only distress.

Virtue uses, exercises and eventually embodies wisdom qualities such as love, courage, integrity, kindness, compassion, equanimity, and integrity. When we deviate from the path of these virtues, we scatter our energies, pollute our social environment and harvest the disconnecting reactions of others as well as ourselves. Virtue as conscious relating, speech and action, supports retraining our reactive habit body into a body of sacred wisdom.

Making distinctions about the way we use the term "virtue" helps to reveal how we can make this idea a support rather than a judgment in shaping our lives and building relationships. At the core, virtue concerns wisdom qualities rooted in our basic goodness, our fundamental wisdom nature. Virtue is also a sacred force that shapes us—a force of the Sacred that finds expression in our conscience and works through us when we seek to be a beneficial force ourselves. As we make this force part of our lives, virtue becomes a personal quality of our character. As we access and use the wisdom qualities of our nature we manifest virtue as a personal behavior through our beneficial presence and our actions that contribute value to the lives of others.

The Virtue of Intimacy and the Intimacy of Virtue

Virtues guide a relationship in creating a supportive environment within which intimacy can deepen its roots, strengthen its trunk and branches, blossom in beauty, and bear nourishing fruit. The virtues in a relationship are not some abstract, detached concept of approval or condemnation. They are guides toward excellences, qualities that are developed through practice.

Virtue supports the environment of intimacy and love and the heart posture of love. The experience of intimacy makes the practice of virtue possible. Our inspiration toward virtue is a kind of love. Our desire to mature and improve the conditions of our relationships and of our communities flows from intimacy with each other and with life itself.

A natural ethics arises when we are true to the nature of being intimate with our own true nature, with life, with our close others, with our communities, and with the Sacred. The ethics that flows from intimacy guides us with the principle of being supportive of other people in their efforts to bring their unique gifts to the world and to live their lives in alignment with the story that surrounds those gifts. To violate this principle is to hinder or diminish their capacity to live out their lives of contribution and the sharing of the blessing of presence. Violations break our connections to their innermost sacred nature and their uniqueness, ripping at the fabric of intimacy that holds relationships together. Ethically, we want to affirm the integrity of who they are and the divine nature of their true mission in life.

To fully support another person in their sacred nature and mission, we must know what that means from having discovered that within ourselves. To be intimate with another requires that we be intimate with ourselves, at least in terms of the experience of being whole-hearted.

The Three Jewels: Consciousness, Participation, Contribution

The foundation for the virtues of wisdom rests on three impulses that we have as human beings. These impulses of aliveness are consciousness, participation, and contribution. From the point of view of the impulses, our impulse to make meaning, grant significance, to be aware and give direction to life is consciousness. Participation is the impulse to "show up," to exist and express aliveness, to "participate" in life. Contribution is the impulse to relate to our surroundings, to belong, and to make a difference. Participation and contribution are given shape and purpose by our consciousness as it defines context, meaning and caring.

When we live in and from our limiting beliefs, distressing feelings, and reactions, we turn consciousness, participation and contribution into fixations of attention that become crystallized and result in reactive patterns of thinking, feeling, and behaving. When our consciousness is reactive, we go numb, deny reality or try to fit everything into what we already understand and conceptually know. Our fixated reactive forms of participation are fear, struggle and avoidance. Our reactive forms of contribution and relating are neediness and attachment. We call these three patterns of fixation the "three poisons." Not realizing that these poisons are contracted forms of natural impulses, we treat the sense of ignoring, fear, and need, as if *they* are the basic impulses.

When we live in a conscious, open way, the three impulses become the jewels of wisdom of consciousness, presence of participation, and radiance of contribution. Our challenge then is to take a path of virtue, namely to use these three jewels to consciously access our wisdom qualities, to become present in ways that manifest these qualities and to enact them by creating benefit and beauty in the world.

Just as we can grow our capacity to *be* intimate, so we can also develop our skills and capacity to *do* intimacy. In the Tibetan tradition of Buddhism, certain practices have the practitioner identify with a particular deity such as Avalokiteshvara, the Bodhisattva of Compassion. This deity not only represents the idea of compassion but is an embodiment of awareness as compassion, and the energy and radiance of compassion. In the practice we not only think about our connection to this deity and the idea of compassion, we gradually imagine ourselves as the deity, as compassion itself. Then we grow to think as compassion, to feel as compassion, open to others as compassion, to walk, talk and breathe as compassion, now and in every moment of the day. We feel the texture of each moment as a compassionate being, aligning our words and deeds, our touch and our gaze, so that a field of love and compassion radiates from us and pervades the atmosphere.

Practicing Virtues

The first step is to practice non-pollution of our lives, our relationships, our communities, and our world. This is what some traditions call purifying intentions and actions. We refrain from habitually reacting in ways that diminish ourselves or others or our environment. We don't dump our uncomfortable feelings inappropriately. We resist speaking ill of others and of life except when it clearly serves a beneficial purpose. We avoid meaningless gossip, habitual criticism, trivial talk and disconnecting communication. Basically we examine our motivations and behaviors in order to get beyond those that derive from reactive fears, insatiable neediness and insensitivity.

In the second step we consciously seek to know 1) our own essential nature, 2) what contributes to the life and environment we know to be good for ourselves, others and the world, and 3) the qualities of character and skill in action that will be effective in creating value, benefit, and evoking these qualities in others.

The third step involves bringing virtue to life by placing attention on the qualities of wisdom and character, aligning our actions accordingly, and opening to feedback on the results. By regularly placing attention in qualities such as praise, kindness, and generosity, we access and cultivate these within ourselves. It is a way to employ everyday life as a gym for using and developing the muscle of wisdom energy. For those of us who share our lives with intimate others, the arena of everyday life provides a great and constant opportunity to practice, exercise and cultivate the qualities that we value. In this way we increase and strengthen our capacity.

In our world where we are so busy and caught up with our reactive habits, we need to be reminded of what is really important. This is the role of learning about virtues and practicing virtuous behavior that is emphasized in all spiritual and philosophical traditions. We must consciously interrupt our reactive behavior patterns and find ways to rework our attitudes, beliefs, and body of habits.

Contemplation and meditation are powerful tools for interrupting reactive patterns and for creating a space where we can examine them. Through inquiry we can discover what is really true about us and for us, what is authentic, and what we really value. Through clarifying true value, virtue can be seen, cultivated and brought from our meditation environment to the rest of life. Meditation also cuts through our polluting reactions and we realize how to be a beneficial presence.

As we practice virtue, over time we cultivate the qualities of being virtuous and become an increasingly beneficial environment for others, not to mention ourselves. We bring out the best in our own nature as our presence radiates a field of wisdom energy, our actions are a skillful expression of the clarity, and we show up as an enlivening, harmonizing, encouraging, supportive, and loving presence. By being and acting virtuously, we tend to bring it out in others and make it more accessible in the world.

Thrones of Dignity

Virtue further develops our heart posture of basic dignity. Our dignity is our intrinsic nobility of character as a manifestation of the Sacred. As we train in wisdom habits, our sense of life, quality of presence and intimacy with each other are transformed into the majesty that was always our potential. Just as in mythologies where the hero or heroine begins as a lowly peasant, makes a journey of challenges that confront their greatest fears, and arrives finally to a position of sovereignty as king or queen, so we must find our own path of dignity. In the traditional stories certain qualities are generally highlighted: loving connection, serving a great cause that serves all of life, humility, honoring, gratitude, courage, compassion, and stamina. These are considered to be the requirements for a successful navigation of the path.

In sacred iconography thrones are used to represent those virtues upon which the others can be built. These thrones include:

- Love that embraces all life
- Discipline that is solid and vital, like an elephant or bulldozer removing obstacles
- Adaptability that is unstoppable in moving towards its goal
- Playfulness as a sense of humor and an attitude of perkiness
- Home in the sense of being a part of life, of a community, of the world
- Freedom in the sense of having choice and thriving in the space of possibilities
- Dynamic engagement in the energy, communications, and activity of interactions

Character: Habits of the Heart

Just as individuals develop qualities, so do intimate relationships. As a couple, a family, or a community, certain qualities manifest more than others and some collective actions happen more frequently than others. These qualities that we personally and collectively do embody and that show up in our behavior represent our character, what Alexis de Tocqueville called "habits of the heart." The term "ethics" derives from the

Greek *ethikos*, that which pertains to *ethos* or character. Character refers to that core interior part of ourselves and our relationship that holds our values, our conscience, our convictions, and the virtues we operate from day to day as well as in crisis. It is not the same as personality and is not developed suddenly. It is character that reflects our capacity to live according to our wisdom nature and how much we have matured. The real strength of character is built on having the courage to become intimate, not in abstaining from life by seeking some personal nirvana.

As is true for us individually, the character of an intimate relationship reflects our experiences, the choices we have made, the lessons we have learned, and the challenges we have faced. The character we have developed in a relationship determines how we engage each other, how we make decisions, and the strength with which we mutually confront adversity, injustice, and chaos. It is value living through us in our presence and our actions.

Conscience, a key aspect of character, is a guidance system that operates internally in each of us personally and within the heart of the relationship. Our conscience senses when we act or even contemplate acting in ways that are contrary to integrity and a basic sense of what is beneficial. Conscience requires listening to deeper callings, particularly in lives that are busy, noisy, and saturated with stimulation and distraction.

All relationships develop patterns of reaction. These habits must be outgrown and reformulated if we are to mature and realize the full potential of intimacy. Virtues as wisdom give us the directions and the tools for changing our reactive habits and developing the qualities of character that are increasingly beneficial for each other, the relationship and our community.

Walking Our Talk

It is difficult to be a saint in the midst of one's family.

ANATOLE FRANCE

In retraining ourselves to be able to walk our noble talk, we initially practice those virtues that do not pollute and limit our restimulation of reactions. We are like infants who cannot digest many foods until we have developed a greater capacity. As we learn to discipline ourselves, our capacity for practicing new habits expands. Gradually we use all challenges as part of a conscious growth process.

The word "discipline" has its root in the word "disciple," one who is committed to learning and growing out of love. Discipline, derived from love and sense of value, is a critical ingredient in retraining our body of impulsive and reactive habits to embody the qualities of wisdom. "Will" gives us the juice to start our work. It is discipline that keeps us going and makes conscious intimacy a part of our lives. Discipline is like a muscle in that the more we exercise it, the stronger it gets.

Without discipline, habits and addictions that are so prevalent in our consumer society will continue to keep us wrapped in a cocoon of self-concern governing our behaviors and our heart postures. The rich potential of our nature will go untapped and we remain trapped in the clutches of comfort, reaction, and fear.

Guided by our sense of value, our discipline can grow in the soil of love, Divine support, community, and the larger contexts that we are dedicated to serve. We align our inner resources with the efforts of others and the sense of serving and being encouraged by the sacred. Discipline is not a punishment for our habits but a vehicle for realizing our deeper nature and a greater joy. Discipline makes us conscious and intimate with each other and life as we seek to manifest love and wisdom moment to moment.

Vows

Vows between people are a living commitment to creating a home in the relationship that manifests the environment we mutually want to live in. Vows articulate the core of shared values and the outlines of a mutual path. They reflect a willingness to integrate and grow with the circumstances that flow from sharing a home in the relationship. In marriage vows, we mutually agree to honor the bonds between us, to continually explore the nature, depth, and expanse of love and intimacy, to celebrate each other, the relationship, and the larger contexts of community and the Sacred, and to navigate the tides of grief and joy that regularly touch the shore of our connection.

Vows align us mentally, emotionally and spiritually with the core of the relationship and our intimacy with each other. They remind us of the path we have chosen, calling us to remember not only ourselves but each other in the dynamic flow of life together.

Ethics

The goal of the path of sacred lover is not to become lost in rapture, the ecstasy of Love for the Beloved, but to be awake in it so that we still hear the cries of a small child, feel the pain of wounds, and taste the bitterness of enslavement to reaction. As long as we are of this world we must also serve this world with the caring of a lover and parent.

It is from this caring that appropriate and ethical actions will flow. Without the core of love and caring, ethics degenerates into rules that polarize rather than connect, that inhibit growth rather than open us to maturity, and that can lead to unquestioning extremism rather than the clarity needed to respect each other and all life.

Ethics based on absolutist moral rules cannot take into account the subtleties and variety of human situations and the full complexity of our humanity. The concern about being "right" according to some formula dehumanizes us and other people into simple behaviors that we approve of or condemn. This polarization loses all sense of the Sacred and reduces society and religion to a system of managed and judged activities rather than a community of relationships.

The result is always failure, alienation and the creation of a spiritual wasteland. The reaction to this wasteland is to regressively long for the sense of connection we had as very young children rather than the mature relationships of a lover.

Part of our challenge, personally and collectively, in our polarizing society is to release ethics from the prison cell of rigid morality and to reclaim the role of sacred intimacy as a guide for ethical behavior. An authentic ethics which builds and reflects our personal and collective character will only emerge when we are rooted in a sacred, yet humanizing, fundamental love and respect and approach each other with humility, courage, and compassion.

Humility, Courage, and Compassion

In most traditions, humility, courage and compassion are key qualities in an intimate spiritual life. "Humility" comes from the word *humus* meaning of the earth or ground. Coming from the earth and sensing our connection to and rootedness in it, in our humility we realize that we are agents, vehicles, and vessels of larger forces and principles and not the source of reality. Humility opens us to learning from everything. If heaven is the state of grace in which we are present with all that is—with God—without distraction or reservation, then humility, being of the earth, the ground, creates the conditions for heaven by opening and strengthening us, overcoming our attachments to material conditions and to identities.

The word *courage* has its roots in French and means "large heart." Strengthening and deepening the heart is what relationships and spiritual practice are about. Courage takes us into the face of all that is and gets us to affirm reality even when it scares us and makes us uncomfortable. Courage gets us to show up, participate, and care.

Compassion draws upon our capacity to take seriously and get inside the reality of others—their pains and inner lives, their emotions, and their external circumstances. It is our impulse to open our hearts and to help and support those in need. In compassion we engage each other in our mutual humanity and divinity. It reflects our ability to invest mental, physical, emotional and spiritual energy in what happens to others and to manifest our caring in action. One of the keys to great intimacy is not great gestures or grand deeds or spectacular feats but small deeds done with great love. It is the heart of moral awareness.

Using the power of awareness and imagination, compassion not only places us in the position of others, it also accesses our own best intentions, caring, and wisdom. We radiate these qualities from our hearts into the world, contributing love and wisdom to the environment of consciousness that surrounds us all. These encouraging and embracing qualities can be sensed even if they cannot be seen, creating an intimate home for all.

Compassion is not an idea but an authentic connective response. It is felt in the core of our body from our belly through our heart center up to the throat. It is what we feel when we see a small child fall off a swing and we want to pick him or her up and comfort them. We want them to feel the warmth of caring so that the heart connection will heal the sense of tearing that the fall and its shock induced in their spirit. We send the loving, healing energy from our being to theirs without condition or hesitation. This is the type of connective, loving energy of compassion that we want to apply to ourselves as well as others.

The Buddha taught that our true nature is inseparable from the nature of all being and is open, radiant and lacking a permanent separate self. In the Buddhist teaching on presence, we are all features of Reality. When our authentic nature is realized, certain wisdom ways of being naturally emerge such as compassion, loving-kindness, equanimity, and generosity (*Brahma-*

viharas). From this profound realization, we develop the heart posture of *bodhichitta*, the desire and dedication to free all beings from suffering.

In Jesus's teachings, love is at the center of all being—love that is forgiving, unconditional, and generously unself-centered. For many Christians, Jesus was a human being whose great gift was that as a human with all our frailties he could incorporate the true nature of the Divine.

For Karen Armstrong, the noted writer on comparative religion, "Compassion is the key to religion, the key to spirituality. It is the litmus test of religiosity in all the major world religions. It is the key to the experience of what we call God—that when you dethrone yourself from the center of your world and put another there, you achieve extasis, you go beyond yourself." She quotes the Buddha: "First, live in a compassionate way, and then you will know." [xxxi]

Reflection and Inquiry

Be patient toward all that is unsolved in your heart and try to love the questions themselves *like locked rooms or books that are written in a foreign tongue. The point is to live everything. Live the questions now. Perhaps you will then gradually, without noticing it, live your way some distant day into the answers.*

R. M. RILKE

Our ability to reflect on our own actions, feelings, thoughts, and nature plays a critical role in the development of conscious relationships and deepening our capacity for intimate bonding. One of the most ancient ways of becoming more conscious and intimate with ourselves is the use of questions as part of conscious inquiry into the nature of our habits, identities, sensory reality, and all existence. We want to penetrate to our very soul, uniting the head and the heart by going beyond ordinary curiosity and intellectual speculation to the very core of our being and the heart of wisdom.

Inquiry not only takes us "home" to our deeper self, it can cultivate who and what we are as human beings. It draws on the ancient traditions of wisdom and fearlessness, which transform the compelling fears of human reaction into unconditional aliveness, intimacy and presence. Then this way of being and sense of presence becomes a hosting presence within which events, activities, and feelings take place.

We want to cultivate three qualities in approaching the soul. Silence opens us to both inner and outer realities of what is. Conscious attention attends to both the world and the sense of what is beyond our concepts of the world. The third quality is dedication, the sense that life is asking us about the meaning we are creating for our life, moment to moment.

Zen teachers often speak of three factors to be cultivated in spiritual practice: great faith, great questioning, and great courage. Faith is not in beliefs but a confidence that it is possible for each of us to realize and embody our true nature through the path of meditation. Questioning as a practice in meditation is a form of doubt that is not disbelief and not wavering indecision that can immobilize and confuse us. It means being fully present, alive, and alert with the mystery of life, acknowledging that we cannot truly know what has happened, what is happening, and what is going to happen. Courage is the determination and strength to be uncompromising in being ourselves as we work to embody the qualities of sacred wisdom even when confronted by the challenges of life and relationships.

Freedom from Being Hostage to Ourselves

In our habitual ways of being and doing, we often experience life as a prison in which we are doing time trying to avoid fears, satisfy longings, and struggle with confusion and boredom. The clearest statement about the nature of our condition was given years ago at a Passover ceremonial meal by my son Micah, who was five years old at the time. As I was explaining the meaning of the bitter herbs in the Jewish tradition as reminding us of the bitterness of slavery, he said, "It seems to me, that we are all really slaves to ourselves."

This process of freeing ourselves from reactive mental, emotional and physical habits that keep us hostage to our fears, wants, longings, and hopes is at the core of reorienting and retraining ourselves for deeper intimacy. We want:

- freedom from confusion to have the freedom of clarity,
- freedom from alienation to be free in the sense of home,
- freedom from contraction to be free to grow,
- freedom from pretension and reaction to have poise and choice,
- freedom from fear to act from wisdom and generosity,
- freedom from reactive self-concern to active intimacy with others, life and the Sacred.

In my own life, I have uncovered countless ways I tried to protect myself from imaginary threats in an effort to secure a sense of well-being. A major agenda in my life has been the need to be highly competent and very "good" in order to feel worthwhile and to have a place in the world. In this struggle, I would use my mental gifts to perform well in the eyes of others.

For example, when I was in my second year at the University, I enrolled in a fourth year class on constitutional law, taught by a brilliant and an extremely tough professor. For the first two or three weeks of the semester, I sat quietly observing and analyzing his lines of reasoning, as well as garnering examples of what to do and not to do from watching others. Only after I was sure of myself did I finally enter into legal arguments with him. I succeeded in winning my point and gaining his respect. It was only then that I felt that I belonged in the class and had something to offer.

Years later, as I struggled to excel at being director of a research institute and a professor myself, I realized that I was hostage to insecurities and my need to prove myself. At that time my first spiritual teacher, Chögyam Trungpa Rinpoche, pointed out that I needed to give all that up including my need to prove myself in spiritual work.

There is always something that holds us back, some image that we are attached to or feel needs to be realized before we can give ourselves over to life and be safe. This is what must be confronted, penetrated, and transformed. In spiritual practice, all the accomplishments, successes, failures, and frustrations are evaporated by the laser of our unrelenting inquiry and our burning desire to live a life of meaning and leave a beneficial legacy.

Freedom arises paradoxically from being what we already are in this divine depth and obeying that nature without getting hijacked by fears, desires for substitutes, and reactions to the challenges of life. When we are divorced from our loving nature, we are seduced by the hope of material success, the promise of intimate pleasure and the possibilities of power. Cut off from the natural ease of being who we truly are, we discharge stress through sex, eating, and emotional outbursts. We worry about how we look, seeking to reveal to ourselves and others the radiance that is our nature. We want to take refuge in a peak experience, the rush of addiction, the ritual smoke, and the mind- and heart-numbing trance of the TV, as if they could offer the simplicity of being that waits in our core but we think we are unable to access.

Our authentic presence is an expression of freedom. We are free when we act in accordance with our deeper spiritual nature, free to be genuine, spontaneous and beneficial without qualification. Spiritual work is based on the view that our ego identities are mistaken ideas about who we are and that each of us can discover the truth. Spiritual teachings work from the premise that a core of wisdom and beneficial intention is basic to the human design. This core is not adopted or imposed, rather it is discovered and nurtured as part of our growth and maturation. The tradition of working with this core has been at the heart of the wisdom and spiritual traditions for thousands of years.

The path of inquiry involves learning how to ask fundamental questions in ways that are fresh and alive. In this way we are training ourselves in a way of being that brings openness, wonder, and a kind of intelligence to the daily circumstances of our lives. In using any of the types of self-inquiry and the various methods developed over the ages, it is vital that the questions open us and take us to the dimensions of sacred being in the moment. The dynamic of wisdom is cultivated by strengthening the inquiry process, following questions with questions, asking with the heart, the senses, and the body as well as the mind.

There are many types of inquiry ranging from those that reflect on the dynamics of our feelings and reactions, to those that penetrate to our fundamental fears and longings to find a core of basic wisdom, to still others that move our consciousness beyond thoughts opening us to pure presence and awareness.

12.

Entity of *We*

There is a saying in Zen, "First there is a mountain, then there is no mountain, then there is." Initially we see majestic heights, the rocky cliffs, and the snowy summit. We walk through the trees, smell their fragrance, and enjoy the colors of the vegetation and the earth. This is the world of our senses, the world of form. This world of form is real and as humans who have bodies and form, we can appreciate and engage this world. At the same time, this is not all there is.

As we open with spiritual practice, we can directly experience the essential nature of all being in which we rest in pure awareness, with no separation between our nature and that of the mountain or the nature of anything else. The mountain disappears as mountain in this boundlessly open embrace. In this experience of oneness, we experience a deeply satisfying completeness and sense of home. Nothing is needed.

Yet we do not escape into this dimension of our being but rather return to daily life, allowing this sensibility of oneness to enliven and illuminate everything in our world. The mountain is now magical in its magnificence as a feature of all that is, in sacred engaged intimacy.

In a relationship we can experience the same dynamic. We

can initially enjoy the sight, feel and fragrance of our partner with all our senses and the depths of our emotions. Then we relax into the unity of "we" in which the sense of separateness dissolves into a sense of a larger whole and collective consciousness. We then bring the radiance of this collective heart posture to the details of our lives together and individually, feeling that everything is enriched by the glow of our collective love.

Buddhism points to our essential nature that is not a thing but is beyond all particular things. The same is true of a love relationship. Love is not a thing, it reaches beyond description in its vastness, openness, clarity, and embrace. Relationship is not a thing either.

Aspects of Relationship

Relationship refers to a number of qualities and experiences. At one level relationship can point to the relative location of two things or people. At another it indicates that two or more people have impact on each other. At still another level relationship refers to the bond that people mutually experience. Further it can also mean the simple act of relating, of mutually opening, being present with each other, and caring.

If we divorce our sense of relationship from actually relating, we diminish the connection. Relationship becomes simply a concept and an intrapsychic phenomenon and not the collaborative act of relating. Upon deep reflection, you can see that the essence of relationship is relating, is an active engagement and is not something to possess or own. Relating involves living experiences together, being aware and sensitive to each other, and responding to the needs of one another.

Experience of *We*

We can be mistaken when we identify intimacy with pleasure, gratification, intensity, and understanding. It is not that we do not experience these in intimate relationships. We do.

Yet authentic intimacy is much deeper and vaster and conveys us beyond our own feelings into the innermost world of the other, into a core of their presence. Something essential in us touches and is touched by what is essential in the other and we are connected. A new entity of *we* is born.

In the experience of *we*, there is an excitement from being more than one plus one equals two. One plus one equals an entity called "we" that is bigger and more inclusive than the energy of two separate people combined. This collective dynamic enhances each individual field of energy and generates a third field, a collective consciousness that encompasses a collective identity, attitudes, values, history, and sensitivities.

Collective Consciousness

We can think of the *we* that develops as a collective being, an entity or larger body that includes each of us and has its own life, dynamics and consciousness, not apart from us but beyond each of us individually. By participating in and nourishing this collectivity, we build a consciousness that has capacities, intelligences, qualities, creativity and powers we cannot have as an isolated, disconnected individual.

The life force of the collective consciousness of relationship is connective intimacy. Through intimacy we experience the vitality, the communion, and the qualitative connection that all parties identify with and feel bound to sustain. It is given form in the body and in the imagination and consciousness of each participant and exists as a sacred field.

This collective entity needs to be nourished. If the sense of *we* dies, the relationship becomes empty, often haunted by the ghosts of hope, disappointment, resentment, grudges, and the stench of its own decay.

We feed the sense of *we* by cultivating a heart posture of inclusion, by developing the sense that we are in this together, by caring about the impact of decisions and events on the other person and on the relationship. We create the *we* day to day by the way we attend to each other and create an environment of love and home. We deepen the connection by sharing from our heart and allowing our partner to touch our innermost being. We build the relationship and make it part of the larger community by working together to welcome others, in participating in community events, in raising children, and in supporting each other to bring our gifts to the world.

One of the wonderful, paradoxical aspects of authentic intimacy is that in the creation of a durable *we*, we find a place where we personally belong and where the integrity and significance of our individuality is respected and maintained. We embrace each other for who we are, without the burden of seeking or giving agreement. We do not depend on each other to validate our value or reality. We are supported in being full participants in the relationship as ourselves. In fact, we are called upon to give our unique gifts to the relationship that in turn supports our bringing these gifts to the larger community.

Relationship as Context and Container

Every *we* and every layer of a relationship is a system or a container. In developing a relationship, we are building a relational container for the intensity of the energies of intimacy. The edge where our two worlds meet is a place of tremendous energy, like the shore where the ocean and the land come together. This meeting can vary from the powerful turbulence of crashing waves to the caress of a gentle surf. Sometimes we feel electric with excitement and at other times relaxed and comforted with the sense of home.

In this sense, intimacy has many of the qualities of a high wire act with both of us as tightrope walkers. We must deal with flux and uncertainty while trying to remain balanced. The act depends on not only maintaining our own equilibrium, but as we shift back and forth to not make moves that will throw off our partner who is on the same thread. This requires dynamic harmony that builds an ever stronger context of *we*.

The relationship grows to contain, accept, and integrate conflictual differences. These differences have the potential to fragment the relationship and dissolve intimacy. We are challenged to build on our similarities, shared feelings and mutual experiences and to identify what the differences really are, using them to learn from each other. The task is often to give boundaries to these differences and tensions within the larger context of the relationship. Then issues do not dominate the relationship but have a place where they can be seen in proportion.

Holding an issue in a larger context of the overall relationship keeps us from being stranded on an island of obsessive thinking and feeling that goes round and round upon itself. Feeling supported for who we are, the radiance and splendor of our own being stands out and intensifies against the background of a luminous relationship, becoming even more intense when beheld against the eternal, clear brilliance of the Sacred.

Boundaries

We are all systems as human beings and we are subsystems of larger systems—physical, social and spiritual. Every system is a container that has boundaries. Boundaries serve many functions. Like our body systems, the boundaries of a relationship contain our potential for action and connection and can mobilize, manage and direct our energy in service to the relationship. They provide clarity about what is internal and what is external to the *we* and can provide definition of the relationship to the larger communities of which our relationship is a part. Boundaries can provide a basis for communication between us, between sets of relationships such as when two couples get together, and with the larger community such as when we participate in religious ceremonies or as parents in meetings with teachers of our children.

How we relate to boundaries often poses real challenges in the modern world where traditional guidelines have been undermined or have even disappeared. Rigid boundaries may feel more secure at times as defenses against a variety of threatening possibilities, but over the long haul they undermine the viability of a relationship because they limit our responses to change and thus inhibit growth. Particularly in intimate relationships, where we want to support each other's development, rigid defenses tend to undermine authenticity and sap the vitality from love. A certain degree of permeability of boundaries supports fresh elements being introduced into the relationship and the sense that the relationship as a collective consciousness can grow as we grow.

In marriage, we forge a container that can hold the dynamic forces and feelings that arise between two people over time and provide a nurturing environment so that each can grow, ripen and bring forth fruit. This container can only be made strong by commitment and discipline. For a marriage to bear fruit both personally and mutually, we must embrace it as the place within which the energies of love and relationship will grow and transform us.

Energy of Intimacy and Relationships

Experientially we all know the feeling of being energized by love. We readily sense that there is an energy that exists between lovers, between parents and children, and between members of a high functioning team.

There are three kinds of energy at work in intimate relationships: flows, fields, and bonds. Flows refer to what goes back and forth between us and what moves in a direction. By giving someone our attention and making efforts to connect with them, we send energy in their direction. It may not be measurable but it can be felt. This energy tends to operate in degrees, namely we can send or receive more or less of it. The intensity of the energy tends to be as important as the character of the energy.

Fields are the spheres of influence we generate through our presence. Our field is experienced more as a quality such as caring, disdain, welcoming, distancing, or love. When we are affected by a field, we tend to be attracted or repelled. Fields set a certain atmosphere. The strength of a field is defined by the intensity of its quality and its reach, how far it extends from its source.

Bonds, or binding energy, define the boundaries and nature of the relationship. Bonds maintain the integrity of the relationship and stabilize the activities of flows and fields. Binding energy maintains the integrity of any entity and contains the blueprint or design when new entities are created.

Binding Energy

I am suggesting that binding energy operates in four ways in a relationship: as pathways, connectors, a container, and a regenerator—as pathway like blood vessels, as connector like tendons, as container like skin, and as procreator/regenerator like the DNA containing an intelligence/blueprint. We can notice that, in an intimate relationship, we have particular ways of getting and receiving attention—pathways. There are objects, activities, and places we are mutually attached to—connectors. We develop a culture of mutual meanings, agreements, and values—container. And patterned ways of doing things and ways of relating tend to shape how we respond to new situations and the ways we incorporate new activities into our mutual lives.

At a personal level, within our self-system, binding energy is what holds our belief systems together—our identities, world views, heart postures, cosmologies. At the level of a relationship, binding energy gives coherence to our collective consciousness of shared feelings, meanings, values, and goals.

Clearly, consciousness and imagination—our awareness, images, thoughts, and feelings—play a critical role in the development and strength of bonds.

We want to cultivate the qualities that enhance binding energy as part of a maturing relationship—love, trust, respect, caring, admiration, willingness to share, willingness to be cared for, sense of sacred, clarity, authenticity, playfulness, and devotion. Being conscious in our personal growth, psychologically, emotionally, intellectually, and spiritually supports us individually in bringing these qualities to our relationships. We also need to mutually work to bring these qualities to the relationship so that we strengthen not only the heart to heart connection but also the environment of the relationship as whole, day to day, hand in hand. Bonding transforms our heart posture from the desire to get or create connection to the felt reality of having connection. The connection becomes a given, a familiar home, and our task becomes consciously growing and caretaking the intimacy that holds us in its embrace.

The concerns of a collective consciousness are naturally collective in directing attention to the development and well being of the whole. Yet, in many cases, there also exists an active awareness and support for individual members. Both the individual and the collective are open and related systems that are dynamically evolving. There is no sense of opposition between the individual and the group because there is a personal and collective sense of being intimately, integrally and mutually related.

In Buddhist practice, we take refuge in the Buddha, the Dharma (teachings of the Buddha), and the *sangha* (the community of other spiritual practitioners). Taking refuge in the Buddha encourages us to grow spiritually and to mature into the realization and embodiment that the Buddha experienced and manifested in his life. Taking refuge in the Dharma encourages us to use the teachings as a path to clarity, encompassing awareness, and boundless compassion. Taking refuge in the *sangha* suggests that we bring our spiritual efforts and realizations into our relationships and use the dynamics of relating to enhance our spiritual maturation.

For monks, the *sangha* is their monastic community and the community of formal practitioners. For lay people it can be our practice community. For those of us in partner relationships, we can take refuge in love, in the wisdom that can be provoked by living with another person if we remain conscious, and in the cultivation of "we."

Creating durable and supportive relationships is made possible by love combined with attentiveness, embracing awareness, and vital presence. Relationships are powerful opportunities to learn about ourselves, about the world beyond us, and how to translate our spiritual life into daily practice.

Relationships call to us to move beyond our self-concern, our desire for control, our self-righteousness, and our self-centeredness and to relax into who we truly are. We become more connected, more integrated with the whole, and more fully our unique self.

As Thomas Patrick Malone and Patrick Thomas Malone say in their book *The Art of Intimacy*, "...few of us could sit in a closet with another person for any length of time without learning a great deal about that person.... In the closet our own awareness is focused on the other while we are close. But in some rare moments, in that shared space of our closet and in the presence of the other, we may experience ourselves in some new, different, and more profound way. This is intimacy. When I am close, I know you; when I am intimate, I know myself. When I am close, I know you in your presence; when I am intimate, I know myself in your presence. Intimacy is a remarkable experience. Usually I know myself only in my aloneness, my dreams, my personal space. But to feel and know myself in the presence of another is enlivening, enlightening, joyful, and most of all, freeing. I can be who I am freely and fully in the presence of another."[xxxii]

Buddhism explicitly encourages us to see how selfish desires and self-preoccupation cause suffering. In a relationship we quickly realize that we cannot always get what we want, since the desires of another person or persons must be taken into account. All circumstances become opportunities to learn and grow.

In working as a family, group, or community we often tap more readily into a deeper process of awareness and dimensions of consciousness than if trying to do it by ourselves. Even when working alone, we can access collective consciousness by sensing our connection to family, a teacher, a larger community, ancestors, and a lineage of wisdom beings. Since a collective conscious, particularly a sacred one, does not conform to the usual limitations of time and space, we can utilize its potential through our heart connection, making our efforts collaborative.

While writing this book, which I do in a separate space within our house, I always begin by sensing my connection to my teachers, my spiritual communities, and the entire wisdom lineage that I am dedicated to. Frequently I experience receiving insights and wisdom that is beyond what I have previously thought or known. During the writing of the book *Opening the Heart of Compassion*, I regularly received teachings from my teacher Dilgo Khyentse Rinpoche, even though he was in Bhutan and I was in the United States. The heart connection seemed to acquire a specific focus when he sent his blessing for the writing of the book.

When we are connected into this collective consciousness, we know in our very being our interconnectedness with others and with life, becoming agents of a larger community. We are participating and contributing to a larger system, feeling a communion through shared understandings, responsibilities and dedication. Belonging to a larger whole, in a mature community, means that we know the value of our particular and often unique contributions.

Relationship as Environment

When we live and work alone, we are often unaware of our habitual patterns because we live inside them without the input and responses of others. Relationships force us to confront our conditioning, stirring up our worst fears and exciting our secret hopes and longings. Intimacy heightens our consciousness making all our peaks and valleys and rough edges more evident. In a loving relationship, we can experience an environment of support for moving beyond our stuck places and our internal quagmire to the flowing nature of the river of life carried by the authenticity of our presence and the connections of caring.

To open our hearts, we all need to work through layers of buffering that were meant to keep us safe from pain and ignorant of our underlying grief. This underlying grief is for the loss of aliveness and intimacy with the Sacred and a vital larger collective consciousness. It includes all the ways we exiled ourselves from life out of reaction, spite, or fatigue. We want to tap all the energy contained in our physical, emotional and spiritual contractions that inhibit our hearts and preoccupy our minds.

A relationship that creates a space for us to share these feelings provides a loving container into which we can place long-ignored pains and begin the journey beyond our personal history. We forgive the pain and reconcile with our past. We grieve what was of value from the past and take that value into our hearts as inspiration. When we grieve fully, the remnants of pain bring forth a confidence and gratitude. We replace ancient sufferings made up of fears, frustration, sadness, and confusion with aliveness, compassion, and a heartfelt tenderness.

When we are loving and conscious in our relationships, we make manifest an inner sacredness, a holy spark or flame. This in turn creates a sacred environment for our partner and others to share their holy flames creating a blessed warmth for everyone, a sacred hearth. Just as we are the environment that others experience, so our relationships are an environment for other people and other relationships.

As we create an environment of love through our presence and the qualities that manifest in our relationships, we implicitly call on others to organize themselves as if they are in the very presence of love itself. Spreading this sacred aspect of intimacy supports the Divine manifesting collectively through the culture and atmosphere of the community. It has even been suggested that the next Buddha may be a community.

In a Buddhist frame, we do not direct our energies to trying to change our partner but more on recognizing their wisdom nature, on knowing how things are with them, and on how we can work together. We enlarge our perspective in at least four ways: by perceiving the fundamental humanity and lovability of our partner; by knowing that particular circumstances are impermanent and will change, placing the particulars of a situation in the context of time and space; by sensing our basic heart connection and realizing that they long for the same happiness and belonging that we do; and by willingly entering their world and opening our own to them.

In Buddhism a metaphor for our fundamental sacred nature is of a bird that flies through the air leaving no traces. This suggests both the freedom of movement and the sense that each moment simply comes and goes and when it is gone, it is no more. Our divine nature is like the sky in that all the passing phenomena leave no traces on its vast original beauty.

While the sky and our essential nature are not impacted by the flight of birds, thoughts, feelings, actions, these phenomena do have impact on each other in the relative world where everything and everyone is interconnected. The relative world is the world of "karma." In this world, every thought, feeling, and behavior leaves traces and those traces make up the conditions for experience and action in our future and the future of other people. Because *karma*, which means "action," has impact, it always presents us with the opportunity to create benefit through our actions.

In Buddhist meditation, we make a choice to be present and attend to the moment rather than get distracted by worries, habitual patterns of thinking, or emotional distress. The present moment is like a lover. Our connection is sustained by committed gentle attention creating an embracing environment of presence and engagement.

All relationships can support us remaining conscious and can encourage a collective consciousness. We need to intentionally act to create a collective ecology where everyone takes responsibility for building a home where we all bring our full presence, a willingness to deeply listen, an open heart, and an unconditional sense of connection and support.

Larger Circles of Intimacy and Relationships

The goal of the community is to make sure that each member of the community is heard and is properly giving the gifts that they have brought to the world.

SOBONFU E. SOMÉ [xxxiii]

All relationships are more than personal. They belong to the community and to the culture. Any relationship, love relationship, friendship, or family, is a gift from the Divine and we have been brought together for some purpose. A mature relationship serves more than our personal happiness. It supports each of us giving our gifts to the world and our realization of our life purpose.

Community is the context and entity where we can collectively make our contributions, help others succeed in their purpose of service, take care of each other, and amplify our sacred celebration. We relate to and feed the larger community as individuals, couples, families, workers, and friends. Our participation and contributions weave the tapestry of connections that make a collective soul that not only supports us but informs future generations in their dance of intimacy and growth.

To serve this larger community well, we need to be aware of its culture, meanings, rituals, and needs and find the time, energy and attention to bring our presence and our creations. We want to ask ourselves "How is our marriage, partnership, family, and/or friendship serving the larger community? What are its larger purposes?" Without our contributions, a community will disintegrate. And with a fragmented community, we find fewer and fewer ways and places to contribute our gifts.

When we become preoccupied and consumed by the enclosed small circle of a complex relationship, we shut out the larger context of which we are a part and the expansive possibilities of love in the community and in the world. Without the larger world to feed it, a love relationship will devour itself over time and we are left with a shell and no substance, a house that is lacking the living presence of sacred love to make it a home.

Our spiritual development and connection to the sacred is nurtured in relationships and in community through our participation in shared feelings, shared vision, shared experiences, shared memory, shared challenges, and shared hope. It is in loving, living and working together that we not only get support and share our gifts, but we also learn about ourselves and the world.

In relationships and communities in which we are supported in giving our gifts, we feel at home and are nourished by our giving. When this does not happen, we feel disempowered, cut off, and empty, leaving us with the ghost of our giving impulse which is an insatiable hunger that is susceptible to addictions and consuming rather than creating. When we hold back our contributions feeling that we have nowhere to have them received, we can experience both the void and the blockage of our natural flow, mentally, emotionally, and spiritually. We feel spiritually impoverished and homeless.

As the fabric of community and extended family becomes thin and weak, we place more reliance on couples, friends, and coworkers for the sense of belonging and deep connection to life, the world, and the Sacred. The absence of an integrated community and of a living relationship to the Sacred leaves us individually and as couples and families responsible for ourselves and for all the things in our lives. In these situations, we try to be a full community to each other and the burden can be more than many of us can reasonably bear.

Today we are rarely a part of the same community from birth, through childhood, through our working years and into our later years and death. We are repeatedly challenged to create communities that are places where we feel at home, have deep connections, can give our gifts, and can receive the support we need. To make all this viable requires a mutual commitment to the larger story of the community, tribe, lineage, and/or nation.

The heart posture of contributing to larger stories opens us to the support of others, to the gift of giving and supporting others, and to the energy of wisdom traditions. These can only be fully opened by our service to that which is beyond us and by our recognition of interconnection, interbeing, and interdependence of all life.

Mutuality of Giving and Receiving

Intimacy involves a *mutuality* of giving and receiving. One of the wonders is that, from the point of view of our spiritual growth, we receive through giving and give through receiving. Our sense of connection and contribution are enhanced by giving and we enhance these qualities in others by opening to receive from them. This giving and receiving principle applies to everything from love, to sharing stories and inner truths, to the gifts of our presence and hard work.

This principle of the mutuality of giving and receiving is at the heart of marriage, family, work groups, teams, friendships, support groups such as A.A., genuine service to those in need and a balanced relationships with the Sacred. Mutuality forms the basis of the heart posture and practice of compassion and addresses a basic question of our belonging by placing us within a community of fellow human beings.

The task of reviving community in our fragmented world may seem daunting. Yet if we do not start here and act now, the process of community dissolution will accelerate. This challenge is part of a larger story that began long before we were born. It has been faced a number of times in the past as humans have had to reform their communities to navigate the changes from hunting and gathering families to tribes, from nomadic tribes to landed peoples who till the earth, to larger scale civilizations, and on into the present era of industrialization, commercialization, and high speed exchange of information.

We can start with the simple acts of kindness and connection that create a collectively supportive environment for all of us to live and work in. When we act for the benefit of others and for our communities, we may operate locally but with results that have global implications. By tapping into and cultivating a sacred sense of love, we amplify its presence in our time and make it a living, radiant legacy for future generations. We keep the sense of the Beloved alive in the world.

We must embrace and do this now if an age of intimate communities is even to re-emerge hundreds of years in the future. We can set in motion the evolution of our relationships and our society so our children can learn, grow, and improve on what we have created.

Vital Communication

Among the many ways we weave the threads of intimacy together is communication—the ways we give voice to our love. Communication is more than the exchange of information. To communicate is "to reveal clearly," "manifest," "to receive communion," and "to be connected, one with another." (*American Heritage Dictionary of the English Language*)

It is said in some of the mystical Jewish traditions that our words are angels that are sent out into the world. Once we create them, they have a life of their own that is beyond our control. Clearly, there are many kinds of these angels, many of them sweet and many that are ugly and bitter. We want to be conscious of the angels we are releasing into a relationship and the world, for these become part of the environment that we and other people live in.

Communication includes more than what we say verbally. It includes our body postures and gestures, our expressions, our silences, our actions, and the quality of our presence. Being mindful in communication that encompasses all these dimensions may seem daunting. The key is really quite simple. The quality of our communications is determined by the way we combine our head and our heart.

When we communicate strictly from our head, our communications are totally dependent on the clarity of our thinking and even the clearest message will lack the depth and soul that can come only from the heart. This may suffice in certain types of functional communications in impersonal contexts such as a business report or a financial evaluation, but it can become deadening if it dominates personal relationships, even in business contexts.

When we communicate strictly from our heart, our communications are totally dependent on the purity of our feelings and the quality of our intentions. In this case, even the clearest emotion stated with the best intention may lack the care of articulation and the intelligence that comes from the head. This can serve certain expressive purposes and is important where there are mental barriers and censors, but it can become overwhelming and self-preoccupied because it lacks the larger vision of the contexts and sensibilities of other people and the quality of the environment we are creating through our choice of words and expressions. Communications that leave the mind out tend to be reactive and are often shaped by the power of our fears, longings, and anxieties about being overwhelmed.

The integration of head and heart can result in communications that authentically connect us to others and create an atmosphere that is aligned with our intentions. When we communicate to create and sustain intimacy, our words, silences, stances, gestures, and deeds reflect our basic heart posture of love.

Like Moses who finds his voice when he discovers his calling from God, so our true voice emerges when we are aligned with our deeper nature, contributing our gift to the world and committed to supporting the participation and contribution of others in our relationships. This is what makes us free. This is what allows us to lead and be led into the land of our true home away from being enslaved by reactive habits, fears, needs, and frustrations. When we dedicate our lives to our mission and to growing into the wisest and most loving manifestation of that mission, our voice, through our true vocation (calling), becomes sacred, expressing wisdom, and our actions spontaneously manifest our celebration and service to the Sacred.

Cultivating Intimacy in Communications

The depth of our connection grows through the quality of our communications and the ways we listen to each other. Good communication is not agreement, understanding or even liking the messages we receive. A partner can understand us perfectly and still say things that we do not like and don't want to hear.

We often think that if our partner only understood our feelings, situation, thinking, or life story, then agreement would prevail. This is often a way of saying: How dare you try to be my lover, my friend, my partner and not see things my way!

All couples have differences. Relationships that maintain intimacy find ways to incorporate those differences into the relationship and give them a place. We turn perpetual issues into annoyances that we live with and work around, not making the marriage or friendship hostage to them as a perceived problem. This presumes, of course, that the issue is benign. Physical and sexual abuse are another matter, for these are destructive problems that need to be confronted.

We all spend years trying to change each other's mind and rarely does that ever occur. Many significant disagreements cannot be resolved and we must find ways of living with that reality and not letting the marriage get hijacked by them. Most disagreements are rooted in basic differences of personality, values, and lifestyle sensibilities. We must learn to accept and even appreciate these differences and center our attention on what builds positive regard and feelings.

Communication involves being fully and intimately present with each other. In sharing feelings, we speak from the heart asking only that our partner witness with their full attention. In listening we open to what is shared even if we have our own feelings, judgments, or do not understand how it is they came to feel that way.

One of the primary practices in Buddhism is giving and receiving. Usually this refers to radiating compassion and taking in the suffering of others. At the same time the underlying principle of the flow of interconnection applies to sharing. We reveal what is true for us to our partner and receive what they share. This sharing cultivates presence, acceptance, openness, listening, and trust. Each person sheds layers of defenses both in the sharing and the listening. The sharer in the process of trusting that what he or she says will be heard and the listener in the simple act of being present without having to respond, defend, or make it better. Each person learns to feel free to simply be who each is, without pretense or agenda.

One of the lessons in the sharing process is that love is embodied and it is clearly embodied in the silence of listening as well as in the words of our speech. The sharing process is an opportunity individually and mutually to experience and embody connection through both speaking and listening.

We speak our own truth. Except under circumstance of the most intimate communion, we are not in a position to speak for each other about what the other feels and how those feelings arose. When we think we know what is really going on with each other, we are usually projecting something from within us. Even if some of it is accurate, it lacks our partner's voice. Even though we always have theories about why our partner behaves the way they do or says what they say, these are our ideas about them filtered through our own hopes, fears, experience, and agendas. This is why it is important to avoid stereotypical, psychological, moral, and prejudicial labeling. These only lead to misunderstanding, depersonalizing conflict, denial of real issues, and escalation of alienation.

Intimate relationships are able to contain and explore differences without criticizing, psychologizing, or blaming each other for ideas, feelings, and positions. Through good communication we find similarities within our differences and further explore the differences in those similarities. We continually support the relationship containing the differences, connecting through similarities, and growing through our ability to host them all.

From this we evolve a critical mass of shared meanings, purposes, experiences, challenges and successes to sustain the relationship. Building on a basic love, we create a home in the relationship in which we are responsive to each other's bids for connection with our attention and presence. We consciously create the environment of the relationship we mutually want through the ways we welcome each other, the ways we say goodbye, the ways we share about our day, and the ways our respect and love are reflected in what we say to and about our partner. We also intentionally encourage each other to grow and share what they have to offer with the larger community.

Strengthening Bonds Through Challenge

There is a Zen koan that goes: "How would you walk straight through a narrow mountain path of forty-nine curves?" This question is meant to awaken us to the directness of our clarity and our vision of the goal of unwavering support, the unity of being and our home in our relationship and the path even as we navigate all the unknown challenges of life.

Maintaining a relationship periodically and unpredictably involves challenges as circumstances change. When an impactful event occurs, we often reactively try to divert the energy released (distraction), to constrict it (trauma/reacting in/repression or suppression), or discharge it (reacting out). Then our decisions are reactions to the tension of conflicting feelings and difficult choices and do not reflect real clarity about the situation or our real intentions. Other times we may fall into ambivalence where we vacillate between choosing sides in our inner struggle moving one way one moment and the other way the next.

In these reactions, we lose the opportunity to learn how to be fully present and even energized by the tension. By living in the middle, we can intensify our sense of presence by drawing energy from the sense of uncertainty and from each of our conflicting possibilities. In this middle place we can experience every feeling and choice openly and fully and explore their meaning, implications, and dynamics. The middle way leads to both personal and mutual growth.

This choice between reaction and growth, while not easy, is critical to the long term well-being of a relationship and our confidence in its potential to endure. When we openly and mutually respond to changed circumstances, such as loss of a job, a family member, or physical health, we find that learning and new forms of integration are possible. Depending on how we frame the challenges in our imaginations, we can even make such challenges opportunities for transformation and deepening of our intimacy.

If we turn to other lovers when things get difficult, or complain to friends about problems without dealing with our partner, or seek escape in work or substances, we make the container of our marriage leaky and the energies that could support our growth will drain away.

"What do I do with these feelings of something missing in my marriage?" This question has been posed to me by many students and clients. One woman, we shall call her Rebecca, had been married for nine years and had two young children. She liked her husband and thought of him as good man. She expressed distress that her feelings were not more vibrant and romantic toward him. She was not interested in someone else, but struggled with the feeling that life was passing her by while she did time with her husband until the children were older and more independent.

Many of us have or had such questions at times in our relationships. For some this is something to accept without having to act upon the feelings. For others it raises questions about the commitment to stay in the relationship. I cannot advise you whether to stay or leave but to become more aware of the source of your dissatisfaction. Is it the result of idealized expectations, a perceptual filter to find what is missing, a habit of dissatisfaction, or in fact a destructive and deadening relationship?

When we define or characterize our life by what we do not have, we are manifesting what Buddha called "wanting mind." This frame appears in obvious and subtle ways. When we want more money to purchase a larger home in a better neighborhood or when we experience irritation with particular habits of our partner, ourselves, or our lives and then compare these discomforts and frustrations with an imagined perfect alternative, we set ourselves up for suffering and a heart posture of insufficiency.

Being grounded in a spiritual practice provides the consciousness, strength and confidence to cope with the challenges that all relationships encounter. In fact we not only deal with the cycles of our connections, we use them to become more aware, more loving, more inclusive and more engaged with each other and with life. The hardest spiritual practice we can engage in is an intimate relationship.

The more we practice consciousness and communication, the more skilled we become and the greater our confidence in our own abilities and in the relationship itself. Through practice we master not only the techniques but also ourselves. Just as a dancer masters body movements to the point of surrendering to the flow of music and creating an ever wider range of artistic expression, so we can master our emotional and interactive life, making our relationships an embodiment of love.

As we relax into the home of the marriage, we release the energy that was captive to our reactive fears and agendas. We then cultivate the deeper qualities of our being and of intimacy. We create new possibilities for each other and for our work in the world, engaging in a sacred endeavor of making the relationship a beneficial presence in the world. We experience an inner freedom and sense of larger contribution as together we provide a nurturing and loving environment for others.

The uncertainties and challenges of intimacy are made more workable when we have a sense of a sacred context for the relationship such as bringing out our spiritual potential, serving others such as children or our community, and serving the world of the Sacred itself. Within this context we want to give central roles to connection, wisdom and growth, making love, consciousness and learning operating principles.

We then weave these new threads of our relationship into the fabric of the whole story of our life together. This expanded story further bonds us to each other and creates connection with others who are inspired by or learn from our story.

13.

Intimate Bonds That Support Relationship Development

Intimate relationships involve love, connection, and a sense of home. The social dynamic and experience of connective intimacy arises in three fundamental aspects of a relationship. Heart to Heart intimacy arises from our sense of "being," engages us through love and passion, prefers face to face interactions, and is refined through transformation. Hand in Hand intimacy relates primarily to "having" a relationship, creating an environment of love, has the sense of being circular, and is supported by virtues that build the character of each of us and of the relationship as a whole. Shoulder to Shoulder intimacy, through our "doing," creates our legacy, individually and collectively, that contributes to the larger community and the future, tends to be linear in that it is more functional and goal oriented, and often reflects our sense of mission/calling in life.

Heart to Heart	Being	Engagement through love	Face to Face	Transformation
Hand in Hand	Having	Environment of Love	Circular	Character
Shoulder to Shoulder	Doing	Creating Legacy	Linear	Mission/Calling

Heart to Heart Intimacy

Heart to heart intimacy flowers when some innermost core of our being is touched by another and we touch their heart in a similar way. We share deep longings, feelings, and caring.

In heart to heart connections we become real to each other as we share the erotic aliveness of sharing with each other verbally, physically, sexually, and spiritually. We focus on both the similarities and differences that make for mutual endearment. The heart to heart brings out the depth of feelings and our potential for intense focused relating. Great pleasure, pain, satisfaction, and dissatisfaction flow from the vibrancy of the feelings and the concentration of attention in heart to heart intimacy.

Heart to heart intimacy, at the beginning of a relationship, focuses on the deliciousness of the experience of connection in the moment. The concentration on each other creates a small circle of "we," now. Other people, things, demands, and considerations are treated as external to the relationship. They feel like distractions. We are fully immersed in the river of our heart connection. We are alive and reborn moment to moment in the rapture of communion, of feeling at one with our partner.

Beyond the initial flush of love, heart to heart intimacy plays a critical role in the special moments that couples and friends have together and at times when the relationship is facing a challenge. The challenge can center around an important event or changes in the circumstances our lives.

Heart to heart intimacy both unsettles us and supports us. It can lead to tears, joy, grief, laughter, wounding, tenderness, healing, and the warmest hearth. This aspect of intimacy contains sweetness, hazard, whole-hearted engagement, and the possibility of ecstasy.

Heart to heart intimacy always involves self-reflection, which can be a kind of self-confrontation, and the sharing of insights and inner dynamics with our partner. In heart to heart intimacy, we encounter the paradox that, as we let someone into the innermost parts of ourselves, we open the door for ourselves as well.

Hand in Hand Intimacy

Sustaining connection requires creating an ongoing way of relating that includes all parts of life—our daily routines, caring for our living space, hosting, being entertained, having friendships, work, navigating life cycles, change, learning, and growing. This daily, weekly, monthly, seasonally, and yearly connection challenges us to create the environment of home, an environment of the relationship we want that reflects the qualities, meanings, and values that we hold dear. The process of creating and maintaining this environment of love and connection establishes further bonds and deepens those that are there.

Mutual engagement in this process gives rise to hand in hand intimacy. We co-create the sense of home together in the way we greet each other, the way we move in a room to be near each other, the way we stand when we are with other people, the way we say goodbye, the way we ask our partner to pass the salt, the way we look at each other, the way we share about our day, the way we respond to bids for attention, and the way we say good night. In other words, hand in hand intimacy is the home we experience in the relationship over time more than in the intensity of our feeling.

The exquisite beauty of the heart to heart connection needs to be framed in the simple beauty of mundane, day to day, hand in hand intimacy. Without that frame, the energies of the heart lack a home, a context, and so have a tendency to wander.

John Gottman, along with many family therapists, argues that the most important predictor of satisfaction and durability in a relationship centers around how people handle hand in hand intimacy, the day-to-day bidding and responding in relationships. The hand in hand relies for its durability on supportive routines and rituals, on an attitude of freshness—doing something again for the first time—and the capacity for delightfully surprising variation. While unremitting change leaves a fragmented house for the relationship, skillfully introducing variations in routines and new activities periodically maintains enough of the edge of the unknown to keep the relationship alert and exciting.

Hand in hand maintains an ecology of all the factors of life in ways that support each of us and encourage a heart posture of love as a defining characteristic of the relationship in all of its dynamics and manifestations. Hand in hand intimacy builds confidence in the relationship itself that can hold all the cycles and variations of our feelings. The daily deposits of attention, kindness, caring, and respect grow a connective savings account that is needed during times of stress and emotional lows and for investing in the work that we individually and collectively do in the larger community and world.

We are the environment for each other in a marriage, a friendship, or a team. Our relationship is also an environment that people beyond the relationship experience. The qualities that we bring to our relationships, that our relationships bring to others, and that get passed on by others to the world shape the collective environment that we all live and work in.

Shoulder to Shoulder Intimacy

Mutually creating a home, raising children, working together, teaming up, making decisions, resolving conflicts, and taking on projects—all these bring us together to accomplish something. Working together to achieve an outcome, whether for one of us, for the relationship, for our family, our friendship, for the larger community, for our company, for our team, or for the causes we support develops shoulder to shoulder intimacy.

We experience this most obviously as members of a team, as co-workers in an organization, and as parents raising children. We also have experienced it as siblings and friends playing together as children.

Shoulder to shoulder is more activity based. We are comrades, brothers, sisters, and companions. The intimacy is deepened as we share activities and experiences at the same time. Meeting challenges and solving problems together strengthens the bonds, like soldiers who have served and fought a common enemy, or neighbors who build a playground, or classmates who study together to prepare for an exam.

In the film *Nowhere in Africa*, the couple reclaims their relationship through the intimacy of fighting shoulder to shoulder against locusts that attacked their crops and threatened their harvest.

Shoulder to shoulder intimacy results from playing, traveling, making and listening to music, dancing, and having adventures together. Celebration also binds us in this kind of intimacy and brings forth collective joy, grief, and praise.

Working together brings out the part of us that wants to make a contribution to life and to create a legacy that will be carried on in the world. The relationships we form around offering our gifts to the world bring both inspiration and satisfaction and play a vital role in creating a home in the world and a home for those in need.

Types of Communication

In a supportive relationship there are three types of communication that are useful to distinguish—sharing, environmental, and dialogical.

Sharing

Sharing involves both speaking and listening. In authentic sharing we speak about what is true for us from our heart, our innermost core. Speaking about the things we want our partner to know about us, we open ourselves to being heard and seen in ever deeper ways.

We listen with our full presence. To fully listen means that we do not get caught up in understanding or judgment. We become intimate witnesses for each other. We take in the presence of the person speaking, as well as the content of what they are saying without becoming preoccupied with the implications about us. As a listener, our job is presencing in an open and interested way.

Sharing enhances heart to heart intimacy. It leads to increasing trust in being able to safely share feelings and speak our truth. We learn how to stay present with each other and hold that innermost truth. Regular sharing frees us from having to carry around the baggage of unspoken issues that could accumulate an intense destructive charge.

It is important in sharing that we authentically disclose our truths rather than get into doing a "presentation" of the self we want the other person to hear or of a point of view that we are trying to convince our partner to agree with. During sharing, it is vital that we maintain a clear sense of ourselves, even when we know that our partner may not like nor agree with what we are saying and that we not try to manipulate them into seeing things our way. Authentic sharing is not about having power over each other's thoughts, feelings and behavior. It allows us to discover both similarities and differences without an agenda of getting agreement. Sharing offers a gift that invites each of us to enter the world and heart of our partner.

The sharing process, like all witnessing, enlarges the frame of reference beyond our inner critic, which in its imperial greed would occupy all our inner space. In a setting of sharing inner stories and truths, we form a community of witnesses. The sense of mutuality grows not simply from what is said and heard but also from having shared the experience of the process.

By listening and sharing and being together, we fashion a mutual story of home. The relationship becomes the context where our ambivalences of thoughts and feelings, our missteps in behavior, and our ambiguities fit in and bridge the personal with the shared, the individual with the collective, and the known with the unknown. The shared story becomes the relationship that can hold the disagreements and challenges that inevitably exist.

There is the famous story of a woman who brings her dead child to the Buddha and insists that he bring the child back to life. He sees her grief and distress and agrees that he will do this, if she would first go to every family in her village and find one that has not had a death. She faithfully goes to each house and listens to each family recount their tale of loss and grief. She not only cannot find one household not touched by death, but is transformed in the process. She returns to Buddha with her new wisdom and matured heart to perform the appropriate ceremonies for her child and to become a disciple.

Authentic sharing moves the energy in a relationship away from blame, fear, anger, withdrawal, and retaliation and toward continually weaving the fabric of the relationship using the thread of current experience and connection. We move away from patterns of avoidance and distraction and toward embracing and affirming what is true for each person, for the relationship, and for the large contexts of which the relationship is a part.

In sharing we also learn two additional lessons—*humility* and *obedience*. *Humility* grounds us in relation to others rather than controlling them. It means we take a learning stance rather than a problem solving position. It engages our heart more than our mind. It respects the truth of our partner rather than insisting on our ideas about them. It treats them as a real person not an object of observation and reaction. *Obedience* means simply to subject our views of our partner to their truth by thoroughly listening with an open heart.

Environment of Love

Love prepares the ground and plants the seed for intimacy to grow. After it sprouts, we intentionally nurture it through actions, caring, consciousness, and loving communication so that intimacy will grow, flower, and bear its wonderfully delicious fruit.

Building the hand in hand environment of a loving home in relationship means we appreciate our partner each day, moment to moment, seeing him or her freshly as if for the first time. We seed and grow the home together through an ongoing process of loving attention, fresh appreciation, a heart posture of praise and abiding affection.

In the home of love, we cultivate appreciation and joy in just being around the house together even as each person engages in different activities and interests. Paradoxically, this sense of home is nurtured by sharing a space together and yet the sense of presence of our partner can be experienced beyond space and time. In this transcendent quality, we can be mutually present with our partner in our hearts even as we are physically separate. Even with distance, we feel bonded.

Integrity in relationships means being true to the relationship, to its spirit, to its energy, to its agreements, to its process and evolution, to the reality of the relationship as it is now and as we mutually envision it becoming. We want to develop the heart posture of a caretaker of our relationships not a proprietor or owner. We are stewards of love not possessors or creators of it. Love is a gift, a blessing that we want to open and it is meant to be shared.

We cannot live in the pretense that we act and feel from our sacred open and loving nature when that is not the case. We all have times of reaction, laziness, superficiality, and unconsciousness. A healthy relationship does not depend on our total consciousness and love. Patience, kindness, regard, attention and support in the day-to-day details of living together are what weave the fabric of a strong relationship.

There are no short cuts to real intimacy. It must be cultivated moment to moment, action by action, and at the same time we must open to receiving its blessing. Each blessing is a seed that must be nurtured to live and grow. This requires work and practical skills in building and sustaining the intimacy in our relationships as we become close friends. John Gottman makes the simple point that happy marriages, for example, are "based on a deep friendship." This friendship involves mutual respect and enjoyment of each other and taking the time to support those qualities.

Supporting Hand in Hand Friendship

In loving hand in hand intimacy we keep moving the overall state of our relationship in an increasingly positive direction. With a high state of caring and loving, the threshold for unbalancing the relationship in a negative direction is set very high. In marriage, we have the sense that we are mutually responsible for creating the relationship we both want to call home, a home for both the romance and sharing of heart to heart intimacy and for mutual endeavors of raising children and participating in larger communities.

Among the dynamics that can most undermine hand in hand intimacy and usually the other two as well, are constant criticism, contempt, withdrawal, feeling at war, closing off to overtures of connection and frequently feeling overwhelmed. When we have passed over a negative threshold, almost everything is interpreted and felt more negatively and feeds our distress with the relationship. Simple feedback is taken as an attack. Judgment and righteousness prevail over friendship and love as we engage in an ongoing undeclared war, turning our partner into an opponent.

Hand in hand intimacy that builds a home of friendship fuels the flames of romance because it provides a loving, positive environment that protects us from feeling adversarial. Our heart posture is one of caring and friendship rather than living in a war zone. The caring atmosphere of home creates a container within which disagreements and annoyances can come and go or even have their own small space within the whole of the relationship. They are like a squeaky door in a beautiful house. The squeak is annoying but the overall beauty is what gets most of our attention and what we enjoy.

The practical suggestions that follow are not a cookbook for relationships. We must remember to listen deeply to the authentic voices of the sacred that are trying to speak and create benefit through each relationship and the situations we face. At the same time, there are specific things we can do, guidelines we can follow, and qualities we can cultivate.

Life and relationships all require consciousness, communication, sharing, vision, groundedness, capacity to nurture one another, peace, reflection, wisdom, reconciliation, purpose, humor, magic, and integrity. To realize the potential of intimacy also requires stamina, tenacity, dedication to a sacred purpose and commitment. Consciousness and communication form the foundation for building an intimate relationship that works.

Kurtz and Ketcham tell a wonderful story:

> "An old Jewish woman was dying of rectal cancer. Her husband sat at her bedside, holding her hand, talking to her, crying with her.
>
> "A nurse came into the room. 'Excuse me, sir,' she said, gently touching his shoulder. 'It's time to change the bandages. If you'll leave the room, I'll be done in just a few minutes.'
>
> "'Excuse *me*,' the man replied with a gentle but determined smile, 'but I'll stay right here. This *tush* and I have had a lot of good times together. I'm not going to turn my

back on it now.'" [xxxiv]

Hello! How Are You? And Goodbye

Environmental communications establish and maintain the qualities in the relationship that are the atmosphere each of us lives in. There are many types of relationship environments. Some may look and feel like a desert, without much growing in it. Others have the sense of being a dump filled with discarded feelings and the rotting waste of resentment and regret. And some are like a garden in which beauty is cultivated, new growth is incorporated, a wildness is included within boundaries, and we feel inspired, nourished, and supported in both mundane and sacred ways. If we want a loving relationship, our communications express support and do not diminish the environment of love. We actively grow the environment of the relationship we want, deepening and widening the reach of hand in hand intimacy between us.

The key principle here is that *we are the environment that other people experience*. The question is always, *what kind of environment are we creating?* Are we polluting or creating beauty and benefit? This principle applies not simply in our marriage, but in all of the contexts in which we are participants. From a spiritual point of view, even in solitude, each of us contributes to the atmosphere of consciousness that we all live in.

Environmental communications range from the way we greet each other in the morning and on coming home from work, to the way we talk when preparing a meal, driving someplace, or relaxing together. These include the qualities of our day-to-day presence with each other, our facial expressions, our body postures, and our gestures toward or away from each other.

Very importantly, the ways we respond to bids for attention play a vital role in our experience of the relationship environment. Do we listen when our partner wants to share experience from the day? Do we give them a hug when they are feeling down? Do we encourage them when they struggle with difficulties in their work?

We want to approach intimacy much like an artist approaches creating a work of art—with clarity, feeling, openness, inspiration, and heart-felt engagement. Hand in hand we infuse our interactions with affection and caring and weave respect and admiration into the ways we respond to and talk about each other. In the active engagement of hand in hand relationships, we each address the deep wishes we have to be heard, to be seen, to connect, to contribute, to receive, and to be regarded in a worthwhile and unique way.

We want to move beyond our attitudes that treat most things as ordinary, unexceptional, flat, routine, of little value, or even boring. We cultivate a sacred view, a spiritual heart posture, that sees the extraordinary beauty and significance of what is, of all reality, of the Divine manifesting in everything, including in each other and in the relationship. To develop this way of seeing, this heart posture, requires great effort and often a model and a mentor.

Conscious hand in hand intimacy requires that we turn down the static of judgments, blame and concerns that are so distracting and distressing. We do not want to overwhelm, control, or stalk our partner with our fears, hopes, dissatisfactions and comparisons. Rather, we scan our feelings and our connections for the beautiful music at the heart of our relationships. We nurture affection and admiration. Often this comes forth when we host other people and mutually create a sense of home for others.

We also create mutual names and rituals for things, activities, and special occasions that are unique for our relationship. We give special meaning to something we share such as a pair of wine glasses that we use to toast each other every evening at dinner or a ritual lighting of candles to greet the Sabbath or a family meal we have after church every Sunday. These are the materials and activities of connection that sustain and grow hand in hand intimacy.

Dialogical Conversation

Living and working together that leads to shoulder to shoulder bonding always supports a greater sense of meaning and purpose that each of us has for our lives. In marriage this involves being willing to accept that each of us has a point of view and values that we believe to be right and that we are willing to invest our time and energy in those. Respect in this case is not agreement but an acceptance of our partner's truths for them. Support means that we will encourage our partner in bringing the gifts that they have to the relationship and the larger world. On teams and in work situations, we respect and encourage members to contribute themselves and their skills to the larger purpose that we are all serving.

Whether in raising children, buying a house and making it a home, working together to support a religious community, volunteering for charitable or political causes, or simply hosting friends and family, we want to discover workable divisions of labor, to experience being responsible together for creating good outcomes, and to appreciate each other's participation and contributions. Being teammates in some sport, buddies on adventures, protectors and defenders of each other in the face of threats from outside, and colleagues in learning, all involve mutually participating in activities that convey the sense of *we*. In this process we create not only shared meaning but also shared experience that strengthens the shoulder to shoulder bonds between us and affirms the entity of *we*. In creating this inner life together, we evolve a culture that has a sense of the purposes that transcend the relationship itself.

Open to Being Influenced

As our relationships grow, we must do more than support

each other. We must also let our partners, teammates, and coworkers influence us. While this is more obvious in team and work situations, although often ignored, it is often difficult in marriage when we have strong ideas of what, why, and how things should be done. Accepting influence is both an attitude and a skill, especially because we want to convey honor and respect.

Accepting influence requires that you are open to possibilities suggested by your partner. It does not mean placating him or her or resentfully going along. It does involve being willing to compromise and mobilize yourself to make the compromise work.

In addition to being willing to accept your partner's influence, you want to find ways that you can meet some of your partner's requests. An attitude of support and mutual contribution is important. Relationships work better when each person avoids turning requests into power struggles.

Mutual Exploration Not Necessarily Resolution

As was discussed earlier, there are many differences between people that lead to issues that are not resolvable that we must live with and there are those conflicts that can reach some accommodations or solution. Happily married couples have loud arguments, even screaming matches, and these do not necessarily harm the marriage. These couples have a confidence in their bond that provides a generally friendly and loving context for the fights that do arise.

In working with couples and families, I have found that it is essential to build the hand in hand bonds of intimacy before or at least along with working on the issues that families have. As Gottman found in his extensive research on successful marriage, "Successful conflict resolution isn't what makes marriages succeed."[xxxv] In terms of marriage therapy, Gottman points out that conflict resolution as such does not work to make marriages more viable and lasting. Finding ways to successfully deal with conflict will vary from couple to couple, but the important piece is that it needs to work for all the people involved. One of the most important tools in working on issues, whether for resolution or fuller exploration is what I call "dialogical communication."

Dialogue

Dialogue includes those conversations and interactions in which we make decisions, explore ideas and points of view, work together on some issue or task, and engage each other in an exchange of thoughts, energies and activities. Dialogue builds shoulder to shoulder intimacy.

Dialogical conversations often involve topics and situations where we feel vulnerable and awkward, where we feel the stakes are high and the outcome uncertain, and where we care deeply about the issue and about the people with whom we are in conversation.

We hesitate to broach potentially conflictual topics because, on the one hand we fear that confronting the issue could make matters worse or get explosive, and, on the other, if we ignore the issue, it will fester and we will have to carry it like a ball and chain without having the opportunity to find something more workable. We fear being misunderstood, attacked or even rejected at the same time we fear hurting our partner in ways that we don't intend.

Disagreements and conflicts are part of life and definitely part of any intimate relationship. How we relate to these differences of opinion and points of view and how we discuss them can enhance or break a relationship.

Nansen's Cat

In a famous Zen story, the monks of the eastern and western halls in a monastery were quarrelling about a cat. Zen Master Nansen, hearing the heated argument, walked

> into the midst of the monks, held up the cat and said, "If one of you can say a word, I will spare the cat. If you cannot say anything, I will put it to the sword." No one could answer, so Nansen cut the cat in two and handed half to each side.

As brutal a teaching as this story seems to be, it reveals that when we get so caught up in our own point of view, we lose sight of what is real and living. Life is lost in rigid arguing and we are lost when we remain stuck in right and wrong without listening. By losing sight of the beauty and vitality of the cat, we kill the subject, which in many conversations with a partner may be the relationship itself. If we get into a habit of fighting about who is right and who is wrong in trying to resolve our conflicts, the sense of "we" is damaged and the intimate bonding is diminished. The way we discuss disagreements is more important in most cases than whether there is resolution. It is also important to keep in mind that many differences may not get resolved and the challenge is to grow the relationship so that it is large enough and sufficiently vital to contain and even grow from the continuing disagreements. We want to make the relationship itself develop the capacity to hold paradox and complexity of divergent viewpoints.

In broaching difficult subjects with your partner, no matter how strong the relationship and deep the intimacy and skilled we are in talking with each other, it will always be challenging. The goal is not to make us completely comfortable with hard conversations but to reduce the level of discomfort and anxiety to the point that issues can be discussed.

Conversation Impasses

Before proceeding to a fuller discussion of dialogical communication, recognizing some of the common stumbling blocks to supportive and intimate dialogue grounds our examination in the realities of everyday life and experiences.

Righteousness

Going into conversations about issues, we often get caught into assuming that I am right and you are wrong. This sense of rightness, even righteousness, is natural and causes enormous grief. We must realize that each of us thinks we are right, that we may simply have differing perspectives, interpretations, and values on the subject, and that disagreements are generally not about truth but about personal meaning.

In approaching dialogical conversations, we must examine our unstated but inwardly held agendas. These often include wanting to prove a point, get our partner to do what we want, or to tell them off about something they did that annoyed us. In cases where the relationship is deteriorating toward a separation, the agenda is often to fire warning shots of blame across the bow of our partner to let them know that we intend to fight or to demonstrate how much evidence there is supporting our victimization in the relationship and all the ways our partner is destroying the relationship.

Intense Emotions are Difficult to Discuss

Feelings and emotions are difficult subjects to discuss. Besides their obvious charge and sometimes confusing nature, they are not really open for discussion so much as sharing. By this I mean that we each are the authority on our feelings and our feelings simply are true for us at the time. It is not a question of whether we should or should not have them. It is not a subject of mutual decision. It is about what is true for us right now and our sharing that with our partner and having him or her listen.

Since the way we feel constitutes a major ingredient in any issue, it is important that we communicate our feelings if we want to work on the issue. In most cases, I have found that couples have great difficulty handling the feelings at the same time they are trying to make a decision or explore the non-emotional content of an issue. The emotions simply overwhelm everything else or get ignored entirely. What I have found works best is to have people share, face to face and heart to heart, the feelings that they have before they try to engage in dialogue (what I call shoulder to shoulder intimacy in a side by side activity) that is intended to produce a decision or even a simple exploration for learning. From this we may begin to understand that each one of us has a particular, possibly even reasonable, way of looking at things and holds different values.

Mindreading

Another common error in discussing issues is mindreading. Mindreading is where we project our own thoughts and feelings onto our partner. If we feel hurt, we attribute meanness to their intentions. We may see their comments as attempts to control us. We assume we know what the other person is thinking and know more about that than what they are saying or willing to admit. Yet we cannot really know the complexity of thinking and feelings of others, and even when they hurt us, it is usually unintentional. We cannot be the authority about the inner workings of other people, just as they cannot know exactly how things work for us. Each of us is the authority on our own views and inner worlds.

Blame Frame

Using the blame frame, talking about fault, is often another dialogue stopper. Blame usually results in disagreement, denial, opposition, and little or no exploration and learning. Focusing on blame and our associated righteous judgments sidetracks us from finding out what is true for each other, what roles we each played in contributing to a difficult situation or issue, and how we can work together to make things better.

The Art of Arguing and Dialoging

As was mentioned earlier, arguments are a natural part of many relationships and are not necessarily failures in the relationship. Over the years of working with couples, I have found that arguing is more comfortable for some people than others. As long as both partners are reasonably OK with disagreement and emotional expression of opposition and they are skilled in the art of argument and repair, these kinds of interaction do not result in damage to the relationship. In the art of argument, it is vital that certain thresholds are not crossed such as threatening your partner, the relationship, acting contemptuously, or physically acting out. Arguments can serve to release tensions, focus attention on each other, energize each person, and create response potential for connection.

What does not flow from arguments that degenerate into shouting matches is listening and understanding. In dialogue we appreciate that each of us has our own way of looking at things that gets us to notice different information, that we know ourselves and our feelings better than anyone else, that we bring different experiential background to issues, that we hold different values and often care about different things, that we have different standards for feeling satisfied, behavior, raising children, and hosting guests, and that we are bound to operate from a great deal of self-interest even when we are not aware of it.

To be successful in dialogical conversations, it is important to have shared the relevant feelings and truths as much as possible prior to the conversation so that we are less concerned about revealing what we feel and can focus on the topic we are mutually engaged in. Even sharing feelings and truths that are not directly related to a particular issue helps to clear the deck of feelings related to other issues and makes a cleaner and more supportive space for connective dialogue on hard topics. It is also useful to have reflected on what the issues mean about us in terms of our fears, longings, self-images, and sense of worth, competence, significance and lovability. All of this helps us get clear about our purpose for raising an issue and the kind of outcome we are working toward.

In dialogical conversation our communications are low on explanation and high on exploration. We place high emphasis on discovery and less on interpretation. We try to avoid blaming in order to move into real discovery and problem solving. The point of dialogue is not to have a forum for making pronouncements but to create a way to have conversations from which we learn, make decisions, and work together, shoulder to shoulder, even on difficult topics.

Just as personal inquiry is a key element in individual Buddhist practice, so collective inquiry supports the maturation of a relationship. We need to approach these conversations of discovery and insight with openness and mutual respect, accepting that there can be multiple ways of viewing things and even a variety of valid solutions to the issues being explored.

Buddhist teaching on personal inquiry emphasizes the development of presence, refined attention, openness, and a willingness to live in the midst of paradox. These qualities also apply to healthy engagement in conversation. We want to be fully present with our partner, be attentive to what is said as well as the unstated feelings and dynamics that are occurring, staying open to each other and other perspectives as we remain connected even when issues and situations have no apparent immediate solution.

A good rule of thumb in deciding what and how to say things in dialogue applies the criteria that statements be necessary, true for us, and kind. These criteria bring consciousness in what we say, avoid a tendency toward exaggeration and generalization, and support the loving nature of the relationship. In the dialogical conversations, we want to engender the sense of being a team together, working shoulder to shoulder to make decisions, accomplish tasks, identify conflicts and resolve those that can be resolved and find ways to live with those that are perpetual.

Helpful Attributes

Some of the attributes we want to bring to dialogical conversations are: open listening, genuine consideration of different points of view and ideas, making contributions without attachment, staying on target in working toward our mutually desired outcomes, respect for each other, self-questioning, questioning each other in ways that maintain our connection as well as move us toward our goal, providing loving reality checks for each other, being clear about outcomes as they change, and staying grounded in ourselves and in the relationship so that we do not take disagreement personally.

For example, in our heterogeneous society with its diversity of backgrounds, opinions, and opportunities, even couples that participate together in some religious community will usually have differing points of view. It is the things we do together shoulder to shoulder by sharing rituals such as grace before meals, participating in holiday gatherings, attending services or spiritual retreats and having shared symbols that all support the structure of intimate bonding as a context that can hold and even encourage our personal differences.

The Bear Costume

Everyone in the village had gathered in the town square and were engaged in serious, vehement debate on the many dangers and challenges of violence, hatred, and fear. They were split into many factions, each with its own adamant ideas about how everyone should be and what they should do. A massive cloud of despair hung over the entire gathering.

A simple young woman, seeing the tensions in everyone's shoulders and the glum looks on their faces, ran home and came back dressed in a bear costume she had worn while working in a circus. She growled playfully to get the attention of the crowd. She struck funny poses, scratched her hairy bear butt, cavorted and danced until she succeeded in making everyone laugh.

By sharing the joy of their laughter, the gathering released the grip of their rigidity and enjoyed the connection of being together. From that place of humor and happiness, they realized that they could deal with the challenges of life more readily from a space of joy and connection more than from the storm of distress.

In all conversations about relationship issues, whether solvable or perpetual, it is critical to convey a basic acceptance of each other's views as being true for them and for who they are. Listen for areas of similarity and try to learn from differences. Contempt and rejection make it nearly impossible to have a conversation. People become increasingly willing to listen to you if you communicate understanding and respect to them.

In problem-solving conversations, keep in mind the larger context of love in your relationship, lead with understanding and caring, make and receive repair attempts when needed, soothe yourself and each other, accept each other's limitations, and compromise when possible. Leading with understanding and caring means that we avoid the blame frame, begin with ourselves, describe the situation as objectively as we know how as clearly as we can, be appreciative if possible, and recall times when we were both resourceful.

What Gottman calls "repair attempts" are statements and actions that keep an interaction from escalating out of control. Some basic phrases that can be used to repair a downward spiral to a conversation or interaction are "I feel," "I need a break" or "let's take a break," "I need to calm down," "sorry," "what I can agree with," "let's agree to disagree," "I appreciate," "we can work this out," and "I think I understand." In situations where we become flooded with emotion that feels overwhelming or that we are being overwhelmed, the act of withdrawing for a period of time to take a pause can be a repair attempt. Be sensitive to flooding, because overwhelm does not produce results and usually makes us feel wounded.

Even in conflicts, try to be supportive and not inflict damage. A powerful exercise to do in preparation or as part of a conversation is to look at yourself from the other person's point of view and see what kind of environment you are creating. You can also examine the dynamics from the vantage point of a neutral, nonjudgmental witness.

As we engage in dialogue and discover all the relevant feelings and points of view on an issue, we find that both positions on an issue contain elements and kinds of truth and that things are more complex than our simple understanding up to that point. We need to personally hold all these conflicting and competing concerns and factors and to mutually embrace the position that multiple truths and feelings are relevant. It is not a matter of simply one side or the other but of creating the space to include both. We learn to live and relate in a shared world of paradox and complexity.

When we are working with impasses on issues, the emphasis is not on solving the issue but moving into sharing and dialogue that explores differences and makes these kinds of conversations a strength in the relationship. I have found, from my own experience and that of my clients and students, that the more practiced couples become in dialoguing about hard subjects, the easier such conversations are to have and the more effective we are at getting results that strengthen the relationship.

Intimate Relationships as Teachers

Relationships are one of the most profound and refined learning environments we will ever have. This learning opportunity demands more than mechanical knowing such as driving a car or playing an instrument. We are dealing with our own nature and complexity and that of another human being with all of their complexities, paradoxes and changeability.

To engage the path of intimate relationships well requires more than a commitment to the relationship. It demands a commitment to personal growth, to the growth of the relationship, to the sacred nature of life and particularly to our lives together.

It is one thing to experience sacred presence within the shelter of our own meditation and prayer, it is quite another to experience the Sacred through our interaction and connection to another person. The former, as wonderful as it is, can limit our sense of home whereas the latter expands our home to include the world. To be intimate with ourselves is only part of the journey to realizing the fullness of the sacred presence in the world and the boundless radiance of the Beloved.

At the same time, human relationships are not only about the spiritual transcendent. A relationship never lives outside the context of time, space and other people. It has its roots in the past that can be traced back to the lives of those long gone and it moves forward creating the destinies of its offspring. The offspring include flesh and blood people, stories, the way we serve as examples for others, and the impact of our actions in the world.

A good relationship is a platform for each of us to grow, to tap the sacred nature of love and meaning, and to cultivate our own divine loving nature for the benefit of all.

At a certain point in a love relationship, or any intimate relationship, it may occur to us to stop trying to get what we originally thought we wanted and what we thought would make us happy and decide to make the relationship we have our teacher. We become a disciple of the relationship.

The demands of full force relating require us to reverse our habits and patterns of self-concern. In the course of a long-term relationship with a lover such as in marriage, our partner will provoke every possible issue, every reactive pattern, all our insecurities, and the sense of helplessness in relation to the unknown.

These relationships generate a great deal of heat and require that we learn about surrender and holding complexity, intensity, paradox and not knowing. In dynamic relationships we are always living on the edge between the known and the unknown. We are pushed and pulled into developing skill and capacity for intimacy. The life force of a relationship is sustained by intimacy. This is the profound crucible of a deep partner relationship in which we can grow and our love can mature.

In a sense we become like a clay vessel that is baked by the heat of love and its challenge so our integrity and being are strengthened and can hold sacred energy. At the same time, another metaphor is also appropriate. We are raw food that is cooked by relationships so that we are transformed into nourishment for the benefit of others. By being cooked, our particularly delicious qualities enhance the feast of life for other people.

Our bodily food is changed into us, but our spiritual food changes us into itself.

MEISTER ECKHART

The Clarity of the Innkeeper's Daughter

Once upon a time, that is still here and now, there was a nobleman who decided to pose a riddle to his leaseholder of the inn on his land to determine whether to let him continue or not. He sent for the innkeeper and said, "I'm going to ask you three questions: What is the fastest thing in the world? What is the fattest thing in the world? And what is the dearest thing in the world? Give me the correct answers within three days and your leasehold will be granted for ten years without fee. But if you give wrong answers, you will need to leave my estate."

The innkeeper made his way home in great perplexity. He came across a friend who tried to help him with his puzzle. The friend suggested that the innkeeper say that the fastest thing in the world was the nobleman's horse; the fattest thing was his pig; and the dearest thing would undoubtedly be the woman he marries. But the poor innkeeper was uncertain about these answers, figuring they seemed too provincial to him. Yet he had no idea how he would reply to the nobleman.

Now, the innkeeper had a beautiful and talented daughter who asked, "What makes you look so worried, Father?" He told her about the questions and what was at stake. "Of course I look worried. I have no idea what the real answers are." "There's nothing to worry about," she said. "They are simple enough: thought is the fastest thing in the world; the earth is the fattest; and sleep is the dearest thing of all."

On the third day the innkeeper returned to the nobleman, who listened carefully to what the innkeeper had to say. "I like your answers very much," he said. "But I know you did not think them up yourself. Tell me the truth; who told you what to say?"

The innkeeper confessed that his daughter had given him the answers.

"If you have a daughter who is that bright, I want to see her," responded the nobleman. "Let her come to me in three days. I want her to come neither walking nor riding, neither dressed nor naked. And, in addition, have her bring a gift that is not a gift."

The innkeeper returned home even more depressed than before. Seeing her father so dejected, she inquired, "What happened, father? Why do you look so worried?" So he told her what the nobleman had requested. "You needn't worry," she responded. "Here's what I want you to do. Go to the market and buy a fisherman's net, a goat, a pair of doves, and a couple of pounds of meat."

He did as she had asked. Then she took off her clothes and wrapped herself in the net so that she was neither dressed nor naked. She straddled the goat so that as the goat moved, her feet dragged on the ground. Thus, she was neither riding nor walking. She placed the doves in one hand and the meat in the other. Neither riding nor walking, she made her way to the nobleman's house.

When the nobleman saw her coming, he unleashed his dogs. She simply threw them the meat, stood up straight releasing the goat from his burden to run free, and walked calmly into the house. She announced herself to the nobleman saying, "I have brought you a gift that is not a gift." Whereupon she released the doves, who circled their heads and flew out an open window.

"You are so clever, I want to marry you," he said boldly. "But I must ask that there be one condition if you consent: that you won't meddle in the decisions I make when petitions and suits are brought before me." She agreed to marry him and promised not to interfere in his decisions. And so dear folks, they were married.

Some time later as she was standing at an open window, she saw a peasant who was extremely distraught passing by. "Why are you so upset?" she asked. He looked up and saw such a kind face that he readily unloaded what was troubling him.

"Oh gentle lady," he began, "I and one of my neighbors own a stable in partnership. I own a mare, and my neighbor owns a wagon. Well, the mare gave birth to her foal under his wagon, and my neighbor claimed that the foal was therefore his. So we appealed to the nobleman to settle our dispute. The nobleman said that the foal belongs to my neighbor. It seems so unfair. That's why I am weeping and so upset."

She paused for a moment, then said, "Let me help you out. I'll tell you what to do. Get a fishing rod, some line, and bait and stand in the sandy area outside the nobleman's window. Pretend that you are fishing in the sand. When the nobleman asks, 'What are you doing? You cannot possibly catch fish in the sand.' You then say, 'If a wagon can give birth to a foal, then I can catch fish in the sand.' "

The peasant followed her instructions, and, when the nobleman heard his reply, he immediately saw that his wife had been involved. Turning to her, he said, "Since you have not kept to your part of our agreement, I want you to leave the house and go back to your father. You are welcome to take with you the finest and dearest thing that you can find here."

"All right, if you insist," she said. "Before I go, I want us to have one last meal together." His ambivalence about having her leave at all impelled him to agreed to this request.

At dinner, she made sure that he had plenty of wine so that he got completely drunk. When he passed out on the floor beside the table, she ordered the servants to put him into their carriage. She sat beside him as they were driven to her father's house.

When the nobleman awoke the next day, sobered by a long sleep, he quickly grasped where he was. "How did I get here?" he asked.

She calmly replied, "You told me to take the finest and dearest thing I could find in your house. I could think of nothing finer and dearer to me than you."

With that his heart broke fully open. He embrace her happily. "In that case," he said lovingly, "let's return home and never be apart. We shall share the governance of my lands."

And, dear folks, from that time on, they grew old together, made decisions together, and were honored far and wide for their wisdom and compassion.

14.

Compassion

A leading disciple asked the Buddha, "Would it be true to say that a part of our training is for the development of love and compassion?' The Buddha gazed lovingly upon the disciple and replied, "No, it would not be correct to say this. It would be true to say that the whole of our training is for the development of love and compassion."

A spiritual mystic once said, "Of what use is an open eye, if the heart is blind?"

One of the arcs of this book suggests that the experience of intimacy connects the self with other, the interior with the exterior, and provides a basis for intimate bonding that connects the personal with the collective experience and the experiential with the functioning of social relationships such as marriage. Compassion, as a form of loving intimacy, is a significant element in releasing the grip of self-concern to teach us the language and ways of the heart. The domain of an open, loving heart has an infinite capacity to reach out and connect. It radiates love through that connection, coloring everything with compassion and it guides that connection with wisdom.

As lovers in the world, we are inclined toward caring. We are incurable romantics of life in our work for a better life for others, in our desire to live in alignment not only with the planet but with the heritage of the past and the great possibilities of the future. We want to contribute our portion to a collective environment of love and peace. This intended union of the personal and communal worlds reveals that we are participating in larger stories of a greater community.

Kinship

Is not this the sort of fast that pleases me
—it is the Lord Yahweh who speaks—
to break unjust fetters
and undo the thongs of the yoke,
to let the oppressed go free,
and break every yoke,
to share your bread with the hungry,
and shelter the homeless poor,
to clothe the man you see to be naked
and not turn from your own kin?

ISAIAH 58.6-8

Compassion is a way of life—a way of being, a way of being conscious, a way of relating, a way of acting, a way of living from the base of interconnection, interbeing, and sharing. Compassion is not a "should," a rule, a commandment, for it is a way of living, a way of treating all there is in life—ourselves, our bodies, our imaginations and dreams, neighbors, enemies, the air, water, the earth, animals, death, space and time. Compassion is a heart posture as if creation matters, treating all beings and things as sacred and as divine.

Compassion involves the feeling of being together as kin. This sense of togetherness opens us to rejoicing at another's joy and grieving at their sorrow. In compassion we let go of separation, of problems, of vanity, of self-concern, and of control in remembering our common bonds and our heartfelt desire to bring about happiness. Compassion as a heart posture perceives others as family that we celebrate, care for, and want to support in dealing with the challenges of suffering. Compassion is our kinship with each other and with the universe; it is the action we take because of that kinship.

Compassion is more than knowing about the suffering and pain of others. It somehow involves an entering into, a sharing, and tasting in so far as that is possible. This requires both imagination and the ability to move our attention into dimensions of awareness that transcend the personal. We allow our heart to be touched and present our love in ways that touch the hearts of others. Compassion implies passion, pathos, deep caring, gut feelings, heart connections and bonding and at the same time a profound understanding of these connections, of pain, of life, of the nature of being and of the workings of the heart.

The practice of compassion puts our own pain in perspective. We see it as a part of life that is not simply personal but also collective and that it is "noble" to work with it in both interior and exterior ways. Building our capacity for compassion for ourselves and for others enhances our ability to live in the world without reservation. In compassion we affirm life and other beings, making everyone and everything matter. We invest the world with significance, realizing that, while nothing has inherent value, in the relative dimension of life, such investments experientially and socially matter in both personal maturity into wisdom and collective development of supportive relationships.

Compassion is the natural and spontaneous response of an open heart. In addition, we are more resourceful and insightful when helping others than when we are concerned solely with ourselves. Compassion as the concern for the well-being and happiness of others and the sharing of our suffering can lead us out of our separate worlds of pain to a mutual sense of connection and understanding.

The cultivation of compassion begins with caring connection, the wish to alleviate the suffering of others as well as one's own, the desire to see reality clearly, and the impulse to embrace all life. In our intimate encounter with pain, our own and others, and joy, our own and others, the impact of the feeling and emotion is magnified and intensified in the encounter.

When we are compassionate, we must be careful to notice traces of separation and condescension in our thoughts and feelings of compassion, traces of pity. Compassion does not hold another as weak or inferior or inadequate. Compassion sees the shared nature of pain and suffering and the strength that flows from the sense of connection.

We need to take care not to confine our compassionate and loving connection to pain, our own or others. We do not want to develop a taste for pain, as if this is the most real and intense part of feeling alive, and become attracted to suffering. This is not a matter of "poor me/poor you/poor us." At root, compassion is a celebration of all life and we share that joyful possibility with others. There is a German proverb that states: "A sorrow shared is a sorrow halved; joy shared is a joy doubled."

Compassion in Action

If a person who was rich enough in this world's goods
saw that one of his brothers and sisters was in need,
but closed his heart to this person,
how could the love of God be living in him or her?
My children, our love is not to be just words or mere talk,
but something real and active.

JOHN, FIRST EPISTLE

Active compassion moves us beyond meditation and introspective contemplation to a way of living that experiences both sacred awareness and pain and gives birth to healing, growth, and remission from that pain. Compassion is not simply heart to heart, it is hand in hand in the building of a collective home and environment of love and shoulder to shoulder in the mutual efforts to relieve suffering and to celebrate together and to bring justice into the world.

To work with compassion means not only to imagine, to feel, and to generate a loving presence, it means to engage in acts of service, an extra reaching out. Acts of compassion are not favors but flow from the obligation we feel for supporting the integrity of mutuality, of community, and of interconnection, of love, of kinship.

These acts include everything from making a stranger welcome to works of peace-making that seek to harmonize the discord among people. In Matthew (25.34-46) Jesus says that what we do for the least among us, "the least of these brothers of mine," you do for me. We are to love God, to love life, to love all being, through the caring and care of others.

Engaged compassion can include specific acts such as feeding the hungry, clothing the naked, sheltering the homeless, breaking unjust fetters, giving drink to the thirsty, visiting the sick, burying the dead, praying for the living and the dead, instructing the ignorant, counseling those in confusion and doubt, warning people who violate integrity of self and community, bearing wrongs with patience, forgiving willingly, and comforting the people who are afflicted with pain, fear and grief.

In the West, many of these acts of compassion are what we consider justice. In many ways we have abdicated the work of justice and compassion to government and politicized the process of deciding whether to act with compassion. Beyond whatever political action we may take on behalf of others, personal acts of compassion manifest our personal responsibility for creating benefit and support the building of a more loving and supportive culture.

Knowing What Happiness and Freedom Are

We cannot comprehend how to relieve the suffering of ourselves or others if we have no sense of what authentic happiness, freedom and spiritual realization are about. The desire is not to release our habit bodies into another form of suffering but to actually find unqualified presence, home, belonging, and fearless aliveness that are characteristic of intimate living. This arises as a way of being that embodies profound wisdom and unpretentious presence.

Compassion trains the heart for service, resilience, beauty, benefit, growth, transcendence, and groundedness. It integrates the above with the below. It integrates the personal with the collective with the universal. It integrates the locational with the spacious, the now with the eternal and the unfolding of the temporal.

One of the components of happiness is meaning, in the sense of experiencing both value and significance. By working on behalf of others, we sense a larger calling to our life. The happy life—what the Greeks called *eudaimonia*—is the life that is good for the daimon, our particular spirit of genius. Not only does it bless us with its calling, we bless it with our style of following.

Supporting the Daimon

In compassion we not only follow our daimon but support others to find the authentic alignment and happiness of pursuing their own calling. Our dedication to our calling or mission pushes us beyond the edge of simple comfort; its principal passion is realization in the world both personally and collectively. Compassion involves us in supporting each person realizing their mission and bringing forth the fruits of their daimon.

Dedication involves the act of declaration. Declaration is different from assertion. Assertion leads the mind to demand evidence, and the mind often listens for discrepancy.

Declaration in a sense creates its own truth by being uttered and creating a vision for direction and future actions.

Receiving and Sending: *Tonglen*

In the practice of *receiving and sending—tonglen*, we consciously and intimately take in the pains of others into our heart center where we sense our intimate connections and apply our basic clarity and wisdom to the nature of these pains and then radiate our desire for relief from suffering and the realization of happiness for others.

The practice of *tonglen* trains us to remain open, loving, and giving beyond ourselves even when our heart reflexively wants to close in order to protect itself from hurt. We can choose to feel the pain and practice staying open, using the pain to remind us of the pain in the world and our own desire to radiate compassion. By opening to pain, our own and that of others, the cycle of reaction is broken and we generate a field of loving intimacy. *Tonglen* is like doing heart-to-heart resuscitation.

This practice can be significant in both your personal maturing into sacred wisdom and love and in the development of a larger atmosphere of encouragement and support. In this practice you work not only with those people who you identify as victims but also with people who you consider perpetrators in some sense. Doing *tonglen* with someone who you dislike and blame opens your heart beyond a sense of victimness so that you are able to live fully without a sense separation from the larger sense of your own soul.

A brief overview of a form of this practice will give you some experience in how this works. Begin by relaxing into the entirety of this very moment. Embrace everyone, including yourself and others. Allow your hosting, beneficial, and loving presence to live through you, realizing that everyone yearns to live in happiness and to blossom as love.

Offer your openness, your love, and your presence to everyone, including to those who have wounded you. Sense a deep heart connection to them as fellow humans. Have a sense of receiving their full humanity, including their desires for happiness, their griefs, and their fears along with their strengths and weaknesses. Sense their fears and longings resonating with your own and inhale them deep into your heart. Also sense the clarity and caring of your basic wisdom nature in your heart and how these dissolve and transform the solidity of pain. Offer and radiate the loving energy of your deepest soul to others. As you exhale, sense the radiance of uniting with everyone in this moment. Repeat this process for whatever period of time you have decided to engage in this practice.

When we grow beyond our self-concerns, the suffering in the world moves us to grow ever higher, wider and deeper. We eventually realize that no matter whether this world improves or it degenerates, we remain dedicated to being a loving presence and creating benefit and beauty. No matter if we are loved or hated, if humans are simply a passing breeze in the trees in the life of the earth, if all our efforts at service are lost in the immensity of world machinations, or if we are appreciated or denied, the only way to live is to be lovingly intimate with what is. We are wholeheartedly intimate with the richness, aliveness, and texture of now, embracing fully this moment. When we are intimately alive in this way, love expresses itself in everything we do.

15.

Deepening Intimate Bonds Through Challenges

Challenge to Mature with Change

In life there is no fixed reality. In creative intimacy, the process of change and pervasive *becoming* suggest that each moment is unprecedented. Even in the continuity of patterns, a freshness radiates from the moment. Both the patterns and the changes pose many challenges for us.

We are not a fixed entity and neither is our partner or our relationship. When we freeze them in our minds, we make them an object that is not quite fully alive rather than a vital subject of our heart. We are not an idea or simply a noun in the sentences of our mind. We are always *becoming*, a process that moves beyond edges, more of a verb.

In our partner and parenting relationships, we are constantly being challenged to be supportive of our lovers and children as they grow, have their feelings, enact their behaviors, and make choices, many of which may feel threatening or seem misguided. Striking the balance of engagement, boundaries, feedback, and support often seems to require the wisdom of Solomon, the patience of Gandhi, the compassion of Buddha, the dedication of Mohammed, and the love of Jesus. We may not always be able to do that, yet holding that intention and working from our basic heart posture of love will bring us a long way in that direction.

Strengthening Through Conflict

One of the more difficult things for many of us to understand is that heart to heart intimacy develops through conflict, grief, the willingness to be authentic without external validation, openness to having our heart broken, and unilateral sharing as well as mutual love. While it is true that the foundation of a relationship is built from shared love, good feelings and caring, it is also true that we need authentic conflicts that naturally arise, for they are the only forces that can test the relationship and make it stronger.

Working with issues and conflicts can strengthen a relationship in two ways. In the first instance, we are engaged in mutual problem-solving, such as dividing up household chores or making a family budget. An issue becomes a mutual topic for discussion that we figure out a solution to or for which we negotiate a compromise. We work shoulder to shoulder to find and implement an agreeable resolution. Success builds confidence in our collective ability to create a way out of difficulty.

Unresolvable Issues

The second way involves those issues that do not have resolutions. Issues in themselves are rarely beyond resolution, but our deeply held values and desires may make an issue beyond the scope of problem-solving at the present time. This would include having a home in one place but an important job in another, or where one person likes to always have many people around and the other prefers to be alone, or when one person connects through doing activities together and the other through hanging out, talking and sharing, or a situation where one person wants constant change and the other is only comfortable when things are the same and familiar.

When we adopt a heroic attitude toward irresolvable issues, we realize that each monstrous issue possesses a treasure for us. Each demon protects something valuable or is itself a great treasure. To meaningfully engage this monster by being present with it, feeling its energy, and extracting its raw power into the heart of our own presence means we can incorporate the energy of the issue into ourselves, and can transform it into a cloak that we wear or a feature of the body of the relationship. We do not resolve the issue or release the energy of its tension. Rather we inhabit it and let it inhabit us as a quality of aliveness. This becoming, this incorporation, this embodying of the tension in a conscious way, intensifies the field of our presence and becomes a bond in the relationship at the same time as it retains an edge of its divisive nature.

Bring Conflicts to Consciousness

Our tendency to become blinded by our stories and understanding of issues makes us hostage to those points of view. As a prisoner of our way of thinking about issues, we tend to reactively go numb or feel like victims. Conflicts need to be fleshed out not resolved. They need to be felt in the physical body of each party and in the body of the relationship itself. Then when the relationship incorporates differences over time, they become strengths in future conflicts.

When conflicts are not fleshed out and incorporated, they become ghosts that haunt one or more people and reappear over and over again in monstrous ways whenever the relationship is challenged. We must be willing to get our hands dirty in all the sordid aspects of our feelings and behaviors and yet not dwell there or make that our world. We must not get defined by our conflicts, only become present with them.

Surviving Disenchantment

All love relationships go through at least one period of disenchantment with the way we hoped our partners would be and the way we thought we would behave once love was realized. Not only do we project our longed for images onto the other, but the early, honeymoon stage of a love relationship tends to bring out the best in us. As we relax into the relationship and the relationship must be integrated into not only our personal lives but also the larger community, many fractures appear in the ideal pictures we have painted in our heads.

As in the story of Eros and Psyche, the arrow of love breaks the skin so that blood, the water of life, can be released and exposed to the outer elements of life, the reality of our full situation in the world. This necessary wound can eventually bond us to each other if we can remain in touch with the source of our love and go through the difficult tasks and stages to build a mature relationship. This mutual wounding, made conscious, can become an unbreakable bond. In many cultures a connection through mutual wounding is made by cutting a hand or arm and co-mingling blood. This bond is considered stronger and more sacred than the exchange of sexual fluids.

Often the areas of our relationship that most threaten us and we want to avoid, hold the greatest promise for bonding in the process of mutually exploring and holding these challenging issues. In the course of this work together we clarify "what is so" in the relationship. We move beyond our fantasy misconceptions, unconscious projections, fears, and hopes to the reality of what is actually true in the relationship now. We discover more of our similarities and face the actuality of our differences.

The cohesive threads in the fabric of a relationship need to be strong enough to hold the non-cohesive forces that naturally arise in the disappointments, conflicts, and disenchantments over time. During disenchantment it is vital to maintain a perspective that includes all the cohesive elements in our relationship. This is particularly true during the initial building phases of the relationship until everyone in the relationship is confident about its endurance. We must internally distinguish between our own sense of disenchantment around a particular aspect of our partner or of the relationship on the one hand and the value our partner brings to our life and the viability of the relationship as a whole on the other.

When the cohesive threads are overwhelmed or cut, the challenge becomes finding ways to successfully be apart. This involves changing the agreements and structure of the relationship even as we try to stay in touch with the bond that does exist and the connections that must be maintained. We work to change the form while keeping some of the value in the relationship.

A break up is not necessarily a personal or even collective failure. We must realize that longevity is not the only measure of success in relationships. In many relationships, we may experience profound connectedness, sense of us, and personal transcendence for extended periods. The fact that we part ways at a later time does not invalidate the value that those relationships had at the times when they were intimate.

Often, if there is enough connection and solid reasons for being together, going through challenging phases can lead to the rediscovery of love as our caring clarifies and reveals our essential bond. A bond is reinforced and elaborated by celebration and praise, but it is in the challenges that we get at the essential core.

With the passage of time and the successful navigation of formidable challenges to our intimacy, an openness and ease becomes evident in relationships that have matured and softened through renewal and sacrifices. We experience grace when that which seems unconquerable opens itself to us, whether this be the heart of a partner, the fortress of unresolvable issues, or the sacred sense of home that we long for and seek to build but seems to come on its own.

Beyond the Problem Frame

When one of us is going through a difficult time, the other needs to simply be present as an intimate witness as much as possible. Difficulty is not necessarily a problem to be solved. What is needed is connection and for that connection to be fully human. We must not be reduced to our problems and our partner to a problem-solver. We need to be seen and to see ourselves as a voyager across the challenging ocean of life, not as something broken and in need of repair.

Of course there are times we want and need problem solving assistance or ongoing help with such things as chronic health conditions. This can be connective as well. The challenge in these situations centers around maintaining each other's sense of magnificence. We do not want to reduce the images we hold of ourselves or our partner to the details of a particular condition such as diabetes or recovery from an addiction. We want to experience the full aliveness, caring and love of each other as human beings who are traversing the turbulent ocean of life. This creates the conditions for communion in which our consciousness includes the experience and world of our partner. We experience what it is like to be inside their being, sensing not only their feelings, but also their heart postures, their deep fears, longings and deep wisdom nature. This communion is the ground for profound compassion and the experience of essential unity.

Renewing Intimacy, Reviving Relationships

Intimacy is kept alive by mutually having the sense of approaching a new horizon and fashioning the outlines of a vision of our future together. Such visions are not blueprints but guides that change with feedback and are reshaped just as we are shaped. They give us a reference point from which to be conscious of where we are and a sense of direction.

All such visions need to be re-visioned from time to time to keep them real and relevant. Re-visioning supports the ongoing freshness in a marriage as well as encouraging the personal re-visioning that we each must make about our lives and our contributions to the world.

One of the driving spirits for lasting relationships is our curiosity, a wondering about each other, about ourselves in the dynamics of relating and about how this will unfold and transform into something never before seen.

When a long-term relationship gets into an uncomfortable and divisive rut, we are challenged to remember the authentic, sacred and beneficial reasons that gave rise to the relationship in the first place as well as those that have emerged as the intimacy evolved. To move the relationship forward and get beyond whatever destructive patterns have developed, we need to take a vacation from our routines that are not working. In vacating our habitual life, we can shed our skins of accumulated habits. This molting makes us open, newly raw, and re-sensitized to each other.

Part of the wonder and mystery in relationships is not quite knowing what the other person is about and what it is that they are doing in bringing their unique gifts to us and the world. We want to keep some of their distinctiveness free of our understanding and expectations in order to protect against the tendency to limit or even smother them. We also do not want to make who they are and what they offer either too small or too cosmic.

As the relationship matures, we approach each other with both the sense of knowing their world from the inside and not knowing, of being open to who we each are in this very moment. Our openness allows us to know each other in this moment, free of what we thought we knew from the past.

Surrender

Surrender in intimacy, rather than being about defeat and weakness, requires that we offer ourselves to experience and each other with our full resourcefulness and power. We release pretensions, fears, agendas, and blockages to giving ourselves openly and fully.

We want to feel into each other's sense of being in deep and loving ways. For this to happen we each need to trust, to open, to penetrate, to feel each other as ourselves, and to engage fully in the intensity of that love, celebrating the intimacy with our rapture. We learn how to do this and to elaborate on its richness by actively and consciously relating heart to heart and by creating the environment of love hand in hand.

To love is to surrender. When we experience the depths of love, we willingly offer ourselves to our beloved. We want them to know that we openly serve them and have them witness our giving of ourselves. To greater or lesser degrees, we entrust ourselves to their care and are willing to be exposed and vulnerable. We surrender to the force of love and tap into the energy and quality of something sacred and divine. In a sense, we entrust ourselves to the divine loving force of our partner and, in this way, we surrender to and affirm the Sacred as Beloved.

In the mutuality of love, we witness the surrender of our partner and our love compels us to treat them with kindness and to wholeheartedly support them and give them a home in our heart. At the same time we find a home in their heart, beyond our own identities. In this home we come to know all the contours of their being and the hidden places of their heart, some of which have been locked away by fear and others that are wellsprings of wisdom and beauty that lay beneath the flooring of everyday consciousness.

The river that flows in you also flows in me.

KABIR

In our modern society, we have great difficulty, psychologically and emotionally, surrendering in a relationship. We often are concerned about issues of power, wanting control over our own lives and even those people we care about. We hate to feel helpless and powerless.

Our culture plays on our fears and needs and encourages taking control of our bodies, our feelings, our thoughts, our lives and maximizing our "personal power." Many people and couples that I counsel struggle with the feelings of being imprisoned by their fears, longings, and overwhelm. They want to break free. At the same time they often think that having more power to control their situations and themselves is the solution. They know they want change and they want to control the change. There is a basic mistrust of themselves and of life. They are so frightened of disappointment and of not being good enough that they do not see how they will survive or be able to deal with opening to deep intimacy and the flow of life. They are hostage to their own horror movies created by their fears, anxieties, and frustrated desires even as they long for rich aliveness, beauty and love.

In our confusion and sometimes desperation, we settle for counterfeit intimacy and superficial substitutes, such as soap opera entertainment and stories of romance. We cannot experience the real thing and live in the world intimately unless we surrender to the requirements of authentic love and do the work that frees us of our reactive conditioning. We must give up our favorite hobby horse so we can move on to relating to and riding a real horse.

Spiritual Surrender

Spiritual development requires that we be willing to be influenced. This involves *surrender* in the sense that we are willing to offer ourselves to the influence and service of someone or something that is worth following. To be open to discovery means that we open, witness, surrender, trust, and love such that we are transported beyond whatever self-centered world views we have held.

It is sometimes said that we must have a strong ego or self-esteem before we can give it up in spiritual work. In fact, we simply need to offer up or surrender whatever identity we have, esteemed or not. The Divine accepts all vanities whether we are filled with a reactive emptiness, inflated with worthlessness, or puffed up by our own insignificance. The strength and true confidence that resides in our nature can be uncovered whether our identity is lofty and grandiose, balanced and well-adjusted, or lowly and wounded.

Surrender is not a one time event or decision. We practice it moment to moment in offering ourselves to the Beloved, no matter what condition we are in. We become one with the reality of now and experience the aliveness of the experience as a profound kind of love. We give up our identity, our sense of separation, our entire world view up to that point. By surrendering, we move inside the moment.

The experience of music, particularly sacred music, draws us inside the vibration and rhythm of its sound. Often when we play an instrument, sing, or openly listen we feel the fullness and aliveness of the moment and openly surrender to where the music takes us in the next moment.

While I am not very musically gifted (I am a rhythmic klutz and without other singers to guide me will often sing in the key of flat), a guiding model for me in life comes from my childhood when I played some piano and had learned a few pieces very well. I got to a point where my fingers, body, and being could play without any thought. I would simply give myself over to the music and as I struck notes, the music played me. It would bring out feelings and states of being that I had not known were there. I became the music. The notes and the silences were inside and outside and any distinction between inner and outer disappeared. Even when I would play to express my feelings, the music took me to another place beyond where I had started. I entered its flow and transcended even my sense of self into a realm I can only describe as sacred.

Spiritual surrender takes two forms. In the first we feel that we are dissolving outward and into the Divine. In this form a seed becomes the entire universe. Nothing is too much for the opening of this transcendence. It is as if the cells of our body and the particles of our being release their grip on each other and our form disintegrates, flying outward into the vastness of pure openness. We no longer exist in a particular way. All being, all forms become our home. We are "hosting" itself beyond our hosting and being hosted.

In the second form, we take in—host—the Divine, realizing the Divine in life. We simultaneously host and are hosted sensing the vital vibration of presence. This hosting presence can include everything and give it form. We live with clarity and beauty, dedicated to cultivating and manifesting benefit in the world. We consciously participate in the details, the flows, and the challenges of everyday life. We walk and converse with our companion in this way, on this path, sensing this wind, and feeling this aliveness and joy. The Divine shows up through us and through everything. The Sacred is manifest.

Freedom in Serving the Wheel of Necessity

We rarely pay homage or give praise to necessity, the great force that shapes the course of events and the patterns of fate. Necessity expresses both sacred reality and sacred creation. Necessity is what is and what is becoming—what flows inexorably from what exists now. We are all held in the embrace of reality and creation, included in the wheel of necessity. Necessity binds everything, it is the interconnection of all things and is that which makes the universe possible.

The bonds of necessity are often represented by a knot or a net of knots that hold everything and everyone. The bonds of love are represented by a kiss. Both the image of the mouth and the loop of a knot are circular suggesting an affinity between them. When the connection of love is most intimately felt, it takes on the quality of necessity, whose knot we cannot untie and we cut at the peril of our soul.

In the hard choices of life and relationships, our challenge centers around using the forces of necessity to bring forth beauty. When we incorporate service to children, family, work, community or the sacred as a part of our lives, we place our bodies and time under the wheel of necessity. We adopt a heart posture that life in its essence is a sacred gift and discover the gift nature in birth, growth, death and mourning.

When we lose the sense of love, the beauty of the net of necessity disappears, and we are left with our hostility to fate and our retaliatory impulse to strike out at life itself. We must somehow deal with the split in our consciousness, as Plato said, "How very different is the nature of the necessary from the nature of the good."

If we are going to be bound by time, necessity, and death, then we want, at the very least, to transform this net of life into a thing of beauty and to dance in it with the freedom that comes with love and presence that transcends time and space. The power of presence brings us into the freedom of *now*. This freedom makes us intimate with time.

Time

In our reactive ways of thinking, we often create oppressive substitutes for necessity. In our excessive concern with time, we lose our intimacy with both the flow of time and the eternal beyond time. Our clocks and dayplanners have transformed themselves from tools as reminders into preoccupations as we run our lives by them. Time has become segmented and choppy and the cycle of our days becomes so busy with the activities and functions in time that we are simply not present. Our mind is always "doing time" until the next thing on our schedule begins. We may even be so caught up with dealing with what comes next—

and there is always a next—that we are living a life of perpetual anticipation. Then our pleasures center around our hopes, and our pains arise from our anxieties and fears.

One way of defining aliveness is the active creation in this moment of the next moment. To be alive suggests that the next moment flows from a creative dynamic in the present. To be consciously alive means that we are intimately creating the future now. We are the Creative Buddha, integrating our Wisdom and Intimate Buddha natures in creating benefit and beauty.

We are confronted with a paradox. While we are actively creating the next moment now, the next moment is also beyond our control. We are engaged and invested in life even as it is engaged and invested in us. When we are so fully present that we lose ourselves in the moment of now, we open to the larger forces of the Sacred. We and the next moment are thereby shaped by the Sacred and we become a vehicle for sacred creativity. We are intimate with both the eternal nature of time and the flow of time.

Being present in the *now* and able to play within and with the unfolding momentum of events, we honor both the transcendent and the perpetually unfolding reality presenting itself to us moment to moment. We become intimate with the heavenly and earthly qualities of time, with the sacred and the mundane. The heart posture of affirmation, of "YES," is empowered in all its dimensions, free of the polarities of struggle with necessity.

Empowerment

Empowerment is the strength of clarity that derives from knowing our true nature. We often do not realize that our true power is the confidence in our own wisdom nature and in our affirming relationship to life by creating meaning and experiencing deep connection. The radiance of our being is strongest when we are lovers, fully alive, open, and surrendering to the moment in a totally engaged and responsive way.

As lovers, we give ourselves over to being shaped by life, in part because our love gives us clarity. We see that the very act of loving makes us fully alive, connects profoundly, and brings us home. At heart, this is what we have been seeking all along and it arises from the ground of our surrender.

The lover has no need to become a monarch because he or she is already an expression of sacred monarchy. Our reign as lover is invisible yet palpable through our presence. We commingle the sensory and the sacred in a natural and affirming way.

Service

In love we are ripe for harvesting. When we approach love and intimacy from the hiding place of fears, we only see the boulders in the landscape that might provide protection. When we actually experience the edge of possible intimacy, we dance with the unknown possibility of freedom, revelation and service to a supremely worthy monarch. This service is to a new master that can vanquish the old lords of fear, self-concern, and alienation.

No one can live our life for us. Only we can bring our unique way of being and kind of presence to the world. We relate both through our commonalities and our uniqueness, offering our particular contributions to each other and the world. If we do not embody our piece of the Divine, no one will.

We are participants in the creation of our own lives. We take the raw materials, textures, colors, contours, and contexts of our lives and weave them into a tapestry of beauty. We both shape and are shaped in the process, as in any creative process. Our lives become the artistic legacy we bring to the world and pass on to other generations.

In our human design is a great need to be dedicated to something that contributes to the larger community and the larger contexts of life, including the Sacred. Holding a deep desire and vision for connecting, being intimate and making a difference gives us guiding stars around which we can always reorient in our path to embody the triune Buddha of wisdom, love, and service. This is made manifest in our dedication to each other and to contributing to our community and the world of the Sacred. In hand in hand and shoulder to shoulder intimacy, we can experience the paradox that, as we participate in collective efforts, our own personal potential can be most fully realized. True dedication always involves learning and being shaped by the feedback of life and other people. We come to realize that our spiritual development is both personal and collective and each can serve the other.

An Intimate Society of Servants

In an intimate society, the individual and the entire community are willing to be vulnerable and depend on each person making their contribution. While it could seem overwhelming for each of us to carry the success of the community, to our soul it is a motivation. It brings forth clarity, determination, and the embrace of our personal significance that derives from the larger significance and vulnerability of our community.

When we are run by a kind of narcissistic sense of powerlessness to change larger realities, we are fleeing from the overwhelming sense that our capacity to influence and change things is far too small for the universe of our caring and concern. We either go numb to avoid the pain and frustration of our projected constant disappointment or we go inside a closed circle of personal despair. In these times it is important to become even more impeccable in our own actions so that we are creating an encouraging and loving environment for each other. Rather than being preoccupied with what we cannot do, we plant the seeds of change through service, political action, and collective dedication to creating a world of peace and generous connection.

To be intimate with our deepest caring for humanity, the planet and the viability of our collective connection to the Sacred, leads us on a journey of creative intimacy that flows with that which generates, sustains, dissolves and destroys and is about change and possibilities.

The sense of dedication to the possibility of a better world in the future, particularly for our children and their children, inspires our vision. This dedication also gives meaning to our efforts to create a beneficial legacy that others can build on in creating a more loving and beautiful environment for all beings.

We are a sacred voice in the politics of our communities when we bring clarity, sanity, and love to the conversation and to the entire process of collective action. To contribute true wisdom, however, requires that we transcend our own reactive feelings and righteousness and tap our core wisdom that can include our concern without demonizing and dehumanizing those we disagree with so that we can include their well-being and humanity in our circle of concern.

We are members of many circles of connection. These range from circles of mutual care and love, to functional circles of sharing responsibilities, to circles of emotional support, to circles of shared concern and vision. Each of these communities invites, in fact requires, our participation and contribution and involves various kinds of intimacy.

In choosing to have a family and participate in a community, it is useful to see these choices as more than taking on a burden. In opening to the unknown dynamics of caring, giving and receiving, we will find ourselves being much more generous than we could have imagined and feeling more blessed than we thought we had room for.

We can be drawn out further and further from our self-concern into an ever richer world of intimacy. Our union as lovers brings forth the entity of "*we*" and possibly children. Our union with others, hand in hand, creates an environment of supportive community. Our work with each other, shoulder to shoulder, collectively produces a world, both visible and invisible, that not only functions in the present but shapes the landscape of the future. Our profound connection with the Beloved gives birth to a myriad of wonders and miracles and involves us in the creation of the essential reality of the next moment. The love invested in that reality transmits to everyone and everything it touches with a feeling, if only fleetingly, of rapture.

We become a willing servant of these unions. This loving service has the potential for bringing out the best in us. Service invokes and evokes basic dignity, sanity, goodness, courage, love, a respect for the unique ways we all grow and mature, honesty, willingness to meet challenges, true friendship, confidence (power of simply being who we are), spontaneity, learning and our sacred wisdom nature. As sacred servants in all aspects, we manifest our loving nature in the full sense of Eros—love as making meaning, connecting, and being energetically and powerfully intimate with life as we find it.

Service is Using the Loving Nature of Reality

A few years ago I studied with an amazing healer named Katsumi Niikura. An internationally recognized martial arts and healing master, he could send an opponent flying through the air without ever touching the person. Besides his own considerable personal energy, he is able to channel energy from his environment and from great distances toward an objective. While this is dramatically demonstrated in martial arts demonstrations, his mission is to use this capacity for healing and teaching others to channel energy for healing.

For Niikura, all energy is a form of love. In his teaching, we first learn to use our breath to tap and direct our own internal energy, to develop capacity, and to draw in the energy that is all around us. It is not a matter of accumulating all this energy in ourselves. The real power in his work involves directing this energy for healing—healing ourselves, other people, and the environment we all live in.

In Niikura's system, we consciously receive energy and give energy and this involves constantly opening and radiating. We use our breath, attention, imagination, sensation and often movement in the body to direct this energy. The real power to heal, to establish harmony, and to bring out our full potential happens in community. In healing sessions, Niikura will often have his students participate in a process of laying hands on a patient and channeling energy into their body as he directs and refines how all this energy is focused in the patient.

In the process of healing, we became very intimate with the energy of our own bodies, the environment, and with each other in the constant process of receiving and giving. This constant give and take of energy as love makes manifest connective intimacy of the Sacred.

Death

The ancient Masters took everything as it came, gladly, and walked into death without fear. They accepted life as a gift, and they handed it back gratefully.

CHUANG-TZU

Transformation and intimacy often take the face of illness and death. As conscious practitioners who are intimate with the Sacred, we sense the larger dynamics of life. We see the processes and phases of life and death and new life.

Life is made possible by death and is enhanced by the presence of death. Without death new life would not be possible. The transformation of death literally prepares the ground and makes the nutrients that sustain life.

With this understanding, we make eating a sacred act. We eat to sustain our bodies and feeding ourselves means that other things must die. To make this process sacred and to honor what has died for our benefit, we celebrate the blessings of our lives and of all creation. Just as those that have died serve us, so we use those benefits in the service of others, of life, of nature, and of the Sacred.

In cultivating a friendship with death in a healthy way, we come to realize that the welcoming embrace of death is boundlessly hospitable because death refuses no one at any time. The god of death seems like a foe to our ordinary mind, but is in reality a lover to our soul.

Death demands that we attend to life as a gift. It insists that we create meaning and value. Making our life a work of art, an example of love, beauty, and wisdom, is what can transcend the stark necessities of death where there is no personal repetition, no future personal redemption.

To be intimate in the moment means that we touch both the miraculous and the temporary nature of now. Being intimately present means being aware that our lives will end in death and that the eternal nature of being is in the moment, beyond time, not in some undefined length of physical life. To live in the moment is to live with a mindfulness of death and a willingness to embrace the moment of death when it arrives. The openness of the living moment is only possible when the moment of death does not haunt the present. There is an old African saying that "When death comes to find you, may it find you alive."

At some point, the present moment will be your last. At the same time, each moment is fresh as the first. You are challenged by the reality of death to deal with the fact that you are alive now. How are you living your moments? If you are living your last moment, are you open to it? Do you feel you are living your life in the way you want to contribute to the next moment whether you are here or not?

As we reflect on death, we can also see that our life is part of a much larger natural process that began billions of years ago and will continue into an infinite future. Much as we would like to control or influence this greater dynamic, it proceeds on its own.

With death as a teacher and ally, we develop the heart posture of affirmation by embracing the gift of the moment and being present with what is. We develop the heart posture of embracing dying by honoring and caring for those who are dying. When our own time comes, we release what is not essential. We share and transmit the essence and radiance of the life that is with us as we are dying. And we create a beautiful example of making the transition. We develop the heart posture of embracing death as a communion with the Sacred, realizing that this can feed life and support the living. With death as an ally, we are constantly reminded to hold the larger visions of life and to act in service to what is of sacred value.

Grief and Loss

Grief also teaches us, if we listen to its chilling call and make the arduous, sorrowful journey. When we have lost everything, we still have our tears. These tears are a doorway into heaven, into the Sacred. To experience our grief fully is to allow our heart to break open and the divine in us can receive the Beloved as a guest even as we are hosted by the Beloved.

Authentic grief holds the heart posture of praise as we connect to the value of what we have lost. Our pain honors this caring and value. In grief we are brought down by our sadness and uplifted by the praise for those who have passed and by the sense that it is now up to us to carry on whatever good they brought to the world.

Grieving provides an opportunity for a sense of intimacy. In the process of grieving, we extract the essential value of a person's life and presence and take into our freshly opened heart that essence. This remembering leaves an imprint on our soul as we carry on aspects of their contributions in our own lives, integrating these with our own unique gifts to the world.

Our heart extends to others by sharing our mutual pain. Heart to heart we share memories. Hand in hand we maintain an atmosphere of sorrow around our loss, of celebration for their life, and of gratitude for life and the support of each other. Shoulder to shoulder we work to create a loving memorial through creating benefit on behalf of those who have passed and for the children and our children's children. As we make our way through the challenges in our lives, the wise support of others can provide a critical energy of connection and concentration of effort to work our way through our pain and to incorporate the wisdom of our experience for the benefit of all.

We realize that this is more than a personal process. It is a collective one as well. Recall the extraordinary fellowship that people experience during abnormal times of crisis. Crisis challenges us to come from our core of what is truly important and we sense that others are affected in a similar way. Crisis, grief and celebration reveal our need for each other—our fundamental interdependence. We sense the bond we have to what is beyond the ordinary, to the Sacred and to each other. We know how vital it is that we play our part and make our particular contributions.

Intimacy of Affirming Action

When we consciously serve a larger purpose with a sense of presence and the intention to create benefit, we are engaged in "affirming action." Affirming actions include simple, individual acts of generosity, support, healing, teachings, and celebration, as well as organized service, work on a job, community development and political activity that leads toward justice, a more compassionate society and a peaceful world.

Affirming action requires that we walk our talk, placing ourselves in an intimate relationship with the rest of humanity and life in all its forms. By enacting our deeper wisdom nature, we train ourselves to manifest a core of love and to embody the sacred qualities of both creative and connective intimacy. Our collective actions, hand in hand, create an environment of caring, love and service. Our collective work, shoulder to shoulder, dedicated to improving life and creating beauty invites all who share our sacred, affirming vision to join us in building an intimate society and a healthy world.

In affirming action we host all life, welcoming everyone and everything into the circle of our consciousness, caring, and love. We give them a home in our heart and express this through our actions on their behalf. We dedicate ourselves to improving the conditions of all life. We serve and affirm our heart connection to the Sacred through acts of celebration.

Intimacy of Celebration

Our affirming action of celebration manifests the awe, gratitude, and praise we feel in creative intimacy. In our service and celebration we are joining the dance of creation that is being played out moment to moment. We add our own unique gifts of value to the whole magical generation of life and beauty.

The creative life force, as if working from a design, brings each thing into being and infuses it with its own intelligence about how to be itself. These energies and awarenesses that inform and enliven particular forms are often regarded as unseen spirits, angels, or deities. Everything that exists has its own deity, its own essence nature, and its own presence. By moving beyond simplistic material views, we can know and become intimate with these unseen forces and with the magic of creation. The heart posture of creative intimacy embraces the reality that things change, people we love die, we change and we will die. By affirming all aspects of reality, we can dance with the sacred creative dynamics with dignity and a sense of home in the wondrous, seemingly chaotic, surprising, and challenging dynamic of life. We merge with the movement of this divine choreography. We dance and are danced by the music of the sacred. Our hearts open with gratitude, love, and praise enriching the world with meaning and value.

The intimacy of celebration transforms our way of being, seeing, and relating such that colors are brighter, lines sharper, energy more intense, and the sense of connection stronger and more profound. Our hearts, minds, bodies, homes, and relationships are filled with the affirmation of life and a vital intimacy with the Sacred.

Collective celebration aligns intentions, participation, and energies such that our dedication is deepened, our actions become wholehearted and the aliveness and love of the community are embodied. We give to each other and are given to. We sit, stand, sing, dance, pray and meditate side by side and become a sacred witness to each other bringing forth the Sacred. Celebration heals our loneliness and self-concern, mobilizes our energies in service to each other and to the Beloved, and retrains our bodymind to manifest the beauty of wisdom. In celebration we merge heaven and earth to create the radiant space of ecstasy.

As we create beauty by our example, our work, and our art, our intimacy with the qualities of creation and wisdom grows. Beauty penetrates to the core of our being which responds with a sense of awe and grateful affirmation. Every form of beauty, whether in our presence, our actions, or the things we make, creates a form for Divine beauty that we can relate to, be inspired by, and grow from. Beauty is an expression of love that brings the creator and the beholder into an intimate love relationship. We rejoice in the experience and our very being says *YES*, embracing the intimacy of this connection.

Our practice, our creation of beauty, our celebration of the sacred, our service to others, our love and intimacy, our presence, our openness and wonder and freshness, and our dedication to growth and bringing our gift to the world—all these protect us from narcissism, self-pity, powerlessness, nihilism, and despair. They not only make for an authentic life, they can give rise to the ecstatic.

16.

Skin to Skin Intimacy: Sex as Model and as Act

"Sex stands as the ultimate symbol because it both signifies and models the erotic experience in all areas of life. The goal of life is to live erotically in all facets of being, and sex is the model par excellence for erotic love."

MARC GAFNI [xxxvi]

As Liangshan handed Master Tongan Guanzhi his robe, Master Tongan asked him "What is the business beneath the patched robe?" Liangshan was awakened and replied "Intimacy." Tongan responded, "Intimacy, intimacy." [xxxvii]

A good marriage is also strengthened and enriched by times of passion, of intense engagement and effort and of spontaneous creativity that brings each of us to immediate, intimate attention. In deep communion, as a lover we open each other into a singular, shared experience revealing that we are simply two facets of the same jewel.

Sexual Love Making as Sacred

Mature intimacy is intensely personal. We experience our presence meeting the actual presence of the other. This can readily occur in sexual love making. The bed is both a place of comforting rest and, in the words of Roberto Calasso, "the playpen of erotic devotion." In a love relationship, sex becomes a dance of mutual trance states. The intoxication of sexual intimacy does not as such promote growth but the energies can be channeled into the growth of the relationship and into the inner alchemical growth of the individuals. Both these kinds of growth can sustain the intensity and duration of the sexual intoxication.

Yet sex without the personal love denies the sacredness of our loving nature and diminishes the possibility of using the powerful capacity for sexual engagement for cultivating our aliveness, our real love, and our connection to the Beloved.

Sex, as one of the great mysteries in life, has the fiery power to generate bliss and pain, love and obsession, creativity and contraction. When sex flows from authentic intimacy, expressing sacred connection, the experience is ecstatic and enlivens the rest of our lives. In a happy and supportive marriage, lovemaking is an expression of intimacy and we engage sexually to support that bonding without taking differences in needs and desires personally. When sex flows from desperation, loneliness, neediness and addiction to pleasure, the experience quickly loses its glow and leaves an emotional and spiritual hangover.

Skin to Skin Intimacy and Love

Love relationships are sustained by mutual understanding, feelings of being supported, the bond of hand in hand intimacy, and the shared purposes that arise in shoulder to shoulder intimacy. Yet the full power of the heart to heart communion blossoms and bears fruit from whole-hearted passion, expressed sexually as the give and take of pleasure, emotionally as the give and take of love, and spiritually as the give and take of sacred celebration and service. This deep intimacy of the heart is based not simply on satisfying desire for skin to skin intimacy but on giving the sacred gifts of our presence, openness, joy, love, and clarity. When we make love physically, passionately, and spiritually, our partner is the embodiment of the Divine, of the Sacred. Through him or her we are making love to the universe and generating a field of powerful, blissful energy.

To experience the full nature of being, we use the nature of body as well as the nature of mind. Our sensory body connects us experientially with other people and the world around us. We transcend the boundaries of our skin to physically interact with the larger world, expanding our awareness into the ocean of integrated, unified awareness. We can make love with life in the moment in all the sensory as well as spiritual dimensions.

Thoughts, feelings, states of mind, heart postures, attitudes, moods, environment, and culture all influence our sexuality and the contexts within which sexual activity takes place. Sex in a healthy relationship deepens and enhances love and affirms the mutual bond.

Lovemaking uses the physical as a gateway into the play and dance of lovers that takes each of us beyond ourselves. If engaged in consciously as a sacred practice, enormous energy and attention mobilizes to carry us on the wings of Eros into the heavens of divine ecstasy and rapture. In wholehearted lovemaking all dimensions of being are integrated and merge into the profound sense of One. Becoming fully present in lovemaking, our attention rides the ever-changing currents of sensations, dives into the pools of our lover's eyes, and licks the sweetness of gentle caresses. We experience this moment as the One.

Misusing sex is symptomatic of a larger confusion about love, intimacy and relationships. Many of us only sense being fully alive and connected in sexual encounters. We live in a culture where romantic love is the only place where we readily access intimacy and romantic love is primarily associated with the sexual. Thus we imprison intimacy in the domain of the sexual and entangle intimacy in all our complicated attitudes about sex and the tendency to be unconsciously indulgent or reactively moralistic and puritanical. Intimacy then is caught up in issues of boundaries, safety, and legality.

This confusion is compounded by the ways our consumer culture distorts and manipulates our longing for love and intimacy and by the impact of certain religious dogmas on public and private attitudes concerning sex and sexuality.

When we mistake a sexual interaction for intimacy, we completely miss the fact that authentic and mature intimacy creates a sacred connection. It involves respect and loving engagement with each other. It creates the conditions for communion. And it is a foundation for serving the larger community.

Using the Power of the Sexual

"For Freud everything is a metaphor for sex. For the Kabbalists, sex is a metaphor for everything."

Marc Gafni [xxxviii]

Sexual energy is used at a psychological level to create a relationship and, at a spiritual level, can be consciously channeled into the transformation of our being into a radiant expression of the Beloved. Sex can be a kind of meditative practice in that it is one activity in life that transports us beyond ourselves. This potential is incorporated into nearly all mystical traditions. In the West this is called Kabbala and alchemy and in much of the East tantra.

From a sacred point of view, sex is not so much an instinctive drive as an expression of the creative force and subtle life energy that has the power to generate new life and transform the material world into something new. In the sacred view of many Eastern spiritual traditions, such as Hinduism, Buddhism, and Taoism, we are made up of subtle, vital energy that takes many different forms. The most obvious form is the physical body which itself is a play of many kinds of energy, some gross and others finer. The body itself contains, produces and refines flows of energy that circulate within it. One of these more subtle energies is sexual energy.

This subtle sexual energy magnetizes our bodies and mobilizes our mental and emotional energies to create connection and emotional exchange. It can be used for ordinary purposes such as releasing tensions, for recreation to engage us in play, or as an escape into stimulation from boredom and numbness. But it is most powerful when it awakens us, plumbs a depth of loving feeling, and carries us beyond ourselves into an unknown with another person. Sex can cut through our normal defenses and facades to bring us face-to-face with a lover, removing us from our separate worlds. It opens us to each other in a dance of back and forth, in and out, up and down, pushing and pulling, thrusting and receiving, and receiving and giving. In profound moments, all forces and polarities and feelings are joined making everything one in the intimacy of communion.

While the open awareness and ecstasy of orgasm is not spiritual realization, it is a glimpse of that profound experience and of its vast possibility. It can be both an inspiration for sacred work and, under the right conditions, a spark that carries our spiritual practice to another level.

Tantra and Sexual Engagement

Tantra as the practice of transforming the energies of our physical, emotional and psychological design cultivates the qualities of wisdom and represents a form of spiritual alchemy. In tantra, the sexual energy is often used in the spiritual process of cultivation of wisdom qualities and of connection to our partner and to the Beloved. Authentic sexual tantra is about ecstasy and rapture not pleasure. It is about the complete experience of sacred love and connection to the Beloved in an act of creation.

Both Western mystery sexual practices and Eastern sexual tantra involve forms of sexual alchemy. In the Taoist alchemy of "dual cultivation," the sexual alchemists mutually tap the energies of their partners to achieve ever more intense inner orgasms and ever greater refinement of the generative energies. These are then gathered and used to create a subtle energy body.

In the tantric view, sexual union represents the ecstatic bliss of wisdom, love, and creation. The female partner is the embodiment of transcendental wisdom, her vagina (*yoni*) being the home of pure bliss. The male partner symbolizes the skillful action of undeniable radiance, his penis (*lingam*) being the diamond hardness of profound truth. The union, by incorporating all polarities, reveals the harmonious, inclusive nature of all being.

In the experience of sexual tantra, the mixing of the generative energies and the intensification of their vibration reach a point where we, as practitioners, transcend the sense of being confined to a physical body. At some points we become androgynous, both male and female, fully energized and completely open. We become the energy and the space in which the energy radiates in all directions. We experience the union of head, heart, body, and consciousness. We seem to exist beyond time and space, boundlessly open and supremely radiant.

Sex engages the entire physical and energetic body. To consciously work with the powerful forces within us and in a relationship, we need another power that can harmonize the various longings, the competing energies, and the cycles of time. The power of integrated multiple attention, the ability to sustain attention in the physical and the Sacred simultaneously, is such a force that can utilize and transform our generative energies into sacred service throughout sexual union.

Sexual communion arises when we practice the most profound love and full attention in the moment as we participate with each other in the most delicious pleasure, completely surrendering to the union, physically, emotionally and spiritually. Our heart posture radiates presence and love, opens with wonder, serves the union with unrestrained joy, and dedicates our entire being to the transcendence and transformation that arises moment to moment. Our affirmation is boundless and our intimacy with the Beloved transports us beyond distinctions, bodies, and feelings into the state of bliss.

In this spiritualization of our bodymind, we transform sexual and emotional desires into the desire for sacred beauty. We consciously use our senses in the act of physical intimacy as a vehicle to transport us to the domain of wisdom. We love the Sacred and are guided by its teachings. We are led into the heart of the Beloved, giving rise to the experience of supreme Rapture.

When totally engaged in an intimate activity such as sex, playing music, creating art, dancing, and singing, we lose ourselves inside the act and enter the boundless eternal moment. Afterward, there is also a deep relaxation and pleasant aftertaste. On some occasions we may even feel born anew, renewed by the experience of immersed intimacy.

The fully erotic sacred provides a foundation for profound wisdom that grows out of the human impulse to live by the deeper, more sacred truths of life. It is that aspect of who we are that embraces intimacy with larger meanings and community. Love and wisdom ensoul our bodymind with sacred energy and enable it to generate a rich universe of divine beauty.

17.

Superficiality and Fragmentation in a Narcissistic Age

If you bring forth what is inside you, what you bring forth will save you. If you do not bring forth what is inside you, what you don't bring forth will destroy you.

THE GOSPEL OF THOMAS

Each human being has the eternal duty of transforming the hard and brutal into a subtle and tender offering, what is crude into refinement, what is ugly into beauty, ignorance into knowledge, confrontation into collaboration, thereby rediscovering the child's dream of a creative reality incessantly renewed by death, the servant of life, and by life the servant of love.

YEHUDI MENUHIN

Busy-ness and Superficiality

We are challenged to navigate a path of sacred development in a world that encourages us to consume life styles rather than create culture, that trivializes authentic spiritual teachings by dismissing them or turning them into rigid dogma, that peddles addictive commodities to fill emotional emptiness, that validates immature and superficial emotional reactions rather than supporting sacred depth, and that focuses everyone's attention on the personal rather than building authentic community. We have become adept at dealing with the surface layer of life to not only survive but also to experience various degrees of comfort. However, survival and comfort depend, for most people, on working not only at a job, but also on the logistics of relationships, the management of all we consume, and absorption of masses of information. All this keeps us on the surface of life rather than the interior of experience. Even profound spiritual teachings get reduced to concepts to be remembered and information to be used in conversation.

Fragmentation

When we do not belong to a community, when we are not listened to by others who are connected to us, when there is no place where our gifts are received, acknowledged, and supported, then we feel homeless and lonely. The modern world is filled with the silent as well as resounding cries of loneliness, of alienation, of fragmentation, of disconnection and of the disintegration of self, family, and society. Our modern consumer capitalist brand of individualism breeds self-concern, personal autonomy, and freedom to engage in life-styles even as it diminishes personal significance and power and undermines authentic connection and culture.

Seeking security, comfort, and financial success has made us wary of the dynamic and unpredictable world of intimacy. Reducing the range of our emotional connections and having little or no sense of the Sacred, we try to exert control over life. We struggle with deep impulses for sacred connection and the fantasies of finding a sense of home in old and outdated formulas or in material belongings, while not facing the real challenges of intimacy in our narcissistic and material age. Often we achieve a simpler, quieter life at the expense of real substance, not realizing how devoid we are of truly grand stories, how impoverished we become without wholehearted engagement, how reactively we behave without a practice of becoming conscious and of growing, how superficial we make our relationship to the Divine, and how thin and insubstantial is our legacy to future generations.

We make nearly all our sacrifices of time, energy, attention, and caring to the material world instead of to each other and to the sacred world that would nourish our soul and give our lives authentic meaning. We give our homage to material security and comfort rather than the requirements of intimacy with each other and with the Beloved. In so doing, we lose touch with the power of these domains and are cut off from the wisdom and maturity that they afford.

Sick at Heart

Our overly romanticized and consumer-oriented society has stripped intimacy of its sacred essence and its spiritual role. We are left with the sense of being shallow, alone and responsible for ourselves. Our sense of loneliness, of alienation, of separation, of fundamental self-concern have made us sick at heart. We try to fill the spiritual void with pleasure, comfort, security, romantic love, food, alcohol, work, sex, peak experiences and many other offerings of life that we consume rather than intimately engage in and connect with.

One root of these destructive dynamics is the loss of a sane, working relationship with the Sacred. In the West the steady growth of secular power and consumer commerce divorced from the Sacred is accelerating. This dynamic leads to and will continue to result in destructive wars, devastation of the natural environment, the increase of mental and emotional illness, depression and despair, the fracturing of communities, the fragmentation of lives, the growth of fanatical movements, and the rise of addictions. While we may come up with partial or temporary technological solutions, analgesics to ease our pain, and programs to slow the disaster, the apocalypse of the soul connection has already occurred, to a large extent without us realizing how impoverished our inner life and larger connections are.

The Prison of Dogma and Rigidity

One response to this fragmentation and desecration of modern life has been a revival of religious evangelical groups. These religious movements often offer its adherents the sense of community, the passion of connection to something beyond themselves, and the caring of a personal God. Combining this with participatory singing, a sense of dramatic mission in the world, and a coherent view of the world can be much more involving and meaningful than the secular consumer culture being pushed by so many institutions on a global basis.

While these movements may be responding to real needs and human impulses, they, in their fanatical forms, often become hostile and destructive to the world of nature, to other people, to the sexual, to the everyday sense of connection to life, and to the very process of life itself. What we often call fundamentalism is really meant to refer to the fanaticism and rigidity of its dogma and certain of its followers. They have become fixated on one image of God to the exclusion of others. Because that image often represents a God of explanation and rules and not a mature sacred vision that integrates the developments of science and complexities of modern, heterogeneous society, their dogma exiles them into a limited domain of the Sacred and sometimes to a hallucination of God rather than the authentic experience of the Divine. They often substitute morality and the fear of evil for true connection and a loving engagement with life and each other.

When we become attached to a *right* relationship to God and one approach to the Sacred, we short-circuit the maturing of our heart postures into all the facets of sacred intimacy. We limit our divine imagination and create false images of God, becoming defensive and even belligerent in relation to other paths and other images of the divine.

At the opposite end of the spectrum of belief are what could be called secular fanatics who would reduce everything to the material and superficial aspects of life under the guise of science, freedom, and individual rights. These vehement secularists consider all discussion of subjective sacred experience, of spirituality, of religion, of the use of imagination to develop spiritual capacities and levels of consciousness, and of reference to a sacred nature of existence as being "irrational" and "ignorant." Such attitudes are not only superficial, they tend to polarize public discourse and demand dominance in the cultural imagination of modern societies.

Narcissism and Self-preoccupation

One of the most devastating characteristics of the modern life to sacred connection, to participation in the well being of the world, and to relationships of all kinds, is rampant, extreme narcissism. The Western sense of self-consciousness, of the supposedly logical distinction between self and other, between subject and object, between individual and society, has perverted natural consciousness and wisdom and created a phantom form of consciousness that haunts all aspects of our thinking, culture, science and religion.

Our narcissism reaches into our intimacy as we seek personal validation and release of the tensions of modern life through another person. We make the relationship a matter of seduction and conquest rather than the meeting of unpretentious, authentic human beings. When our relationships lack the ground of shared experience, larger purpose and real commitment to depth and growth, we often limit intimacy to sexual engagement. Thus we diminish the domain of intimacy from the full erotic experience of all of life and connection to the

Beloved to the sexual. Then we further diminish the possibilities of the sexual by rules, attitudes, and conflicting feelings and meanings.

This narcissistic preoccupation with "I," "me," and "mine" contaminates even our beliefs about what a human being is about. We mistakenly think that alienation and withdrawal are largely matters of self-esteem, self-worth, and victimhood, rather than realizing that such issues arise out of the preoccupation with self and the fragmentation of relationships. The long term issue is not how high or low our esteem is but whether we can be fully present as who we are and as members of a community that is willing to be present with us. We, from the time we are children and as adults, need to be seen as significant members of a community, not in terms of getting whatever we may want, but in terms of the gifts we can bring to the world.

As a pastoral counselor, therapist, and spiritual teacher, I witness countless people who were rarely if ever told that they were loved and that what they had to offer was important, even by their parents. This is a tragedy of enormous proportions, that so many of us have become so self-preoccupied, so busy and cut off from our own loving nature, that we do not give our spouses, our children, and our friends the support and loving expression that makes them feel seen and loved.

When we try to get some help in navigating this confusing terrain, we are often presented with therapies, groups, and advice that keeps our self-knowledge centered in our narcissistic self-concern. This can result in even more profound alienation and self-deception.

This narcissism is so ingrained that we hardly know where to begin in a journey beyond it. How do "I" break free of the fortress of concern with myself? Is not this concern with my relationship to the Beloved a form of narcissism? It is true that I need to take a personal journey and at the same time, I must realize that this work, at its core, is not simply about me.

True intimacy can draw us out of our narcissistic world of self-concern. Intimacy supports and provides a vehicle for self-transcending and self-transforming action. The challenge centers around using intimacy as a path beyond ourselves but not in narcissistic ways. In this we must not get caught on trying to find the perfect relationship in order to have true intimacy. When we make our commitment to intimacy contingent on perfection, we are blinded to the opportunities for connection and love that are being presented to us all the time. There is no perfection according to some standard or concept. There is only what is.

Reactive Habits and Barriers to Intimacy

Our narcissistic tendencies cut us off from reality, the living presence of all that is. This ignorance of our own sacred nature and of our connection to life keeps us stuck in patterns of reaction based in fear, longing, and overwhelm. These reactive habits imprison us in our limiting identification with our body, our ideas, and our feelings. In our reactive heart postures, we often feel threatened, needy, and wounded by physical pain, disagreement and emotional distress. This in turn maintains an ongoing struggle with the flow of life and a sense of suffering. The contracted and rigid imprints of past reactive experiences get perpetuated in this struggle and they appear to validate our heart postures of separateness, dissatisfaction, and overwhelm.

When our heart postures are confined to our reactive habits, the eyes of our heart peer through the veils of our fears, needs, and numbness filtering out what does not fit our reactive habits of mind. These veils obscure not only what we see in other people and the world, they distort what we see in ourselves as well. The challenge is to remove these veils and to see with the clarity of fresh eyes, an unfettered mind, and an open heart.

Our reactive habit body is a bound energetic system. When

challenges arise, we often do not know how to be present with them and so we react out or react in. We may divert the reactive energy by finding a distraction. Or we may repress and suppress the feelings reacting in on ourselves. Or we may discharge the energy of the feelings by reacting out verbally and behaviorally.

The three primary constricted reactive habits that keep us superficial and away from authentic intimacy involve fear, longing, and overwhelm. Fear in the sense of insecurity and distrust leads to withdrawal, aggression, or even hatred. Longing in the sense of neediness and insatiable wanting results in possessiveness and frustration. Overwhelm and confusion contract us into patterns of denial and numbing out.

Each of these reactive habit patterns can lead to anger. Anger from fear is protective. Anger from longing and neediness arises from the frustration of our desires. Anger from being overwhelmed attempts to exclude and simplify what is overwhelming.

These reactive contractions also freeze us into roles that require us to keep up superficial pretenses that placate our bosses, our spouses, or our children. Or we reactively and aggressively fight against the apparent demands of others and get trapped in the role of victim and rebel. In these roles we unwittingly settle for the counterfeit intimacy of identifying with others who we see as oppressed. We get frozen in role patterns of parent/child, authority/resistance, abuser/abused, and blamer/scapegoat.

Some years ago one of my students approached me obviously anxious and upset. I knew she was having difficulty with some of my teachings, particularly the suggestion that holding onto an identity as a "victim" was a barrier to being fully present in relationships and to further spiritual growth.

As she opened our private conversation, tears formed in her eyes and her lips quivered. She started out telling me how much she loved the teachings, sitting in the community, and how much she had learned over the years of studying with me. Then she launched into how important it was for her self-esteem to feel her indignation at the way her mother treated her as a child and that she did not want to give that up.

I simply listened to her. When she had finished telling her story, I simply said she did not need to give up what she knew about her childhood. Then I asked her "What kind of person do you want to be now and in the future and what do you need to know in order to be that way?"

She seemed surprised that I did not try to repeat the teachings to her in some rephrased way (something I am prone to doing) and that I was not upset with her attitude toward my work. She seemed relieved that she did not need to defend her position of righteousness and began to examine the challenges she faced in the present and her vision of herself for the future. Her position on being a victim did not change so much as she began to be inspired to move forward in a positive way.

This was a great learning for me as well. I had generally thought that we needed to free ourselves of limiting beliefs and identities before we could seriously pursue the cultivation of spiritual qualities. In our conversation, I realized that, if we indeed all have buddha nature that is unaffected by our reactive habits and feelings, then why not access that immediately and cultivate it even as we work with our fears, wounds, and longings.

The movement toward an authentic intimate relationship takes us across the mine field of reactive imprints that include issues of humiliation, shame, shyness, embarrassment, dread, despair, fear of falling apart, fear of disappearing, fear of the unknown, distress with chaos, and intimidation by the requirements of personal change that go with building an environment of mutual intimacy. We confront our tendencies toward possessiveness, righteousness, victimness, hatred, comparison, contingency, entitlement, jealousy, control, and grandiosity.

The development of reactive habits happens for everyone.

It is part of our design as human beings who learn and grow from the time we are born. As children we do not have the cognitive, emotional and psychological skills and capacity to place things in perspective and to integrate all the experiences at the time. As adults, we need to bring to consciousness the nature of these reactive patterns and to outgrow them.

The work of intimacy requires that we become present with our own patterns and trust ourselves, our partner, and our relationship to support us in moving beyond reaction. In this process a psycho-spiritual discipline of patience, reflection, meditation, prayer, and authentic communication can help us relax and surrender to the guidance of intimacy. We build a confidence that allows us to fall apart, shedding the shell of old habits. This frees our heart to deeply feel and connect, as we sense our relationship to the Beloved and the nature of unconditional love.

Addictions

We can also think of our reactive habits as addictions based in a core addiction to narcissistic self-concern. All other addictions grow out of this primary addiction.

When we are cut off from a sense of sacred presence and sacred intimacy by our reactive habits, we seek connection and fulfillment through body pleasure, physical intoxication, intense peak experiences, accomplishments, acquisition, success, acclaim, children, beauty, taste, sex and needy love. Each of these can be experienced in ways that affirm life and the Sacred, but in themselves are not the true source of intimacy and happiness. Dependence on them turns them into drugs, addictive substitutes for authentic connection to each other and the Divine.

Addictions give a curious sense of knowing and a superficial sense of intimacy. We feel like we are intimate with whatever we are addicted to. It is familiar. It has a feel of home, even if it is a dysfunctional one. Addictions provide a momentary experience of feeling before they numb us out. They seem to relieve us of the tensions around our fears, longings, and overwhelm.

For example, sexual addiction and romantic love addiction are really habitual use of counterfeits to feed the boundless appetites of our imprisoned longing and our loneliness. They substitute pleasure and intensity of feelings and an insatiable neediness for the authentic, for the true place of touch, for the connection of love as bond and of desire as a guide from our deeper nature.

Whether we are addicted to a substance, to sex, to romantic love, or to our own "rational" mind, we cannot experience the richness of life or the intimacy of the moment because addiction limits our experiential repertoire and propels us to repeat old patterns.

Neediness and Romantic Love

Our lack of intimacy with all of life and with God as Beloved propels us into seeking that sense of sacred connection in romantic love. For many of us, we think "if only I could fall in love with someone who is in love with me, then I will feel complete and connected." Romantic relationships in our society tend to be driven by longing for a home, by our desire to prove we are lovable and worthy, by wanting the power over another to ensure personal security and satisfaction, and by the hope of a permanent connection that will overcome our fear that we are doomed to always feeling lonely.

When we approach romantic love and life from our neediness, our demands for safety, or our fear of being overwhelmed, losing our balance and center, we short-circuit deep intimacy. We remain closed to the promise of home, of communion, that flows from intimacy. Intimacy includes but is not defined by needs, sensations, dependency, autonomy, and esteem. It is not about getting and having love and connection but about being love and connecting. When we embody love and connect from the nature and radiance of that way of being, we experience the communion of intimacy with life, whether in sexual lovemaking, conversing, nursing an infant, canoeing in nature, making music, or walking the dog.

Romance can and does lead to deeper intimacy, but frequently we do not get beyond our insecurities and neediness. We do not use the opportunity of connection to build a relationship with life itself. Romance tends to go through phases of euphoric enchantment, disappointment and doubt, disenchantment, conflict, temporary truces and conviviality, and finally indifference or separation.

Sometimes the apparent perfection of an intense lovemaking experience can become a golden band that constricts the heart with its magnificence. If we make this memory the model for love, then the difficult terrain of building a long-term relationship feels like a betrayal of this initial promise. We can feel caught in a cycle of being swept away by love and then trapped in the deceit that we think has been perpetrated upon us. We do not realize that our inner chemistry of euphoria literally becomes chemically neutralized over time by constantly being metabolized, like any drug, so that the soaring heights of romance fall away from the daily experience of each other.

Some of us marry out of the hope of salvation. We mistake the intensity of romantic feelings for the real inner strength that is needed to break the cycles and circles of addiction, reaction, and trauma that we think have imprisoned our family. Even during the period of disappointment, we often do not realize all the ways we have projected our hopes and longings onto the relationship and our partner.

We have an amazing capacity to become attached to the familiarity of a projected love—love that exists in the imagination even after it has departed in reality. This is not the environment for sustaining authentic intimacy. It becomes another obsessive prison for reactive hope, fear, sadness, jealousy, and depression. Instead of feeling the living energy of inspiration we are haunted by the false hope and the constant frustration of disappointment.

In this projection, we try to find the fullness of intimacy with all of life within the confines of a single relationship. We want the relationship to be everything or at least the center of our personal universes. Eventually we will feel imprisoned in this restricted room and overwhelmed by all the things that do not work because they belong elsewhere. At the same time we may not be able to see that this room is only a part of the larger house and the frustration of such a limited life results in the loss of the sense of home, even in the relationship.

Our obsession with romantic love has driven us to relationship fatigue, numbed by disappointment, resentment and regret. We, sometimes reluctantly and often willingly, trade the comfort of life-style pleasures for our familiar struggles and pains.

When marriage becomes a defense against curiosity, growth, other people, our work and the world, something vital has been lost and our aliveness, our intimacy and our future well-being are probably in danger. Possibly even dying. Our real happiness can no longer find a home in such a situation. In a love relationship, the equivalent of death is exile, banishment from the home of the relationship, of intimacy.

When we find ourselves in this kind of situation, it is time to pause and become present with the reality of what is. However our relationships got to be the way they are, we must become present now and work to create something of value from what is. Blaming, resentment, and regret simply keep us stuck. Opening to even the smallest possibilities for growth and creativity brings us onto the path of responsibility and connection. We move to create what Stephen and Ondrea Levine call *harmonic love*. Harmonic love is about attuning our hearts with each other in ways that are present and awake so that a deeper commitment emerges to make ourselves and our relationship an expression of love itself.

Mundane Power in Relationships

When we let our fears, needs, and confusion run our relationship, we either become manipulative and controlling or withdraw and isolate. Either way we feel the separation and loneliness, the tension of having a relationship without the closeness and support of connection, and the sense of something being wrong, out of balance, and displaced. We become exiled from the home of the relationship itself as we realize that intimacy is being closed down.

One of the most challenging issues is the struggle for power and control—power over our own lives, control of the ways in which we are supported, the power to manage the lives of others we care about so they will become what we want them to be, and the power to create an environment that is physically and emotionally safe and supportive of our needs.

Examining the remains of our previously disappointing relationships, we often see that we were working to make our partner what we wanted them to be and often could not be ourselves. We haunted them and ourselves with expectations and the constant shadow of our dissatisfaction, sadness and frustration.

Some therapies see all the issues in a family system as ones of power. Yet, what I am suggesting here is that, even in those situations where power is an issue, it arises because of the loss of intimacy and the failure to engage in the processes and communications that keep intimacy alive and help it to grow. It involves losing sight of the sacred nature, possibilities, and mission of intimacy. When we are cut off from the aliveness we feel when we are truly intimate, we reactively try to create patterns that are familiar as a substitute for the greater home that comes when we are open to the unknowns of the journey of intimacy. From the point of view of authentic intimacy, our monarchy, our royalty, come from our qualities of being and grace and not from our power.

As we become familiar with a natural intimacy, we gradually relax from our urgent efforts to control and simply allow intimacy to arise. We open to each other's joys, pains, and longings, restraining our impulse to be "right" rather than connected and to shout our wounded pains and griefs that drown out the melody of love. We become unwilling to continue patterns that divert us from the present with ghosts of the past and fantasies of the future. We move beyond the need to be loved and the desire to be without needs. We see relationships as the opportunity for aliveness on the edges of our comfort zone as we move into the territory of the unknown.

Sacred Longing

Without desire, one does not desire material welfare. Without desire, one does not wish for virtue. Without desire, there is no desire. Even the sages practicing asceticism are governed by desires. Therefore desire is very special. Desire, or Eros, underlies all human activity. In fact the activity and connection in the universe are the domain of Eros.

MAHABARATA

Sacred longings are flares sent from the soul into the sky of our awareness to attend to the deeper nature of our being and to the possibilities for real intimacy. Longings challenge us to feel and to become wholeheartedly engaged in the journey of love to our natural home.

By being intimate with our longings, we clarify them and engage them. This does not mean that we let them go or push them away. Rather we walk a razor's edge of being guided and informed by them, involved in them, and experiencing them on the one side while not being hijacked or seduced by them on the other. We are both intimate witnesses of them and intimate actors in the world without becoming captive of the world. We become wholehearted and yet remain open and free.

Longings can powerfully connect us to our aliveness and our core wisdom ways of being. By relating to them openly and consciously, we explore their basis in our desire for a sacred sense of home. Our longings for intimacy are a driving force in our spiritual growth and maturity.

If we listen to these sacred longings, they will indicate the directions we need to take. We are constantly being called by them to always find the authentic core of belonging that has the energy and richness of the complexity of life and that can deepen and intensify our presence in the world.

Rama's Battle with Ravana

The *Ramayana*, the ancient and magnificent Sanskrit epic that symbolically reveals the dramatic evolution of the Soul, contains this story of Rama.

> One day Rama (the prince of spirit, akin to Eros as a god of love, sacred erotic pleasure, the seventh incarnation of Vishnu, one of the supreme deities) pursues a magical gazelle. He does not know that he is being drawn away from home by Ravana (monarch of the demons, king of reactive desires). Ravana carries off Sita, (the fertility of the earth and Rama's love bride). He usurps the place of the Beloved. He keeps her captive among his women in the kingdom of Lanka.
>
> Rama, wild with despair and grief, searches madly for his wife, vowing to annihilate her abductor. He is aided in his quest by an eagle in his service who points out the trail to follow and by Hanuman, the monkey king, and his nation of monkeys. The always remarkable Hanuman leaps the ocean and walls that separate Rama from Ravana's fortress and

brings Rama news of Sita.

Rama goes through trials and challenges to enlist the support of the Ocean so that he may cross the expanse of sea to reach his beloved and overcome the might of the King of Desires. When he reaches the shores of Lanka, he and his monkey army engage in many battles and he performs many feats of great heroism. His journey and willingness to risk all reveal his dedication to regain the light of his heart no matter what the consequences.

The final battle is joined when Ravana attacks Rama. Having purified himself and given homage to Vishnu as the sun god, Rama personally took on the challenge of destroying Ravana. With his powerful bow that came from Shiva, he shot his arrows cutting down Ravana's ten heads one by one. Each time fresh heads sprang up. Rama then pulled from his quiver a sacred arrow that had come from the gods. Its wings were moved by the wind, its point was made of sunlight and fire, and its force was the weight of mountains. Placing this sacred arrow in his bow, Rama shot it. The shaft flew straight to its aim, pierced Ravana's chest, touched the ocean, and, dripping with blood, returned to Rama's quiver. Ravana was slain.

The next day the "stone letter" was delivered to Rama by one of the *Rakshasas* (demons), a vassal of the slain king. Breaking it open, Rama reads the letter that Ravana had written the evening before the final battle. Ravana praises Rama's extraordinary commitment to the sacred world. He reveals that although he had thrived in the shadow realms of desires, even finding the power to enlist the beasts of the mind, he was still unable to experience the vastness of the heart. Feeling that he had gone as far as he could go in the unsatisfying quests for power and control, he declared that his work was done. All that was left for him was "to be killed by God." He further explains to Rama that his original intention in kidnapping Sita and the fierce battles that followed, were all so that he would be slain, freed of his reactive desires, by the force of sacred love, by the Beloved.

18.

Meeting the Challenge: Taking Responsibility

To respond to fragmentation, narcissism, and cultural shallowness with despair and nihilism, as if nothing matters, is to miss the point. That too is a symptom of narcissism. All great spiritual traditions point out that nothing is secure or promised in life except the Sacred, that death is inevitable, that pain, loss, grief as well as joy, connection and beauty are part of life. Cultivating heart postures that lead to intimacy is based on neither optimism nor pessimism. Life has both. Our task is to consciously, lovingly, intimately, openly be present and dance on the fierce edge of the unknown and create benefit from the challenges we are given and work together in these efforts as we all surrender and celebrate forces greater than us.

In our stressful world, we often live so frantically that we constantly feel the edge or full force of exhaustion. While it is true we need to slow down, the real issue is that we have gone numb with overwhelm and are thus cut off from the source of our living energy. We need to pause and find our true interest, our passion, our wholeheartedness, our love. This will renew us and make everything vivid again.

The path is actually simple. It involves a sacred affirmation from the heart. The path is presence, openness, wonder, celebration, grieving, praising, sharing, creating benefit, serving, loving, intimacy, clarity, dedication, authenticity, beauty and connection.

When we dedicate ourselves and even risk our life for a stranger, we are acknowledging a deep connection between all of us. In the sacred connectedness of us all, the joy and the sorrow of any one of us is, if we open to it, the joy and the sorrow of all of us. Rabbi Hillel said: "If I am not for myself, who will be? If I am for myself alone, what am I? And if not now, when?"

Planting Seeds of Sanity

In meeting the challenges of modern life the question we must answer is not simply how do we teach about these challenges. How do we plant the sacred seeds in the soil of our spiritual wasteland? How do we minister to people in their noble attempts to create a life of meaning, sanity, beauty, service, and depth? It is this ministry that will create the foundations of love, compassion and sacredness that can give rise to a better future.

To establish a dynamic that can redirect the forces of devastation based in narcissism and its attendant qualities, we must look to something in the human design that has the same powerful potential but in the direction that is more integral to the entire design and to all life in the world. It must have the capacity for evolution, unfolding and reorienting the other personal and collective forces over time, including self-concern.

It is possible this powerful dynamic is authentic intimacy. By reclaiming the full power of intimacy from its prison in romance and sexuality, we tap a sacred quality that can resonate through all dimensions of our being and engages the depth of our soul. We are challenged to become carriers of sacred wisdom and supporters of those who make a similar commitment.

Intimate relationships provide an opportunity to discover ourselves in more complete ways, including much about our most authentic and sacred nature. We also learn about others in deeper ways. The challenges of fully engaged relationships and the experience of love involve us in the great powers of life. In conscious relating, *intimacy is a path for emotional and spiritual awakening*.

Each of us is being called to engage sacred intimacy with presence and love. Our passion for cultivating the heart postures of intimacy not only carries us along this sacred path but it inspires others by our example and our encouragement. Our loving presence creates an environment that can renew, recreate, and heal the world. The powers of connection and presence can move our civilization from devolution into evolution. The power, intensity, depth, and openness of our individual and collective efforts at sacred love may be the only way we can make our fragmented relationships whole and can create the beauty that keeps our connection to the Sacred alive.

Tilling the Ground of Reaction

Working with reactive emotions takes practice. To spiritually grow we want to experience the connection, the intimacy at the core of our feelings. Opening to each other is easy in ways that feel safe, such as when we prepare a special dinner, give a beautiful anniversary card, massage each other's back, and make passionate sexual love.

The challenge is holding the heart posture of love when we are angry, feeling rage throughout our body. The key distinction between reaction and intimacy centers around love. Are we absorbed in our neediness for love, power, sex, control, and understanding or can our deep sense of love be present? Are we moved by need in seeking connection or by our heart posture of love? Can we keep our heart open and know the loving connection in the midst of our frustration, our disappointment, and our unmet needs?

These are times to remember the depth of love and the embrace of intimacy. We sense the connection and breathe the intimacy even as we share our most intense feelings. We request each other's presence and openness in working with the energy of emotions. We radiate the qualities of whatever love we have, offering this love so that it contributes to the environment of love in the relationship.

Investing Meaning and Significance

Intimacy deepens with our investment of the time, energy and attention. Attention establishes our connection and we enshrine that connection through meaning. We sense the beloved nature of what we relate to by investing meaning and love. In this way, we bring people and things to life in our consciousness and sense their reality with our being.

Normally our attention is like a dim lamp giving off diffuse light that randomly illuminates the surfaces it happens to fall upon such as a picture, a flower, a squirrel, a person, a sound, a sensation or an idea. The light is not strong enough to reveal much of the details of what it passes over.

When we make attention conscious and intentional, it focuses the light of awareness into a bright beam that can reveal the darkest and most hidden corners of ourselves and the world. Concentrated attention makes us present and open to the presence of whatever we attend to.

In our everyday life, what we do not notice and give meaning to does not exist for us. If we think of somebody only in terms of their opinions, or actions, or their possessions, or their pain, we do not see their full humanity. When we know their name, their feelings, their stories, their hopes and fears, they become much more real for us.

We establish an ongoing relationship with objects by giving them importance, making them significant to us and being willing to learn about them. This may be a guitar we play, a favorite walking stick we hike with, a necklace we wear, or a mountain we live on.

The same is true for unseen beings. As soon as we sense their presence, give them a name, and create some form in our mind, we can begin to relate to them and they acquire existence in our world. Rituals are a powerful way to sense the power of unseen sacred presences, to give them names and forms, to communicate with them, and to establish a relationship with them.

Investing all our relationships with sacred meaning and love builds our own capacity for love, respect, and joy.

Investing with significance also means being willing to enter into each other's being and world. We each sensitize ourself to the feelings, desires, and sensibilities of the other so that we can empathize and know their deepest longings, often in ways that they do not realize. Uninhibited by their fears, denials, and reactive patterns, we see and feel the deeper nature of who they are and can bring that to consciousness. In the same way, they can do this for us. In knowing the reality of the other, we reveal dimensions that may have been hidden or unacknowledged. This interknowing is a face of intimacy and profound love.

Soup Glorious Soup

A great wisdom master, Zaharia, was leading a final retreat for some of his more advanced students, for he was dying and wanted to impart his final teachings to those who would carry on. The disciples all excelled at sitting meditation, performing ceremonies and rituals, and at demonstrating their understanding of the teachings. Yet he could see that something essential was still lacking in their practice.

He called upon his most senior follower Gita. She asked, "How can I serve you my dear teacher?"

"Please go to the bar in the next town and ask the barmaid who works there if she would be so kind as to come and make her special soup for our retreat. I have eaten there several times and the taste of her soup comes directly from heaven. It would be a delight for all of us to taste her soup."

Now let me tell you just how strange was this request. Zaharia was very disciplined and never drank or spent time in bars. Gita was puzzled but loyally set off to fulfill her teacher's instructions. Sure enough in the next town she found the bar and approached the barmaid.

Gita told her that Zaharia was leading his last retreat as he was dying and of his desire to have the barmaid cook her marvelous soup. With a broad smile, the barmaid not only agreed, she wanted to set out for the retreat immediately.

As they walked, Gita asked the barmaid how she knew the wisdom master.

"Well," replied the barmaid, "I met him many years ago. He was passing through town and came into our simple bar to rest for a while. When your teacher entered I knew immediately he was a great spiritual being. In fact I loved him from that moment I first saw him and I wanted to do something special for him. But what could I offer him. He does not drink alcohol and we do not serve food. He sensed my dilemma. He came to me, asked my name and ordered some soup.

"He knew we had no food so he said 'Put everything you have in it and it will be wonderful.' But I had nothing. So I boiled water and put in salt and wept and wept as I prepared the soup. I wanted to give him so much and I had so little. When I brought him the soup, he was very gracious. He picked up his spoon and took a taste. Well, I cannot describe the joyous look on his face as he ate. He even got up and began dancing, announcing to everyone 'The true taste of Heaven!'

I thought he must be joking or being kind to a poor soul like me. However, he had me taste it. I could not believe it. It was the most heavenly soup I had ever tasted. With tears in our eyes we danced and thanked each other. He comes back periodically and we share this wondrous soup."

As the barmaid finished her story, both she and Gita were

drenched in tears. They wept tears of love for the teacher, tears of grief for his approaching death, and tears for how moving and sacred life can be. With these tears they made a great pot of soup together for the dying master and for all those who followed his way. And so this alchemical brew transformed everyone's hearts and minds. And the taste? We should all be so fortunate to experience such rapture. For now, we can only imagine.

Mutually Invested Meaning

The temple of intimacy is built with love, shared experiences, words, rituals, gestures, space, objects, and meanings. As we share more experiences with each other and create a mutual story together, we become increasingly invested in the other's unfolding. We care about the gift that our partner offers to the world. We carry pieces of each others past, caring, vision, and responsibilities. In this process we make contributions to each other's development that we are uniquely able to offer, enhancing the richness and completeness of the other person's life and work.

As a teacher and writer, I know that my work depends on my students and readers for the teachings to manifest in the world. As a student I feel acutely the responsibility of carrying on the teachings that I have been given by my teachers and the requirements of maintaining the integrity of their legacy even as I make my own contributions to the lineage stream of wisdom teachings. As a lover, I also sense the profound responsibility for encouraging and supporting my wife in bringing her many gifts to the world.

Eating Our Tail

When we unconsciously play out a mood, try to avoid conflict by not taking a stand, or assert ourselves from an insecure place, we may notice that people we care about frequently feel bruised, confused, or battered. Our seemingly innocent actions, inactions, feelings, and fears impact others both materially and energetically, and we are often surprised and astounded when we learn what has happened. It is like being a large dog vigorously wagging a long tail in a living room of precious objects unconsciously knocking things over all around us.

This tail in humans is not physically visible yet is very important. It is part of our energetic presence in the world. It includes habits of mind and body that come from our personal history, the patterns of our family, our genetic inheritance and our cultural heritage. It includes the aspects of our personality that we reject or do not own, remain ignorant about, or do not know how to relate to.

In many shamanic traditions, it is said that we have a tail made up of the energy of our past and that of our ancestors. This ancestral tail supports us when we are growing, but in adulthood our task is to make it conscious and draw the energy of it into our body so it serves us. Otherwise it swings wildly behind us striking others and wreaking havoc in our family, social and spiritual environments.

This energetic tail is an *apraxic limb*. "Apraxia" means the loss or impairment of ability to recognize stimuli or to execute intentional movements. In psycho-spiritual terms, apraxia occurs both 1) when we fail to recognize an aspect of ourselves such as our past, unconscious habits, rejected choices that still haunt us, and the energetic impact of our behavior that is out of our attention, and 2) when we know something is there but do not know how to use it and have it serve our life purposes. The energetic tail is an apraxic limb that we simply have not brought into consciousness and learned how to use.

Our conscious work must give special attention to this limb. We need to bring it into awareness, find out what lessons it has for us, and extract the energy from it to nourish the present. It is like uncovering the stranger within us and welcoming him or her so that no part of us is denied or exerting hidden destructive powers.

Other people are an important source of information about our apraxic limbs. Getting feedback from them can accelerate our growth as we treat even strangers as opportunities to discover the parts of life that have remained hidden to us. By ourselves we may have to work harder to bring those elements into consciousness. Intimate relationships bring all of our hidden qualities to the surface. Supportive relationships insist that we deal with and grow from what is revealed.

Intimacy Within

All intimate relationships in the natural course of interactions and connection will bring out and provoke our unresolved issues, wounds, fears, longings and traumas. We then have the opportunity, if we are somewhat conscious, to experience the emotional charge and contraction that is bound to these issues. We can even process them in ways that releases their grip and allows us to live and love more openly, intimately, and freely—authentically.

Over time, the growth of intimacy in a relationship tends to involve a growing intimacy with ourselves. The demands for personal presence in interpersonal interactions push us to heal and transform the splits within ourselves. There are sacred seeds and hidden potentials that live in secret chambers of our heart, apart from the battles that rage within us and the ways we react to them out in everyday life. We carry these treasures until our heart is somehow opened by grief, love, an existential crisis, or even the simple tears of a lost child. From that opening a great spirit can emerge and redirect our life.

As we become intimate with ourselves, we discover the core fears and longing that have been driving our reactive habit body and created a personal history, our story, that we tell ourselves and each other. Like works of art, our story reveals not simply the contents of our lives but underlying themes and directions that make it a farce, a melodrama, a tragedy, a comedy, or a mythic guide that takes us beyond ourselves into the larger stories of life, the greater dimensions of being, and the wisdom of the Sacred.

When our story is told out of self-concern and preoccupation, it becomes a prison for our soul and cuts us off from the world and each other. In the confines of this small place, the interactions of the story are reactive and there is really nowhere for it to go. Even though we may try to fill it with great detail and numerous events, it always remains a short story in what it encompasses rather than an epic that takes in the whole world, life, and the outer limits of the Sacred.

As we dig beneath the layers of fears and longings, of wounds, pains, pleasures, successes and failures, we find an aliveness, a wisdom, a creativity, and a love at the heart of our particular story within the greater stories of family, community, peoples, life and the unfolding of Divine manifestation. Our story moves beyond the ordinary into the extraordinary, as our particular struggle is a pathway leading us ultimately and intimately to our true mission and role, what Joseph Campbell called our "bliss." We discover that our journey is about bringing our unique gift to the story of humankind, of the planet, and of being part of a supremely sacred community.

Intimacy with ourselves involves confronting our aloneness. In working with that aloneness, the sense of separation, and being left on our own, we join the vast community of others who have taken and are taking that journey. We find a special communion on that path. We learn how to be connected in solitude, to speak through silence, and experience the beauty of stillness. We discover the threads of the Sacred that bind us to ourselves, to life, to others, and to the world.

This inner journey works from the principle of exploring and experiencing the entire process with an open mind and full body engagement. This means we are not particularly concerned with explanation, interpretation, and analysis. We do want to be fully present emotionally and spiritually with whatever arises. We use our capacity for witnessing and hosting all the materials in our story to arrive at the deeper sense of our authentic self and basic wisdom nature that resides beneath the layers of intense reactive feelings and thoughts. In the process we establish an intimate relationship with all the parts of ourselves without reaction and attachment so that our deepest relationship with our authentic self is spontaneous, fresh, and open.

Hosting

To be open does not mean spaced out where substance is denied and nothing is fleshed out. This simply leads to an escape from life, not an engagement in it. To be open to life and to all that is, means to be involved and unattached, to be connected and not merged, to live beyond self concern and preoccupation and still have personal autonomy and responsibility.

This openness is best reflected in the quality of hosting. When we host all that is in our awareness, we are spacious, inclusive, and welcoming. We actively relate to everything that arises in the space of our awareness. Hosting excludes nothing. Hosting is what makes it possible to work through our fears, longings, and overwhelm. In the experience of hosting, we realize that, as we host everything, we are being hosted by all that is.

To be fearless in relationships does not mean we have no fears but that our sense of being and presence is large enough to include all our feelings, our wounds, our losses and griefs, our joys, and our conflicting impulses.

The same principle applies in our intimate relationships. When we host each other, we create a welcoming and encouraging space for the other to show up, to be just as they are. In that hosting space we also hold the desire to be of service to them and for them to feel at home in our presence. In addition, we also experience being hosted by our partner and by the relationship itself.

The sense of inclusion resides in the heart and is an aspect heart to heart intimacy. At the same time hosting in a relationship is more than a heart space. It is an environment of welcoming that we maintain hand in hand, day-to-day, and it involves working together shoulder to shoulder as we include others as guests in the home of our relationship. Hosting as a shoulder to shoulder endeavor invites the guest to become temporarily part of the hand in hand family of the relationship and to partake of the overflow of the intimacy of our heart to heart connection.

Working Together

Colainn gan cheann duine gan anamchara

(A person without a soul-friend is a body without a head.)

IRISH SAYING

Doing our spiritual work with others, particularly those who are conscious and have discovered wisdom through their encounters with life, is critical according to all the spiritual traditions. John of the Cross, a sixteenth-century mystic, pointed out: "The virtuous soul that is alone and without a master is like a lone burning coal. It will grow colder rather than hotter."

Responsibility

Our words, deeds, and interactions all have effects on others and on the world. This is expressed in the idea of karma in the Eastern spiritual traditions. One of the most widely misunderstood ideas in Buddhism is the theory of karma. *Karma* simply means "action" and, in this context, refers to our intentional acts. These may be physical, mental, verbal, or even feelings, all of which have impacts. Every action has an impact and creates the environment for the next moment in time. Thus everything we think, say, and do has some kind of impact or effect, even if that effect is in our own psyche. These effects give rise to further impacts creating a chain. Intrapersonally they create patterns, setting in place or reconfirming reactive habits. These chain reactions have not only personal impact but have effects in our relationships, in groups, and in our community. They can affect others directly such as when we say something harmful or indirectly by way of example or simply the kind of climate we create in the relationship.

Karma in its essential meaning is simply the result or effect of any action. All actions have an effect and those effects are their karma. We then have to live with the environment of effects of previous actions, our own and that of others. Every interaction contributes to the creation of the atmosphere and reality of the next moment and future moments. Looked at from a negative point of view, karma presents a burden. From a positive frame, karma offers us the opportunity to create benefit and beauty from our current situation.

Sustaining and deepening intimacy requires that we take responsibility in the relationship. "Responsibility" can mean many things ranging from blame, to control, to an attitude of creation. From the point of view of spiritual maturity, responsibility involves creating benefit from what is. It does not matter how things got the way they are, whether by our hands or those of others. The fact is that right now, all that we can do to take on responsibility is to work to create benefit now and in the future. This is not to suggest that we have control, only that our efforts and skills must be mobilized in the direction of improvement, love, beauty, growth, and wisdom. This represents our manifestation of the Creative Buddha.

All relationships must deal with differences of opinions, feelings, and attitudes as well as periods of discomfort. Taking responsibility means that we work with whatever is happening to make it better or to create something of value out of the situation. The heart postures of blame, regret, guilt and shame all keep us stuck in past patterns of self-preoccupation, victimhood, and control. The heart posture of responsibility actively moves us and others into larger perspectives, current possibilities, and greater futures.

We create benefit by acknowledging and owning the consequences of the past, by grieving what is lost, celebrating what is here now, by opening to being worked by the experience, and by dedicating ourselves to acting in ways that are beneficial.

The Amy Biehl Foundation: A Story of Forgiveness, Reconciliation, and Benefit

Barely able to contain their grief, Linda and Peter Biehl comforted each other on the long airplane ride from California to South Africa. Their daughter Amy had been stoned and stabbed to death in Cape Town by a mob that did not realize that this white person had been registering black voters for the country's first free election. Until that fatal night in August 1993, she had devoted her young life to working in Africa for democracy and rights with such people as Kofi Annan and Jimmy Carter. Just 26-years old, she had dedicated herself to improving the conditions of people in the emerging democracies of Africa and had been active in working for the release of Nelson Mandela.

Linda and Peter were now going to Africa for the first time, on the occasion of her death. As a way of dealing with the shock and intense sadness, Peter wrote Amy a letter in which "I told her I thought she'd done a great job with her life and that her mother and I and her family would try to honor her with some sort of action."

In 1994 they established the Amy Biehl foundation in the United States to carry on Amy's work and in 1997 set up a sister trust in Cape Town. Their actions did not stop there.

They attended the hearings of the Truth and Reconciliation Commission, a powerful process designed to heal a traumatized nation. In this process those who had committed acts of political violence could testify, express remorse, and ask for amnesty. When the four young men who had murdered Amy testified, the Biehls supported their request for amnesty. Linda Biehl put it this way: "Obviously, it was a mob situation, it was really not a personal thing. You have to remember the context. Amy was always describing the condition and plight of black youths in the country...not knowing they would be her killers."

The four men had detailed their parts in the killing and apologized to the Biehl family. In July 1998, they were released from prison. The process of repentance and forgiveness had moved a number of giant steps forward. And there was more.

The Biehls would be considered a fairly typical suburban family up until the time of Amy's death. Peter was a business consultant, Linda managed a couture department at Neiman Marcus, and they had a son still in high school and two other grown daughters. The couple left their careers and comfortable life to get into the unknown business of international aid. They began splitting their year between Cape Town and the United States, spending much of their time in the U.S. giving speeches and raising money for the foundation which has educational programs in both countries.

In 1999 Easy Nofemela and Ntobeko Peni, two of Amy's killers, returned to their home townships to begin working with the problems of aimless young people who were getting into trouble, like they had. A visiting anthropologist suggested to the two men that they might approach the Biehls about getting help in starting a youth program. "I wanted to see them so I can say I'm sorry," Nofemela said. "It was not enough at the Truth and Reconciliation Commission." When they met, he told the Biehls: "I know you lost a person you love, I want you to forgive me and take me as your child."

And so a new and deeper process began that wove

together the fabric of a family from California and two young men from South Africa. Nofemela and Peni started a training program at the Amy Biehl Foundation. By 2003, Nofemela coordinated the after-school sports programs for the foundation that has five schools in the area. Peni also worked for the Foundation. They call Linda Biehl "*Makhulu*," the Xhosa word for "grandmother" or "wise woman." They called Peter, who died of cancer in 2002, "*Takhulu*," "grandfather."

When Peter died, Linda bought two small plots of land in the township in his memory and gave them to Nofemela and Peni so they could build homes for their families. Both have young daughters. The relationships reflect mutual respect, caring, and love. As Linda says: "I have a lot of love for them.... Everyone says, 'You just forgave them.' My husband and I talked about this a lot. Yes, forgiveness is part of it, but the real challenge—and what I think South Africa is about—is the reconciliation aspect. And reconciliation is about work. You can forgive someone and walk away and go on with your life...but if you're going to make a real difference and work at changing conditions, it's more the reconciliation process, the coming together and going forward mutually. It's taking things that are negative and turning them into positive energy."

19.

SHAPING THE EVOLUTION OF COLLECTIVE CONSCIOUSNESS AS A BODHISATTVA

...And I have felt
A presence that disturbs me with the joy
Of elevated thoughts; a sense sublime
Of something far more deeply interfused,
Whose dwelling is the light of the setting suns,
And the round ocean and the living air,
And the blue sky, and in the mind of man:
A motion and a spirit, that impels
All thinking things, all objects of all thought,
And rolls through all things...

From "Lines Composed a Few Miles above Tintern Abbey"
WILLIAM WORDSWORTH

Path of the Bodhisattva

In his article "Come Together: The Mystery of Collective Intelligence," Craig Hamilton poses the questions: "What if, in the face of this knowledge of our permeability and interdependence, the ground of our identity were to shift away from our cherished sense of separate individuality to the whole in which we are embedded? What if our overriding preoccupation with our personal welfare—the ego's endless chain of wants, desires, and fears—were to pale to insignificance in the face of a concern for our larger, collective identity and destiny? What kind of human world would come into existence then? Freed from the moorings of self-concern, what could our individuality express? And more importantly, where could we go collectively that we could never reach in our present, fragmented condition?"[xxxix]

Service and spiritual work are sacred paths of the bodhisattva, a Buddhist ideal of becoming awake and being dedicated to the awakened happiness, growth and freedom of all sentient beings. The word *bodhisattva* can be translated as "one who embodies wisdom." The essential wisdom that characterizes this path includes the qualities of self-transcendence, loving-kindness, compassion, profound understanding of the nature of the mind, the deep sense of the interdependence and interconnectedness of all beings, and the dedication to creating benefit and beauty in the world for everyone. The bodhisattva contributes to the awakened evolution of the collective into becoming an embodiment of the Sacred. The bodhisattva principle includes not only manifesting wisdom and compassion but also the creative nature of the Triune Buddha.

The enlightenment of the bodhisattva is integrally tied to the realization of sacred wisdom, love, and service in all humanity and all life. The fruits of personal intimacy with each other and with the Divine are given to the world to nourish others who hunger for happiness and belonging. This notion of our personal and collective role engenders a passionate, emotional and dedicated intimacy with everyone in his or her potential for sacred wisdom and in being an integral manifestation of the Divine.

"...the bodhisattva, the being who takes on the suffering

of all sentient beings, who undertakes the journey to liberation not for his or her own good alone but to help all others, and who eventually, after attaining liberation, does not dissolve into the absolute or flee the agony of *samsara*, but chooses to return again and again to devote his or her wisdom and compassion to the service of the whole world." Longchenpa.

The world calls us to become active servants of peace, "clothed," as Longchenpa said, "in the armor of perseverance," dedicated to a bodhisattva vision and to the spreading of wisdom into all reaches of our experience.

Bodhisattva Activists

We need bodhisattva lawyers, bodhisattva artists and politicians, bodhisattva doctors and economists, bodhisattva teachers and scientists, bodhisattva technicians and engineers, bodhisattvas everywhere, working consciously as channels of compassion and wisdom at every level and in every situation of society, working to transform their minds and actions and those of others, working tirelessly in the certain knowledge of the support of the buddhas and enlightened beings, for the preservation of our world, and for a more merciful future.

Do your best to be intimate, to breathe closeness, to open to the presence of others in this moment, and to receive their love however awkwardly it is expressed. As you prepare food be intimate. As you arrange your house, be intimate. As you kiss your lover, be intimate. As you hug your children, be intimate. As you share stories with friends, be intimate. As you labor over a project with co-workers, be intimate. Radiate the gift of connection.

Even as you feel lonely and self-comfort with chocolate, become intimate with the fullness of the moment of pleasure and dedicate that pleasure by radiating it out as a gift to the world, sensing that gifting through your entire body and in the depths of your being. Become a chocolate-eating bodhisattva.

As Teilhard de Chardin said: "Some day, after we have mastered the winds, the waves, the tides and gravity, …we shall harness…the energies of love. Then, for the second time in the history of the world, man will have discovered fire." [xl]

The collective wisdom that the bodhisattva taps and contributes to is a sacred wisdom. It is useful here to distinguish between conventional wisdom which is the ability to judge soundly and sagaciously about facts and how to manage the functional details of life and profound or sacred wisdom that arises from enlightened or spiritual awareness and informs our very way of being.

20.

Arc of the Sacred

Relating to Unseen Sacred

To see a world in a grain of sand
And a heaven in a wild flower,
Hold infinity in the palm of your hand
And eternity in an hour.

WILLIAM BLAKE

Seeds and formations
Both have the nature of interbeing and interpenetration.
The One is produced by the all.
The all is dependent on the one.

THICH NHAT HANH

In a Zen koan, Master Hoen says, "Even Shakyamuni and Maitreya are servants of that one. Just tell me, who is that one?" Shakyamuni was the name of the historical Buddha and Maitreya is a future Buddha. This statement and question point to the idea that everyone, even Buddha, is a servant. In Mumon's commentary on this koan, he says, "If you clearly recognize that one, it will be just like meeting your father at the crossroads. It is not necessary to ask others whether it is he or not." [xli]

The question, what is the Sacred, challenges us to look for ourselves, to uncover, beyond words and concepts, the nature of being. In the West we have called this "God." Here we are encouraged to arrive at our own experience and understanding of this "one." We want to come to not only see clearly, but know the One with our skin, in our hearing, in our bones and in our heart. Then we are, without doubt, servants of this greater truth, the profound wisdom nature of life.

In speaking of the Sacred as the world of divine qualities and energies, we are always walking a fine line between the abstraction and the concrete. These qualities and energies manifest concretely and yet cannot be reduced to the material, to the sensible. Whether speaking of our own nature or that of the world around us, the Sacred resides in a felt more than a seen dimension. The fact that we cannot see and measure such forces does not mean they are not real. They really are there and are important to us.

We are making a distinction here between the superficial and the sacred ways of perceiving, thinking and feeling. As we discussed in earlier parts of the book, the superficial constitutes the surface level of what we can see and hear in the material realm as well as our reactive, unconscious thoughts and feelings. The Sacred reveals itself when we experience being conscious of the vaster dimensions and greater forces that operate in the world and make up the authentic nature of life. While the sacred dimension includes everything from dynamic forces to pure being, we realize that, other than pure being, the Sacred is totally relative, everything that is is of everything else that is. This totally relative and radically relational nature of all things is sometimes called "interdependent being" or "interbeing."

Because we are designed to actively relate and create

relevant connections that organize our sense of the world, we need to see beyond the surface to the forces of presence and creation that are always operating in reality. We make the richness of reality manifest in our innermost world of experience and meaning through our conscious use of our mental and emotional capacities.

Our poetic imagination and perception brings forth the soul as lover to become intimate with the objects of our world, the people in our lives, and the experience of aliveness. The eyes of love see the entire universe in a grain of sand as Blake says. We see the extraordinary in the ordinary, the beyond in everything that presents itself to us here, the eternal in the moment of now.

By seeing the extraordinary in the ordinary, we invest events, objects, activities, people, and experiences with meaning from the very depths of our being. The only way to see in this way is gradually to learn how to care, how to create beauty from what is available to us, and how to take care of what we create. We can make the invisible Sacred visible through story, action, image, and song. In this way, using our imagination and our capacity to love, we bring the worlds of the sensory material and the soul together.

Imagination as a Divine Capacity

Imagination is one of the great qualities of our design and is essential to all forms of intimacy. There is no mind without imagination. Imagination is what gives form to our experience, to our part in the larger whole, to our sense of connection, to our future, to insights and deep truths, to the Sacred, and to life itself in ways that we can relate to and work with. Imagination has the capacity to transcend time and space. Far from being unreal, we cannot get a grasp on reality without it. Imagination may not be the reality of an object but it has its own qualities of reality that have impacts and that give us access to multiple dimension of life, of being and the sacred that we cannot enter without it. Imagination allows us to see what is hidden, to enter dimensions of the world that are very powerful yet unseen.

Rabbi Marc Gafni points out that according to the biblical tradition, man was created in the image of the Divine. He argues that this cannot possibly mean a "fixed and idolatrous copy of divinity. God has no fixed form."[xlii] He suggests that humans are created in God's imagination and that we participate in this sacred capacity through our own imagination, a God-given gift that is sacred, making us "*homo imaginus*." Gafni quotes Rabbi Nachman of Bratzlav: "It is for this reason that man was called Adam: He is formed of *adameh*, the dust of the physical, yet he can ascend above the material world through the use of his imagination and reach the level of prophecy. The Hebrew word for 'I will imagine' is *adameh*."[xliii]

Creation is Basically the Possibility of Possibility

Imagination must remain both free and yet be trained. This is the paradox of training the mind to get some control of the disjointed and often reactive mental activity and at the same time open it up to new possibilities. We want to imagine a journey that will take us to the heart of love, of the sacred, and of our true longing. Our identity, concerns, fears, longings, personal history, attitudes, likes and dislikes are all produced in our imagination, a kind of visualization. Conscious spiritual work uses this capacity of the imagination to visualize and to retrain it in relation to the Sacred and the values that reflect our wisdom nature.

In deep spiritual work we visualize ourselves not as a collection of reactive self-concerned habits but as a wisdom being. As a wisdom being we are alive, alert, open, warm, loving, harmonious and hosting. The world that is hosted is not our old perceptual and conceptual ideas about the world, but a world that radiates the qualities and energy of wisdom.

Imagination takes us beyond what we already know. Through the divine gift of imagination, our senses can extend to the further reaches of possibilities and of intuition of truth. It is imagination that makes it possible to know what other people's lives are like. It is imagination that creates memory. It is imagination that is the basis for learning and being able to build a body of knowledge and insight.

Part of what keeps us imprisoned in dissatisfaction with life and the relationships we have, is our inability to envision something new, to envision the sacred dynamics at play, and to imagine what is really going on with our longings and our sense of living in a spiritual wasteland. Without imagination we cannot be intimate with the possibilities of our own becoming, our potential, and our home in the world.

Imagination can take us to a vision of how things can be improved and how we can be of benefit in the world. Without imagination, we cannot take true responsibility, the creating of benefit from what is. This intention to create benefit is useless without the ability to envision the possibilities of benefit that will guide our efforts to actually create something of value.

Connecting to the Reality of the Sacred

Just as we relate to the objects of our material world through imagination, so too we also use imagination to relate to the Sacred. Our having a mental image of a chair does not take away from the reality of the chair in the material world. In the same way, having imagined forms for the Sacred does not make the Sacred less real.

The ways we imagine the qualities and energies of the Sacred is often referred to as magical thinking. Magical thinking is important in relating to the world of invisible connections and forces because it has the possibility of evoking the appropriate sense of wonder and meaning. While we often denigrate and oversimplify magical ways of seeing and thinking, the magical can convey the living dynamics and meanings of what is beyond our material senses and beyond time and space. The appeal of the magical, rather than being a regression into childhood, can reflect those aspects of our being that seek expression for what cannot be conveyed literally and conceptually.

Metaphoric images, mythological figures, story characters and animal images are often better than concept words in describing inner dynamics and sacred phenomena because they capture more complexity and subtlety. We tend to reduce the rich world of nature and the Sacred to concepts hoping to capture the essence of phenomena in a theory or an equation. Such attempts are also exercises of imagination and have great utility. At the same time they may not capture the fullness of what occurs in the world nor convey the same sense of connection. The concept of solar power does not evoke the same multidimensional reality that the stories of Apollo do. The myth elaborates on the impacts of the physical qualities of the sun by exploring its role in relation to other physical forces and to the configuration of human experience and the structure of our psyche.

Concepts are even more limiting when describing nonphysical phenomena such as relationships. The mystery, wonder and subtlety of human connections begs for images, stories, and imaginative creations that are adequate to represent the reality of human experience. The metamorphosis required in the imagination to begin to comprehend the deeper forces and energies of a relationship has become more and more difficult as our modern, material society has become increasingly dependent on abstract theories and statistical measures.

Getting Beyond To Be or Not To Be

To be or not to be—that is not the question! In Western modern thinking, we become so concerned with identity and definition, that we overuse the powerful verb "to be." The word "is" limits the subject of a sentence to what follows this verb of identity. This verb tends to shape our conceptual framework into an absolutist mentality. By saying "I am a good person," we are attributing an inherent reality to ourselves when life is more nuanced and relative, depending on circumstances and contexts.

When used in speaking about our emotions, "I am" tends to make us self-referenced, self-preoccupied and caught in limiting beliefs about ourselves. It also disconnects us from the reality of everything else that is happening which has not been included in the implicit equation of "to be" sentences. These statements also tend to be static and diminish the dynamic aspects of living and growing. The verb "to be" carries a sense of completeness, finality, and time independence. In other words, this particular verb form brings along associations and implications of identity, permanence and static existence that do not reflect either the larger world or the world of our experience.

For many specific purposes and in many situations, the verb "to be" conveys important information and a sense of presence in the moment. This dual condition of adequacy-inadequacy seems characteristic of this verb, providing both its attraction and danger.

To experience life with a sense of intimacy involves more of a way of being rather than questions of whether we exist or what we are. Our challenge centers around finding language and actions that elaborate and deepen our relationship to life and the Sacred rather than define it.

Sacred Forces of Intimacy

Intimacy originates and develops as a gift of the sacred dimension of life. The soul dimension drives us toward real connection, meaning, and durable bonds. It is from this that we relate to ourselves, other people, and to the sacred source from which this drive arises.

In a sense, a relationship of intense intimacy aligns us with the larger and ancient forces of the Sacred—love, creation, and a sense of destiny. These forces are presences that are part of a story beyond our personal history and drama. This larger story shapes not only our world today but the worlds of future generations. In this grand theater we are acting in two realities simultaneously—the concrete personal relationship and the psychic, mythological relationship between divine energies.

When we bond with a friend to share our mundane and profound experiences, we are participating in a phenomenon that has existed for tens of thousands of years. When we fall in love and couple, we are giving personal and mutual expression to the force of love that has always shaped human relationships. When we work together to build a house, to play a game, or to make music, we are following a path of collective action that has its roots in the most ancient communal activity. When greet each other and host friends in our home or simply sing as part of a ritual service, we create an environment of home in the ways people have always done.

Every act of connection is part of a larger dynamic built into our individual design and the nature of human relationships. Love, sharing, bonding, and creation are all more than personal forces in the world, just as greed, fear, loneliness, pain and pleasure are also great forces that shape both personal and collective experience and direction.

Our personal process of creating meaning and the sense of connection through that meaning leads to feeling at home in the world. A truly satisfying home comes when these meanings are shared, the connections include other people, and the home is warmed by an abiding sense of the Sacred.

In recent times it has become popular to distinguish spirituality from religion with the idea that religion is inherently rigid, dogmatic, exclusive, and controlling while spirituality is fluid, based upon practice and experience, inclusive and encouraging. I am sure that this reflects the experience of many people with traditional churches, synagogues, mosques, and temples that they may have grown up with as opposed to the more open spiritual programs such as meditation groups, spiritual support groups, and twelve step groups.

At the same time, we can realize that fundamentally religion is about connecting to the Sacred, to each other, and to a community in shared worship. Spirituality is about transcending the limitations of ordinary life and self-preoccupation and connecting to forces larger than we are and becoming a carrier of sacred qualities into the world. Religion can include spirituality and spirituality can include religion. What unites them both is the sacred nature of being, of conscious action, and of loving relationships.

Naked Truth and Resplendent Story

A great sage of Dubno, replying to a question about why a mythic story is so powerful, said, "I explain the difference by means of a story.

"Once upon a time, that is also now, Truth walked the streets as naked as the day he was born. As a result, no one would let him into their homes. Whenever people caught sight of him, they turned away or fled. One day when Truth was sadly wandering through the world, he came upon Mythic Story. Now Mythic Story was dressed in finely tailored clothes of beautiful colors, showing off her very attractive figure. Story, seeing Truth, said, 'Tell me brother, what makes you look so sad?' Truth replied woefully, 'Ah, sister, things are bad. Very bad. I'm old, very old, and no one wants to recognize me. People are constantly avoiding me.'

"Listening to sad Truth, Story responded, 'People don't ignore you because you are old. I too am old. Very old. But the older I get, the better I seem to most people. I'll let you in on a little secret: Everyone likes things to be disguised and dramatized a bit. Let me lend you some wonderful clothes like mine, and you'll see that the very people who would not acknowledge you will invite you into their homes and welcome your friendship.

"Truth took Mythic Story's advice and put on the borrowed clothes. And from that time on, Truth and Mythic Story have gone hand in hand together and everyone loves them. They are a happy family."

21.

Breath of the Sacred

Kissing and Breathing: Symbols and Forms of Intimacy

And YHWH, God, formed the human, of dust from the soil, and blew into his nostrils the breath of life, and the human became a living being.

GENESIS 2:7

The mouth functions in important ways for us both physically and symbolically. It is integral to both kissing and breathing. The area around the mouth is also where the brain devotes a high percentage of its sensory receptors. When we include in our attention the sensations of the kiss or the breath, we are automatically brought into the present, now.

The kiss and the breath both model intimacy in the qualities of mutuality, dissolution of inside and outside, and connecting with what is beyond us. Kissing conveys the heart posture of love. Conscious breath conveys the heart postures of presence, openness, service in the sense of giving and receiving, and love in the sense of constantly inhaling from the heart of the universe with gratitude and exhaling from the heart center (the chest) relaxation, peace, and love.

The process of breathing is a living metaphor for expanding our narrow sense of ourselves and being present to the wondrous energies and qualities that are in us and all around us. The air we breath is the same recycled atoms that are inhaled by others, not only in the current era but in the past, including Moses, Christ, Buddha, Mohammed, and Lao Tzu.

Breathing is one of the primary ways we can take in the vital energies that sustain our body and nourish our deeper sense of well being. We extract the energy of the air and use it to feed all our organs and our nervous system. Just as the oxygen of the air is carried by the blood to all parts of the body for growth and maintenance, so the energy of the air is circulated in energy channels through our system to provide vitality and strength. Similarly, just as the oxygen is used up by the activities of the body, so the supply of energy can be used up by our thinking, willing, acting, etc. We need to constantly replenish both.

To inhale completely is to fill ourselves with the energies of life, literally to be inspired. To exhale completely is to empty ourselves, opening to the unknown, and to be expired. It is through this primal process that we can awaken to the energy of wholeness and sense being the rhythms of life itself.

The mystical traditions such as yoga suggest that in ordinary breathing we absorb and extract a normal supply of *prana* (energy), but from controlled and regulated breathing we are able to extract greater energy and store it in energy centers, organs, and the nervous system for maintaining vitality, health, and for making qualities of wisdom manifest.

Breath is a link into larger ecologies, a part of nature's complex metabolic system of exchange of substances, and conservation and transformation of elements. It connects our inner world with the vast outer world and all of organic life. It is the moment-to-moment process of letting go of what is no longer useful and opening to what is fresh and nourishing.

From the standpoint of the wisdom traditions, one of the

fundamental truths of life is "as above, so below." The bodymind is a microcosm of the universe, just as we are a particular expression of all being. Not only is the body "in the world," but the world is "in the body." We realize this when we are conscious and sensitive to not only ourselves but also of the rich environment of the outer world of which we are a part.

Becoming Intimate with the Sacred through the Breath

Breath is critical to us for life. We can go without eating for some time and even without water for a shorter period, but without breathing our life span is only a few minutes. The quality of our breathing also influences our overall sense of vitality and health.

Breath works continuously and is unconscious and yet can consciously be controlled. Breathing involves both expansion and excitation on the inhale, and relaxation on the exhale. And breathing converts energy into matter and connects us both inside and outside ourselves.

Conscious breathing can bring us into an intimate relationship with each of the five sacred intimacies. Breath brings us into presence and through presence inside the Sacred. Our presence meets The Presence, allowing us to be simply who we are and everything else to be simply as it is.

In the act of breathing, we create an emptiness, an openness so a new breath can enter. By consciously breathing and using our exhalation we can follow the breath infinitely out into space, connecting to Essential intimacy. The movement of the breath connects us to the underlying, dynamic motion of all creation and the creative life force that energizes all of us. By being conscious of the cycles of breathing, we enact, in the universe of experience, the larger seasons of time, reflecting our capacity for creative intimacy.

When we are conscious of our breath, we can experience

the unconditional support and love of the Beloved in sustaining the gift of our lives. We can use our breath to consciously receive the conditions of others and to send out our loving and compassionate energies to those in need. We experience the loving interconnectedness of all being.

The transitions between inhalation and exhalation has a pause in it. This natural pause places us inside moments of eternity, simply being. As we relax and open, a basic clarity arises in insightful intimacy.

Heaven and Earth

The purpose of spiritual work cannot be reduced only to transcend our earthly nature. It includes being fully alive and intimately present in it. Engaged intimacy brings us into a fullness of presence with the inclusive face of the Sacred that is all reality. We are reminded that each moment is inclusive and what we have to work with.

Attempts to only transcend "what is" simply stumble on the path of reality. They take side trips into conceptual realizations and try to grasp "peak" experiences. It is not that we cannot have transcendent experiences or realize our potential for Essential intimacy. We want to go beyond the self-images of our reactive bodymind and become more present and awaken to the transcendent and immanent nature of all being. The point is to integrate and embody all the aspects of sacred intimacy.

The spirituality of intimacy is not spectacular, requiring our meeting challenges with drama about life-threatening encounters or guilt-ridden confessions. It only calls upon us to live, be conscious, and relate in a sacred way beyond our reactive habits of mind and body.

Spirituality is characterized by an inclusive view, one that is beyond oppositional thinking that polarizes the world into battles of two competing forces. Often our predisposition favors dividing reality into neat and distinct categories such as black and white, good and bad, problems and solutions, right thinking and wrong thinking. We want certainty and often settle for simplistic thinking as a substitute for a more nuanced, usually paradoxical perspective that more closely resembles the realities of life. We shy away from the challenges of sacred view and *want to be God* in our righteousness. Yet, we are not either-or, not one-way-or-the-other. The paradoxical nature of reality and of the Sacred suggests that we are both—wise and ignorant, skillful at some things and clumsy at others, loving and angry, caring and self-concerned.

To bring sacredness to our relationships is not simply thinking about the Sacred, or feeling it, or sensing it around us, although these may be involved. We live it. Sacredness permeates all reality, the core of being human and the heart of intimacy. To make that conscious and active, we bring sacred view to the way we perceive our relationships, the way we experience those relationships, and the choices we make based on those views and experiences.

Earth is the grounded world of action, of creation, of aliveness, and of the diverse, rich, beautiful, continuously dancing, delicious, fragrant, constantly changing, ever-present, and always embracing world of form. It is vitality, life force, activity, energy. When we embrace the earthly nature, we are in the world of cultivation, creation, and transformation. Our dance is not a matter of learned steps so much as the authentic movement with the beat of life and the melody of celebration.

Heaven is the realm of being. Heaven is the open, spacious, inclusive, and luminous nature of things. It is awareness, learning, and qualities. Heaven is not about transformation, it is about abiding. We abide in the nature of Nature, in the essence of awareness and energy, in the sense of boundlessness and beyond. Heaven is encompassing and universal and not particular. Heaven, because it is beyond particular form, can be infinitely vast or infinitesimally small. It can be luminously colorful as light or radiantly dark.

The intimate union of heaven and earth creates conscious aliveness. The human connection adds the element of experience and states of being. In the marriage of heaven and earth, we can know our connectedness fully, to each other, to God, to nature, and to all life. We are intimate with the expanse of the oceans as well as the beauty of a tear drop.

When we marry the qualities of heaven and earth in our heart, we become an agent of love. We host all that is in the embrace of our inclusive and actively welcoming awareness. We celebrate and serve the miracle of creation and the inconceivable sense of beyond—surrendering to, radiantly praising and serving the Sacred. We live in both ordinary life and extraordinary sacred aliveness simultaneously. In this marriage we dance spontaneously, creating an environment of beauty and intimacy.

As we live in the world of sacred intimacy with the qualities of wisdom, we still experience the pushes and pulls of ordinary life. The difference is that we relate to them differently, now from a heart posture of affirmation, Yes, and choice about action, rather than from reactive obsession and compulsion.

In this intimate marriage of heaven and earth, we are aflame with passion, aliveness, and clarity that derives from our basic divine nature and the experience of the sacred nature of all reality. The fire of dedication provides a special energy for us to manifest the sacred in everyday ways that serve each other, life and the Divine. Our love and dedication continuously ignite and enrich themselves turning us into a solar generator radiating kindness, understanding, encouragement, and compassion.

Being intimate with life means being constantly engaged in transforming one thing into another, in a kind of alchemy that takes the lead of everyday experience and turns it into the gold of the Sacred. Just as the earth takes the basic elements and combines them to create life and the rich diversity of its landscape, so we, to be intimate, need to follow the example of the earth and create from our experiences the beauty of ever present living moments.

Creating Beauty

Beauty is one of the great pathways of intimacy. Modern life tends to confine the creation of beauty in art, in music, and in writing to the activity of a few professionals and emphasizes the consumption of beautiful things much more than the production of beauty by everyone. Creating beauty is a way of making love to life, to the world, and to each other. Beauty gives expression to the Sacred as Beloved.

We want to relate to beauty in a sacred way. Unlike the trivialization of beauty as a vanity and self-preoccupation or simply as a comfortable way of feeling good, in a sacred view physical beauty evokes the greater and wondrous invisible beauty.

The materials from which we create beauty in life are extracted from the loves, joys, griefs, pains, and wounds that we experience. We are challenged to transform these into a sacred landscape. Often our pains, "mistakes," and wounds define the edges and lines from which we make something of value.

When we self-righteously repeat stories of our past wounding over and over again even to ourselves, we turn something of potential beauty and insight into the sticky, hostile bogs of obsession, addiction and endless hunger, frustration, and aggression—sometimes against ourselves, sometimes at others, sometimes aimed at God and frequently all of these. When we constantly describe and explain ourselves, our wounds and accomplishments, we are reciting our litany of despair and exile—despair about who we are afraid we are or have become and exile from our own true nature, life and each other.

Shedding our habits of telling our woeful stories and not living as if everything is always a survival issue, we show up and engage others in a dance and conversation that is fresh and reveals even to ourselves things we did not know we would say or do.

We realize that something is always sacrificed and that all choices have unintended consequences that create tears in the fabric of our relationships, even in the most skillful acts. The trick is to acknowledge this and weave it into the tapestry of those relationships. We cannot prevent all tears but we can include all of them in the beauty of the relationship such that the relationship becomes richer.

Often what has been ignored, denied, or tossed aside in relationships, the detritus, the "waste," is where we find the materials to take intimacy to the next level. The waste of today may be the ground from which tomorrow's flowers and trees will grow. In a sense, our failings, our particular struggles, our awkwardnesses, our existential questions all require a willingness to be compassionate with ourselves and each other. Even our clumsiness is part of our beauty as we move toward our core nature, our real element, in which a natural grace will emerge. We make all these the stepping stones on our path to the Beloved, to the Sacred.

22.

Welcoming Heaven and Earth in the Home of Love

Everything that lives, lives not alone, nor for itself.

WILLIAM BLAKE

A disciple complained, "You give us teachings and tell stories but you don't tell us how to understand the teachings or reveal the meaning of the stories."

The master smiled kindly and replied, "How would you like it if a generous farmer offered you a deliciously ripe pear and chewed it up before giving it to you?"

Living in the Earthly and Heavenly Domains

We diminish our relationships when we treat them as simply personal stories, personal feelings, and personal pleasures and pains. We do not respect the holy in us, around us, and that operates through us. When we deny the Sacred, it becomes a ghost that can haunt the relationship, our families, and future generations.

By ignoring the Sacred, we are left with a constant emptiness, a hollowness that we long to fill. Instead of being filled by being open and creating space for the Sacred, we contract our sense of ourselves into feelings of loneliness and frustration.

This shadow of the holy space is then experienced as hollowness.

Only by expanding our view to include the richness of what is and our fundamental relationship to Reality can we see the illusory nature of the hollowness. In other words, we must live out our stories in both the earthly and heavenly domains. When we relax into our sacred natures and participate fully in a life of love and engagement, an ease arises that comes from living in the eternal moment. In the full embrace of intimacy as a sacred connection, we experience belonging, peace, freedom, and a vibrant aliveness and presence.

When we authentically engage in intimacy we transcend the requirement of merely enduring the necessities of life and begin to use them to create something extra—beauty in life. Intimacy rides the razor's edge between the lightness of love and experience beyond time on the one hand and the inexorable change and challenges that characterizes the temporal on the other. We exist simultaneously in both the eternal and the temporal, and intimacy bridges those worlds.

Intimacy with the Divine puts us in touch with the core or innermost nature of ourselves and all existence. It embraces our own sacred essence and that of life at the same time.

Holding Paradox in Our Embrace

Intimacy with life necessarily involves embracing paradox. In the paradoxical view, the world is both impersonal and personal. It is simultaneously what it is, as well as what it is becoming. Life is simultaneously closed and open, calm and tense, struggling and peaceful, maintaining equilibrium and destabilizing, creating and destroying, sustaining and dissolving, evolving and devolving, and richly complex and exquisitely simple.

Harmony is the encompassing field of connections that binds forces, impulses, and feelings, even their opposition, to each other within a more inclusive whole. A paradox of intimacy is that we are called to be in common and unique at the same time, to be a "we" and an individual, to be vulnerable and strong in our participation, to make the effort and let go of the results, to surrender to what happens and to take responsibility for creating benefit from those results.

When we learn to hold the complexities, dualities and paradoxes of intimacy, we do not need to go through a continual dance of death and resurrection of a relationship. Conflicts no longer seem fatal and the cycle of tearing and mending is transformed into a process of integrating the holes and blemishes into the beauty of the fabric of the relationship as a whole.

A Final Word: Completeness of Intimacy

Intimacy gives us the sense that experience is complete in itself, not simply as a function toward something else. This may seem paradoxical from a conscious work point of view. We intentionally practice meditation, mindfulness, retrain our body of habits, and consciously communicate with each other to become more fully a lover that embodies the heart posture of love as a way to deepen relationships and to connect with the Beloved. At the same time, each action can connect us experientially to the fullness and eternity of *Now*, in this very moment. We are inside the fullness of the Sacred, and life is complete. There is nothing missing, nowhere to go, and nothing else to do *Now*.

When we are present in this way, we see a beauty in everything and we are totally in love with that beauty. When we engage the moment with presence, openness, praise, love, and clarity, we invest our actions with something extra, with the affirmation of the Divine, creating more than a physical reality. We are involved in creating a new sacred reality that awakens the soul and vitalizes our being. Our heart posture of sacred intimacy takes us beyond our ordinary self-concerns into the heart of all sacredness and it is from this place that we are able to create beauty and true benefit in our relationships and in the world.

Seven Principles of Intimacy

Over the nearly half century that I have reflected on intimacy, I have come to realize that at least seven essential principles apply to intimacy.

The first is that intimacy is essentially spiritual and is vital to life, connection, and growth and thus is different than what most people imagine it to be.

Second, there is a vast difference between the chemistry of attraction and the experience of the mystery and miracle of the closeness of intimacy.

Third, intimacy is not a thing, it is a process of relating that can be developed and strengthened.

Fourth, we are the environment that others experience and the question before us is "what kind of environment are we creating through our presence and our actions?"

Fifth, responsibility is not about blame but about creating benefit from what is, however it got that way.

Sixth, the soul is a lover and is nourished by intimacy through meaning, caring, sharing, and being wholehearted.

Seventh, intimacy pervades all true spirituality, because of its open heart, its transcendence of self into what is beyond, its profound sense of home, its natural impulse to serve, its mutuality and sense of unity, and its wild closeness to the unknown.

Intimacy of all kinds places us on the inside of our experience, opens and connects us beyond ourselves, encourages praise and gratitude, engenders service to our loving connections, and evokes from our depths a dedication to aliveness and giving our gifts as gestures of love and manifestations of our mission. Ultimately, we embrace the Beloved as we are embraced by the Beloved.

Story of Two Brothers and the Foundation of the Sacred Temple

The sacred nature of intimacy shines through an often told story of two brothers who shared a field and a mill and worked together in harvesting and milling their crop. Each night they evenly divided the fruits of their labors. One brother lived alone and the other had a wife and a large family.

One day, the single brother thought to himself: "I really only have myself to feed and my brother has an entire family. It is only fair that I give him more so he has enough for everyone." So each night he secretly placed some of his grain in his brother's granary.

At the same time, the married brother said to himself: "It isn't really fair that we divide the fruits of our labors evenly, because I have my children to provide for me in my old age and my brother has no one." So every night he secretly took some of his grain to his brother's granary. Each morning they awoke to find their supplies replenished.

As you might expect, one night the brothers came upon each other halfway between their houses and realized what had been happening. They embraced each other in profound love and gratitude.

In ancient versions of this story, it is said that God witnessed this blessed event and proclaimed: "This is a holy place—a place of sacred love—and here is the place for my temple to be built." And so it was. The holy place, where God is revealed, is in the intimacy where we discover each other in love.

Endnotes

i. Chögyam Trungpa, *The Heart of the Buddha* (Shambhala, 1991), p. 6.
ii. Chögyam Trungpa, *The Heart of the Buddha* (Shambhala, 1991), p. 142.
iii. James Ishmael Ford used this quote from Mark Epstein in a Dharma talk on September 14, 2002.
iv. Lama Anagarika Govinda, *Buddhist Reflections* (Samuel Weiser, 1991), p. xviii.
v. Lama Anagarika Govinda, *Buddhist Reflections* (Samuel Weiser, 1991), p. 90.
vi. Lama Anagarika Govinda, *Buddhist Reflections* (Samuel Weiser, 1991), p. 93.
vii. Lama Anagarika Govinda, *Buddhist Reflections* (Samuel Weiser, 1991), p. 94.
viii. Lama Anagarika Govinda, *Buddhist Reflections* (Samuel Weiser, 1991), p. 94.
ix. Lama Anagarika Govinda, *Buddhist Reflections* (Samuel Weiser, 1991), p. 94.
x. Lama Anagarika Govinda, *Buddhist Reflections* (Samuel Weiser, 1991), p. 93.
xi. Ellen and Charles Birx, *Waking Up Together* (Wisdom Publications, 2005), p. 46.
xii. Chögyam Trungpa, *The Heart of the Buddha* (Shambhala, 1991), p. 6-7.
xiii. Alan Watts, *The Book: On the Taboo Against Knowing Who You Are* (Vintage Books, 1972), p. 11
xi. D.H. Lawrence, "A Propos of Lady Chatterly's Lover," from *A Selection from Phoenix*, Middlesex, England (Penguin Books, 1971)
xv. Stephen and Ondrea Levine, *Embracing the Beloved* (Anchor, 1996), p. 6.
xvi. Mordechai (Marc) Gafni, *The Mystery of Love* (Atria Books, 2003), p. 118.
xvii. Rainer Maria Rilke in Stephen Mitchell, *The Essence of Wisdom* (Broadway, 1999), p. 10.
xviii. Russell Lockhart, *Words as Eggs* (Spring Publications,

1983), p. 89.

xvix. John Welwood, *Journey of the Heart* (Harper Collins, 1990), p. 60.

xx. Marc Gafni, *The Mystery of Love* (Atria Books, 2003), p. 19.

xxi. Marc Gafni, *The Mystery of Love* (Atria Books, 2003), p. 147.

xxii. Marc Gafni, *The Mystery of Love* (Atria Books, 2003), p. 171.

xxiii. Dalai Lama, *The Universe in a Single Atom* (Broadway, 2006), p. 24.

xxiv. Johann Wolfgang Von Goethe, translated by Robert Bly, *The Soul is Here For Its Own Joy* (Ecco Press, 1995), p. 209.

xxv. Marc Gafni, *The Mystery of Love* (Atria Books, 2003), p. 283.

xxvi. John Welwood, *Journey of the Heart* (Harper Collins, 1990), p. 41.

xxvii. Martin Buber, *Tales of the Hasidim* (Shocken, 1973), p. 251.

xxviii. Zen Master Dogen, *Moon in a Dewdrop* (North Point Press, 1995), p. 70.

xxix. Stephen R. Covey, A. Roger Merrill, Rebecca R. Merrill, *First Things First* (Simon & Schuster, 1994) p. 19.

xxx. Ellen and Charles Birx, *Waking Up Together* (Wisdom Publications, 2005), p. 77.

xxxi. March-April 2005 issue of the *Utne Reader*, p. 53

xxxii. Thomas Patrick Malone and Patrick Thomas Malone, *The Art of Intimacy* (Simon & Schuster, 1987), p. 29.

xxxiii. Sobonfu E. Somé, *The Spirit of Intimacy* (Berkeley Hills Books, 1997). p. 36.

xxxiv. Ernest Kurtz and Katherine Ketcham, *The Spirituality of Imperfection* (Bantam Books, 1992), p. 242.

xxxv. John M. Gottman and Nan Silver, *The Seven Principles for Making Marriage Work* (Three Rivers Press, 1999), p.11. [See also: John M. Gottman and Joan DeClaire, *The Relationship Cure* (Crown, 2001).]

xxxvi. Marc Gafni, *The Mystery of Love* (Atria Books, 2003), p. 45.

xxxvii. Ellen and Charles Birx, *Waking Up Together* (Wisdom

Publications, 2005), p. 3-4.
xxviii. Marc Gafni, *The Mystery of Love* (Atria Books, 2003), p. 59.
xxxix. Craig Hamilton, "Come Together: the Mystery of Collective Intelligence," in *What is Enlightenment*, May–July 2004 issue, p. 77.
xl. Quoted in *The Tibetan Book Of Living And Dying* (Harper Collins, 1992), by Sogyal Rinpoche, p. 364.
xli. *Gateless Gate, Case 45* (Wisdom Publications, 2004), Translated with Commentary by Koun Yamada, p. 212-213
xlii. Marc Gafni, *The Mystery of Love* (Atria Books, 2003), p. 90.
xliii. Marc Gafni, *The Mystery of Love* (Atria Books, 2003), p. 90.

Index of Subheadings

THE DEDICATED LIFE INSTITUTE (DLI) supports spiritual exploration and growth and is dedicated to making the essence teachings of many traditions accessible in a Western idiom. Incorporating the principles of the mystic way, we promote both recovery of our wisdom ground of being and development of our capacity to use our daily conditions as a means of growth and the opportunity to manifest our true wisdom and loving nature. Our dedication to living as an expression of wisdom and love serves to encourage both personal and social transformation. The Institute offers meditation groups, retreats, workshops, and a home study program. For more information please visit our website at www.dli.org.

MARTIN LOWENTHAL, Ph.D. is an ordained senior meditation teacher, founder and mentor with the Dedicated Life Institute. Dr. Lowenthal is the author of *Alchemy of the Soul*; *Dawning of Clear Light*; *Embrace Yes*; *Heart to Heart, Hand in Hand, and Shoulder to Shoulder*, and is coauthor of *Opening the Heart of Compassion*. In addition to creating and teaching trainings, workshops and retreats internationally, he serves as a pastoral counselor, consultant, and writer. He has been on the faculty of Boston College and Harvard University Extension and has studied with Buddhist and Taoist masters for forty years. Dr. Lowenthal received his doctorate from the University of California, Berkeley in 1970, has worked as an applied anthropologist in Botswana, Africa, and directed a research institute from 1970 to 1977.

Made in the USA